ROUTLEDGE LIBRARY EDITIONS:
HISTORY OF EDUCATION

THE COMPREHENSIVE
SCHOOL 1944-1970

THE COMPREHENSIVE SCHOOL
1944-1970

The Politics of Secondary School Reorganization

By

I. G. K. FENWICK

Volume 6

Routledge
Taylor & Francis Group

LONDON AND NEW YORK

First published in 1976

This edition first published in 2007 by
Routledge
2 Park Square, Milton Park, Abingdon, Oxon OX14 4RN

Simultaneously published in the USA and Canada
by Routledge
711 Third Avenue, New York, NY 10017

Transferred to Digital Printing 2007

Routledge is an imprint of the Taylor & Francis Group, an informa business

First issued in paperback 2013

© 1976 I. G. K. Fenwick

British Library Cataloguing in Publication Data
A catalogue record for this book is available from the British
Library

Library of Congress Cataloging in Publication Data
A catalog record for this book has been requested

ISBN13: 978-0-415-43219-1 (hardback)
ISBN13: 978-0-415-86055-0 (paperback)
ISBN13: 978-0-415-41978-9 (set)

Publisher's Note
The publisher has gone to great lengths to ensure the quality
of this reprint but points out that some imperfections in the
original copies may be apparent.

I. G. K. Fenwick

T HE comprehensive school 1944–1970
The politics of secondary school reorganization

Methuen & Co Ltd
London

First published in 1976 by
Methuen & Co Ltd
11 New Fetter Lane London EC4P 4EE
©1976 I. G. K. Fenwick
Filmset in 'Monophoto' Ehrhardt 11 on 12½ pt by
Richard Clay (The Chaucer Press) Ltd, Bungay, Suffolk
and printed in Great Britain by
Fletcher & Son Ltd, Norwich

ISBN 0 416 65910 1 hardbound
ISBN 0 416 83500 7 paperback

Distributed in the USA by
HARPER & ROW PUBLISHERS, INC.
BARNES & NOBLE IMPORT DIVISION

to my father

Contents

Preface   ix
A note on abbreviations   x
Introduction   1

1   The government of education   5

2   The background to policy-making in
    education   23

3   Defining secondary education: the
    Labour government 1945–51   43

4   Bringing politics into education: the
    survival of the comprehensive school
    idea in the early 1950s   59

5   A time to experiment: the develop-
    ment of secondary education under
    the Conservatives   82

6   Bringing education into politics:
    Labour takes the initiative   104

7   Theory into practice: the Labour
    government 1964–70   129

8   The development of educational
    policy   150

    A note on sources   64
    Notes and references   166
    Index   182

Preface

The bulk of the material for this book was presented in a rather different form for the award of a Ph.D. degree in the University of Manchester. The responsibility for the statements and conclusions of the book is mine alone, but it nevertheless represents the fruits of three years' work in the Department of Government at the university under the supervision of Professor W. J. M. Mackenzie. I shall always be grateful for the stimulation of those three years.

My grateful thanks must also go to Mrs Irene Daly and Mrs Hazel Attwood, both of whom showed endless patience in typing and retyping the manuscript.

I.G.K.F.

A note on abbreviations

The following abbreviations are used in the text:

AEC   Association of Education Committees

AHMI   Association of Headmistresses (Incorporated)

AMA   Assistant Masters' Association

AMC   Association of Municipal Corporations

ASE   Association for Science Education

CCA   County Councils' Association

IAAM   Incorporated Association of Assistant Mistresses

IAHM   Incorporated Association of Headmasters

NALT   National Association of Labour Teachers

NAS   National Association of Schoolmasters

NEA   National Education Association

NEC   National Executive Committee (Labour Party)

NEF   New Education Fellowship

NUT   National Union of Teachers

The view that all is blind drift is largely a fatalist projection of one's own feeling of impotence and perhaps a salve of guilt about it. The view that all is due to the conspiracy of an easily locatable enemy is also a hurried projection from the difficult effort to understand how structural shifts open opportunities to various élites and how various élites take advantage or fail to take advantage of them. To accept either view is to relax the effort rationally to understand in detail how it is.

C. Wright Mills, 'Liberal values in the modern world', in I. L. Horowitz (ed.), *Power, politics and people: the collected essays of C. Wright Mills*, Oxford University Press, 1963, p. 194.

Introduction

Those who framed the 1944 Education Act thought that they had provided the key to 'parity of esteem' in secondary education. The recurrent calls to bi-partisan political unity which accompanied the bill through Parliament were no less genuine for being in part the product of fears that the national and local dissension of 1902 might be aroused again. And yet the next twenty-five years produced little satisfaction, much disappointment and considerable opposition to developments in secondary education.

It is the purpose of this book to chart and account for the growth of expressed dissatisfaction, to examine the canvassing of particular proposals for reform (and for resistance to reform) and to consider the impact opinion had on policy through the processes of power and influence.

Studies in education which cover a substantial period of time find themselves the victim of changing fashions in vocabulary. To some extent the title 'multilateral' has been used by educationists and politicians synonymously with 'comprehensive'. At the present time 'multilateral' is hardly used at all, but in the 1940s it had considerable currency and was often used to denote the grouping of different types of secondary school on the same campus. By this arrangement it was thought that the advantages of limited aims within any one school could be combined with the advantages of cooperation and ease of transfer between schools. To the extent that supporters of comprehensive schools would not now be satisfied with such an arrangement, and few of them would be, the title 'comprehensive' has substantially different connotations of common curricula and common aspirations throughout the ability range. Because the users of these words do not always make clear quite what they imply by them, and because precise definition is not possible, the reader needs to be aware of this ambiguity of quotation and interpretation.

All studies of contemporary policy-making suffer the disadvantages of lack of access to government files and this study is no exception. The innuendo of élite domination could only be seriously tested against reality with access to persons and papers, the second of which only become available when the first have retired to the safest distance. Organized groups are often more accessible, perhaps because they make a more generous interpretation of public relations; the difficulty here is the plethora of documentation available and the mass of groups providing it. It has proved necessary to concentrate on the main partners to educational policy: central government and the political parties which run it, local authorities and the organized groups of teachers.

Despite recent growth in political studies, which has stemmed partly from the realization that constitutionally unrecognized institutions play a most important role in the making of political decisions, its impact on the study of educational policy-making has been small. Few studies have been produced, or published, in this country which make use of material from contemporary educational controversy. By far the best research is historical despite all the limitations of conceptual inexplicitness that so often accompany historical investigation. The one exception to the statement that students of politics have ignored education is the issue of secondary reorganization since 1945.

If one looks, on the other hand, to students of education for theoretically based studies of contemporary educational policy-makers, such studies are again difficult to find. In their place are implicitly or explicitly polemical accounts of developments and strategies, perhaps particularly on the issue of secondary reorganization.[1] I have no wish to decry such studies in principle, but a diet restricted in this way may produce satiety while failing to provide nourishment. Nor am I intending to offer in their place any comprehensive and elaborate theory of educational policy-making; rather, less pretentiously, I hope to communicate my own conviction that the theoretical notions implicit in any study of policy-making need to be made more explicit and nowhere more so than in the field of educational policy-making.

The key word in most accounts of the government of education is 'partnership': it summarizes a great deal about the division of power between central and local government, between teachers, administrators and professional politicians. But it is not a purely objective term; it undoubtedly carries an overtone of approval by its users and it may serve to disguise problems in consensus and to distort analysis with legal fiction.

The aim of this book is to recognize the force of 'partnership' as a summary description of the relationship between many of the agencies and organizations participating in policy decisions, and to examine the way in which power and influence have been exercised on a particular issue. A pluralist analysis has immediate appeal to students of educational policy-making, habituated as they are to the plethora of sectional organizations that claim the ear of government. But this no more implies acceptance of the balance of power and influence existing at a particular point in time than it implies approval or disapproval of the reorganization of secondary education.

The fullest account of secondary education policy since 1944 would take account of the demands made by all those formally eligible in a democracy to participate in decision-making. As the notion of *in statu pupillari* loses force it becomes difficult even to limit the theoretically participating population to the electorate.

Even a more restricted scope, dictated as much by expediency as by a more realistic assessment of the participating population, needs to take account of the effects of the largely negative role played by large numbers of legitimate participants. For the most part it is necessary to concentrate on interested groups, parties, Parliament, bureaucrats and the Press as being, in this country, the most active and well-established gatekeepers of the political system. In education, the role of teacher, parent, school manager or governor and academic serve to widen the range of active participants; but, again, for the most part the direction of their activity is towards the agencies mediating between government and governed rather than directly with the government. By far the most important element among these mediating agencies in day-to-day educational policy-making are the organized interest groups representing teachers and the political parties in education. The extent to which the policy decisions of the government are limited to the demands made depends, in part, on the efficiency of these organizations in recognizing, assimilating and prosecuting such demands. In turn, the distribution of demands among the various organized groups depends on the characteristics of these gatekeepers

> as related to their socio-economic origins, the processes through which they arrive as gatekeepers, the ideological perspectives within which they operate, the motivations underlying their actions, the

communications processes through which the wants of others may be impressed upon them, the resources for conversion at their disposal and their differential responsiveness to the wants of others as compared to their own goals.[2]

The emphasis, then, will be on the activity of certain organized groups who constitute the major elements of the population actively interested in education, the education public.

A social activity such as education, which is centrally directed and locally administered, which involves colossal financial outlay and creates employment for hundreds of thousands, and which affects the life of every citizen as child or parent at least, admits no peremptory analysis. While no final answer is provided, the question 'Who has influence in education?', which is posed in the following pages, is potentially of considerable interest not only to historians and political scientists, but also to all those currently active in education.

Chapter One

T HE government of education

The state first became involved in the provision of education in England in 1833, when the House of Commons agreed that a sum of £20,000 should be 'distributed in aid of subscriptions for the education of children of the poorer classes'. A committee of the Privy Council was set up in 1839 'to superintend the application of any sums voted by Parliament for the purpose of promoting public education'. In 1856 the government, with the agreement of the House of Commons, created the paid post of vice-president of the committee who would be responsible to the House for the proper distribution of grants. The 1870 Elementary Education Act empowered the central government actively to remedy deficiencies in educational provision through the agency of school boards. The Department of Science and Art, responsible for technical education, grew up independently during the same period; it was not until 1900 that the central government's interest in education was channelled through one department, with a political head called the president of the Board of Education.[1] This central unification was considered a 'necessary preliminary to the constitution of any satisfactory local organisation'; this latter need was met by the Education Act of 1902.

Until 1944, the central administration was statutorily responsible only for 'the superintendence of matters relating to education in England and Wales' and was not usually in the charge of ministers of the first rank.[2] The central government's powers were severely limited, and it is only since the 1944 Education Act that there has arisen, other than among local authority associations, the fear that the powers of the central government are too great.

The most obvious change that the 1944 Education Act wrought of itself was in the officially recognized language of education. The 'statutory system of public education shall be organised in three progressive stages to be known as primary education, secondary education and further education';[3] the distinction between different educational institutions for older children had gone, and the most favourably connoted term, 'secondary', was to be used quite generally. But such a change of vocabulary would have had little impact on the reality of the state education system if it had not symbolized a reorganization of statutory rights and duties in education in central and local government. This reorganization of education unified the government of education under the umbrella of state control, making the issue of church versus state and public versus private education peripheral to the development of a coherent state system of education,[4] especially state secondary education.

It would be unwise to over-emphasize the importance of statutes in the development of state-organized services, even when they are as institutionalized as education. The main burden of this chapter is to outline some of the other elements relevant to a full analysis of policy-making in education. But it would be similarly unwise to ignore statutes, especially the 1944 Education Act, when they extend, restrict and re-distribute or redefine responsibilities; their effect may be to accelerate the rate of change, and to alter the direction of activity.

The statutory basis of educational government

Even within central government, presumably most closely attuned to statutory limitations, administrative discretion may foster internal recognition of desirable developments in anticipation of statutory sanctification.

The Board of Education gradually moved towards greater 'territorialization' of its organization, that is, to an organization based on responsibility for all education within a given geographical area. This was particularly marked after the departure of Robert Morant, the permanent secretary. After the 1918 Education Act, officers of the board up to and including the rank of principal were given responsibility for elementary, secondary and technological education in a particular area, thus simplifying liaison and superintendence of particular education authorities. Within the board, important problems would be referred by the territorial officer to the appropriate assistant secretary.[5]

The 1944 Education Act symbolically upgraded central administration of education by giving its head the rank and title of 'minister'. Titles mean little, but it brought education into line with the current fashion.[6]

More important, the general responsibility of the new minister was radically different from that of the president of the Board of Education. The minister was to 'promote the education of the people of England and Wales and the progressive development of institutions devoted to that purpose and to secure the effective execution, by local authorities under his control and direction, of the national policy for providing a varied and comprehensive educational service in every area'.[7]

The remit is perhaps of more political than administrative or legal significance. It attempts to tie the minister's hands in two ways: it makes it difficult for him to argue that any educational matter brought to his attention is not his responsibility, and it characterizes his positive responsibility for a 'varied and comprehensive educational service in every area'. This section of the Act serves its purpose in providing a rationale for the minister's actions. Other sections of the Act give specific content to the minister's overall responsibility: Section 99 gives him the power to enforce the discharge of any duties placed upon local education authorities by the Act; Section 68 gives the minister power to act at his own discretion against any local education authority which, again at his own discretion, he considers to be acting unreasonably.[8] Sweeping though this power is, in 1945 it could still be no more than a symbol of a deliberate change in relations between central and local government in education which was made clearer in the gloss given to it by Lord Selborne, speaking for the government in the House of Lords:

> . . . we should all agree that the Minister should have some power of reversing an unwise or an unfortunate decision. My noble friends say that the Minister himself ought to be subject to the check either of Parliament or of a judge. But this is a matter of administration. . . . You could not administer this or any other Act under procedure of that kind.[9]

Even within the terms of the Act, the new minister of education was not expected to formulate his educational policy unaided; a Central Advisory Council for Education in England[10] took the place of the consultative committee of the Board of Education. This earlier advisory body had not fulfilled the hopes of some educationists that it would act as a safeguard against departmental bureaucracy, but it had survived forceful arguments against any diminution of ministerial responsibility.[11] It had produced in 1938, under the chairmanship of Sir Will Spens, a report on secondary education which had provided in part the inspiration of the official reformers, and was reprinted in 1947 when it was thought it would be 'of value to administrators, teachers and students at a time when the new policy is being developed in practice'. Nevertheless it was said that the consultative committee, composed completely of professional educationists, never dared to ask for as much as was in fact given in the 1944 Education Act.

The new advisory council's duties were to

> advise the Minister upon such matters connected with educational theory and practice as they think fit, and upon any questions referred to them by him.[12]

A new independence contained in the phrase 'as they think fit' was not lost on educationists. Sir Fred Clarke, the first chairman of the advisory council, described the prospect thus:

> They would learn to understand the aims and the possibilities of the scheme of national education as set out in the Act, would watch over its development and take the best evidence they could get towards plans for its future improvement. Then in the form of advice to the Minister, they would announce to the country their conclusions, and so help to create a well-informed public opinion.[13]

Butler's anticipation of the role the advisory council would play was more restrictive: it would 'pay some attention to what is taught in the schools . . . and to all the most modern and up-to-date methods'.[14]

The considerable debate in the House of Commons on the constitution and terms of reference of the advisory council indicates that many of the interested members, none of them particularly naïve, saw in the council an important element in policy-making in education. They saw it as one of the main sources of information and advice for the minister, on which he would generally be expected to act. But the information and advice was not only to be that of practising educationists, and it was in anticipation of the role of link between political leaders and the public, and as the holder of a watching brief on the 'national interest in education',[15] that the Education Act laid down that the council should include 'persons who have had experience of the statutory system of public education'[16] without restricting the membership to such professional educationists.[17] The intention of Parliament had certainly been that the council should contain representatives of a wide range of interests, and Butler, as president of the board, had had difficulty in preventing the specification of particular interests to be represented.

In February 1945 the minister ruled that the newly appointed chairman of the advisory council should hold office for three years and the other members for six, one-third of them retiring every two years.[18] The stage was formally set for the Central Advisory Council to play a crucial revised and expanded role in educational policy-making.

If the reorganization of central administration might mean only a change of names and an opportunity for action on a wider front in education, reorganization at local level under the 1944 Education Act interfered much more drastically with established interests. Three hundred and fifteen local education authorities were reduced to half that number, although pressure from the authorities that were to be abolished[19] led to a compromise whereby some of their long-standing concern with education was preserved.

From 1 April 1945 there were 146 local education authorities, 62 county councils, 83 county boroughs and 1 joint board. It was the county authorities who benefited from the reduction in the number of local education authorities; otherwise the 1944 Education Act consolidated the functions of those local education authorities that continued to exist.[20]

The statutory powers of each local education authority were the same, but in almost every other respect there were very great variations in the characteristics of the different authorities. The role of central government remained, in part, the minimizing of the effects of discrepancies in competence and resources on the uniform provision and development of education.[21]

The existing education committees, statutorily required under the 1921 Education Act, took over the new responsibilities with, in many cases, only minor reforms of membership and sub-committee structure. Part II of the first schedule to the Act makes it clear that the membership of an education committee must include 'persons of experience in education and persons acquainted with the educational conditions prevailing in the area for which the committee acts'. Co-opted members were already common on many education committees, the proportion averaging just under a third in the late 1940s. The majority of the committee had to be members of the local authority.[22]

Every education committee works under a scheme approved by the Ministry of Education. These schemes are embodied in the standing orders of the council of the authority, and they indicate the composition of its education committee and the delegated powers it is to exercise. Within the committee formal power may be variously distributed; it is common practice for authorities to make use of the provision of the

Education Act that an education committee may authorize a sub-committee to exercise functions of the committee on its behalf.

The extent to which the council delegates powers to the education committee varies between authorities. Great 'potential power' lies with the council and can, on occasion, be used to control committees. Only the power to raise a loan or levy a rate is reserved to the council, but power over expenditure may be and usually is made subject to the approval of the local authority's finance committee, and considerable control is exercised. On the other hand, decisions of the education committee may have to be ratified by the council but will in practice almost invariably receive approval.

The compromise effected between the Board of Education and the Part III authorities required the county education authorities to prepare schemes of divisional administration which would give some executive and advisory powers back to single or grouped second-tier local authorities, without making them in any way independent of the education authority. In addition, some of the very large second-tier local authorities could claim to exercise some delegated powers in education. The Ministry of Education issued some guidelines in its Circular No. 5, *Schemes of divisional administration*, and to this extent most schemes were uniform. Lancashire's initial thirty-seven was the largest number; some divisional areas were co-terminous with second-tier local authority boundaries, some reflected educational catchment areas, and the minister exempted thirteen English counties from the necessity of operating divisional schemes. Where the divisional boundaries coincided with those of a second-tier authority, as in the case of excepted districts, the administrative services of the divisional executive could fit quite neatly into the general pattern obtaining under the particular local authority; otherwise, as in the majority of cases, the county provided the administrative staff to service what was effectively an *ad hoc* committee.[23]

Until the 1944 Education Act, local education authorities were not compelled to appoint an education officer. Many of them, however, had done so with the permissive powers granted in the 1921 Education Act. The new Act went a stage further in restricting the freedom of local education authorities as to the means employed to discharge their executive duties in education. No chief education officer could be appointed without the approval of the minister, who was empowered to scrutinize short lists and prohibit the selection of particular candidates.[24] Of course in most cases there was no immediate effect, since previously appointed officers continued in their posts under the new Act.

While the terms of the Act indicated the importance attached to the choice of a chief education officer, his formal position is nevertheless very much that of a subordinate. The historical origins of the post lay in a period of much less complex administration of education. The functional parallel between the clerk to the governors of a school and the chief education officer is drawn in the white paper *Principles of government in maintained secondary schools*.[25] In this paper the central government seems as much concerned to consolidate the powers newly concentrated in a smaller number of local education authorities as to assign specific areas of responsibility to governors and managers. Preparations of estimates, appointment and dismissal of teaching and non-teaching staff, and general discretion of the conduct and curriculum of the school are all formally within the terms of reference of governors, but all with the proviso that ultimate responsibility lies with the education authority and day-to-day responsibility with the head of the school.

The context in which the parent is mentioned in the 1944 Education Act is that of allocation of duties among the various bodies and persons having authority over the child. Parents have two main duties closely related: first to see that their child attends regularly the school at which he or she is registered, and secondly to see that the child receives 'efficient full-time education suitable to his age, ability and aptitude'. Various mechanisms for appeal are built into the system whereby the parent's choice of education for his child is not wholly subject to the dictates of the local education authority. The right of the parent to educate his child according to his own lights is severely restricted under the Act; only the negative rights to have the child excused from attendance at religious worship and religious instruction within the school remain inalienable.

Most of the important rights of the parent in the formal administrative process are available to him in his role as citizen; there are numerous specific rights of appeal to the minister in relation to the establishment of existing schools, and development plans. None of these limit the right of the citizen to ask for action by the minister under the general powers of the Act.

An act which gives central government so much discretionary power over the education system while leaving the execution of policy largely in the hands of local government necessitates a large body of regulations defining in detail the procedures, policy targets and various standards thought appropriate to a particular point in time. These regulations, officially described as statutory rules and orders (now as statutory instruments), have the force of law, though the process of changing them is much simpler, quicker and more frequent than that of the law itself.[26]

Educational administrators

The Ministry of Education is one of the smaller government departments.[27] Until 1919 the Board of Education had recruited its staff independently of the Civil Service Commission. All the evidence[28] shows that the senior staff of the board in the early part of the century had very similar educational backgrounds, public school followed by Oxford or Cambridge, and the last of those recruited under pre-1919 arrangements retired by 1950. Not that this assimilation to the rest of the Civil Service meant any sudden broadening of the educational base of recruitment:

> If we look at the bureaucratic hierarchy, we find that the higher the administrative rank, the greater the correlation with the level of parental occupation and the school attended. In 1950, nearly two-thirds of the Permanent Secretaries or Deputy Secretaries of Government Departments had been educated either in boarding schools or in independent day schools.[29]

However, the mere fact of a complete lack of personal experience of the state education system does not necessarily mean that these administrators lacked either educational or executive vision. But just as earlier educational administrators complained of the poor quality of local inspectorates, whose members were drawn from elementary school education, it is worthwhile noting the narrowness of the personal educational perspective in which central administrators viewed – and view – the statutory system.

On the other hand, a specialized interest in education had been encouraged by Morant:

> it is incumbent upon every Assistant Secretary and every Examiner, as well as upon each responsible head of a Branch, to use every endeavour to keep himself abreast of the best that is written and said from day to day on the subject of education. The Officers of the Board of Education ought to be, and can be, a body of experts in the general problem of education.[30]

Of the two senior chief inspectors in office during the period 1944–64, one had received his secondary education in a state grammar school, the other in an independent school. The gradual amalgamation of the secondary and the elementary inspectorate had removed by the post-war period most of the social and intellectual suspicion between administrator and teacher that had last erupted with the unintentional publication of the Holmes–Morant memorandum of 1910.

The inspectorate are the only group of professional educationists in central administration, recruited almost exclusively from the teaching profession. Their functions are to inspect schools, both state and private; to act as a communication channel between central and local government; and to advise the local education authority, both in their formal reports on schools and informally. They are not able to give orders, and are not directly concerned with the day-to-day administrative intercourse between local authority and ministry, but they may have an important role to play in the planning and scheduling of major educational developments and in long-term educational development.

Administrators in local authorities are 'professionals' in their particular fields. K. C. Wheare characterizes chief officers as 'general practitioners' and their subordinates as 'experts', specialists in some area or functional sub-division of the department's work.[31] But unlike administrative class civil servants, local government administrators, such as the chief education officer, the medical officer of health, the borough architect, and others, cannot be interchanged. To the extent that the law in education, as in other local government fields, restricts the choice of a chief officer, and to the extent that these officials insist upon their professional status, then they are experts. The roles of administrator and professional adviser are combined in local government, while remaining formally separate in central government.

Once appointed by the education committee, the chief education officer is in a strong position to impose his ideas on the authority. Subordinate to him in the larger education offices will be a range of specialists who can supplement his own expertise in dealing with the education committee as professional adviser. In the execution of policy his discretion is equivalent to that of the head of a central department, with the added freedom that there is no established equivalent of the minister in the daily administration. The extent to which the chairman of the education committee fulfils this latter role depends upon the personality of both men.

Little is known about the provenance of chief education officers: research covering the pre-war period provides a picture of the various avenues to senior positions then common; a background of teaching and apprenticeship in local educational administration is now the regular pattern.

Of course, some chief education officers may find their positions made intolerable by a hostile committee, but they have the advantage of permanent tenure – committee members change quite rapidly.[32] Perhaps the most anomalous position created under the 1944 Act was that of the divisional education officer: he was responsible both to the county who employed him, and to the divisional executive whom he might have had to advise in their dealings with the county while carrying out their instructions on matters delegated to them.

Apart from the problem of an adequate general level of expenditure on education, local control has always produced the problem of variations in resources and needs from area to area:

> The parishes in which the richer people live are necessarily those in which there is least need for a primary school; and the districts in which the poor most abound are not infrequently the districts in which the Church is most slenderly endowed and in which voluntary subscriptions are raised with the greatest difficulty.[33]

In its aid to local authorities, central government has sought to raise the general level of expenditure and to minimize the difference between needs and resources. In 1954, the average subsidy to local educational expenditure was 60 per cent, but between areas it might vary from 30 to 75 per cent.

If the Education Act was intended to give the central authority greater powers to induce the local authorities to increase their educational expenditure, then it seems to have succeeded. Vaizey claims that fluctuations in the economy have little effect on real educational expenditure, and:

> behind the ebb and flow of money expenditure associated with transitory economic events lies a rising secular trend of real expenditure which accelerated its rate of growth after the war.

Even more important, he finds that:

> it is striking that both capital investment and current expenditure after 1945 have risen faster than the rate of increase of the national income; the post-war period has therefore marked, since 1949 at least, an era of educational progress proceeding under its own dynamic.[34]

Much of central government's control of local education authorities is exercised through this financial stake in each authority's current and capital expenditure. Building programmes drawn up by the local authority are submitted to the ministry for comment, modification and eventual approval. Thus financial control gives the ministry an opportunity to influence the educational ideas of a local authority. When, as usually happens, the total of building projects submitted exceeds a centrally acceptable level, the choice of projects to be eliminated may have to be made by the ministry.

Political parties and education

Even the simplest sketch of the institutions of educational government could not fail to include some account of the paraconstitutional role of political parties in policy-making. They have their most obvious effects in the partial structuring of political debate inside and outside Parliament, but the interrelationship between party power structure and governmental power structure also has its impact on education.

The title of 'minister' implies no powers in itself, only status. The powers of central government specified in the 1944 Education Act, and the growing perceived importance of education economically, socially and politically, are the factors consolidating that prestige. Nevertheless the ministry has usually been seen by aspiring politicians as an intermediate stage in a ministerial career. For R. A. Butler it turned out to be a stepping stone to higher office both in government and in his party. Of the two Labour ministers, Ellen Wilkinson was Attlee's second choice for the post, and on her death, George Tomlinson, who was not to survive the defeat of Labour in 1951 very long, was translated from the Ministry of Public Building and Works. Of the five Conservative ministers of education between 1951 and April 1964, only one, Sir David Eccles, moved directly to higher office as president of the Board of Trade, and he returned to education in 1959. Florence Horsbrugh, minister of education in the first post-war Conservative government, was not at first given a seat in the cabinet; like Miss Wilkinson before her, she was the second choice of the prime minister, who failed to persuade Clement Davies to take the post with a seat in the cabinet. Miss Horsbrugh's ministerial career came to an end in 1954. Geoffrey Lloyd, who had filled various posts in pre- and post-war Conservative governments, became minister of education in 1957, but was dropped from the government after the 1959 general election. Out of five parliamentary secretaries to the minister of education in the Conservative governments of 1951–64, only one, Sir Edward Boyle, eventually became minister himself. It is perhaps significant that when the Ministry of Education's role was further expanded and its increased importance again recognized by the appointment of a secretary of state in place of a minister, the post did not go to the incumbent minister. Sir

Edward Boyle remained as minister of state, under Quintin Hogg, secretary of state; both had a seat in the cabinet. Thus in 1964 education was recognized, but in 1945 to be a minister of education was an indication of middling rank in the hierarchy of ministers; the contemporary context implied concentration on administration rather than political innovation, and the capacity to maintain political consensus.

But the parliamentary upheaval occasioned by the 1945 general election was not particularly conducive to immediate consensus. Three hundred and twenty-four members were elected for the first time, more than half the total membership; only 204 members had more than ten years' service in the House of Commons. Over half the Labour members of Parliament were products of the elementary school system, the main proposed beneficiary of the 1944 Education Act, compared to an insignificant proportion of the Conservative opposition. This proportion of Labour members with a relevant, but limited, educational background was very considerably higher than the average for the period 1918–51, and it represented the crest of a wave only surpassed in the 1929 membership of the house. Nevertheless almost a quarter of Labour's members in 1945 had attended secondary schools (i.e. all selective schools which were not administered under the Elementary Code nor were members of the Headmasters' Conference). Over four-fifths of Conservative members were products of schools which were in membership of the Headmasters' Conference.[35] Only among the Labour Party members of Parliament was there to be found any substantial experience of state education; and if conflict was to be structured around the traditional cleavage within that system, then Labour members acknowledging loyalty to their educational origins were as likely to find themselves in conflict with each other as with the Conservative members. This is not to say that Labour members saw clearly any alignment of this nature at any time; it merely suggests, with the benefit of hindsight, that while controversy over the independent sector of education might well fit snugly with other political divisions between the parties, the nascent issue of comprehensive secondary education was one about which the Parliamentary Labour Party was potentially confused and certainly unprepared.

The 1945 election was significant for education also in that teachers and lecturers became for the first time the largest occupational group on the Labour benches, ousting the miners. Forty-nine Labour members were teachers or lecturers before their election to the House of Commons, compared with only five Conservatives. (This bias may explain the common but erroneous belief that teachers tend to be left-wing in their political sympathies.) Finally, the record of experience in serving on major local authorities administering education was much greater for the Labour members of Parliament elected in 1945 than for the Conservatives.[36] It is not clear how this experience related to personal educational experience, but it is reasonable to conclude that it tends to confirm the commitment to education, one of government's major concerns, and to indicate that it would be a further source of conflicting loyalties as plans for secondary education development emerged.

This picture of a Labour membership of the House of Commons unprepared for the dominant educational issue of the post-war period is confirmed by an examination of the debates on the education bill as it went through the House in 1944. The debates are concerned more with the ending of an era of religious and social division rigidly embedded in the administrative system of education than with precise formulae for the future development of secondary education. In part this was probably a matter of tactics on the part of government spokesmen and back benchers: tactics to ensure maximum progress with the administrative reforms which were thought to be the precondition of any educational reform. They nevertheless served to make reaction more extreme when the generalized vision did not materialize and the precarious conservative consensus was breached.

It can be misleading to over-emphasize nominal similarities between national and local politics when the institutional, cultural and functional contexts are so different. Such studies as there are refer to the current situation, although it is clear that political attitudes in local government have changed and hardened during the period since 1945 partly as a result of the controversy over secondary reorganization. Bulpitt[37] makes it clear that party politics were not introduced into local government by the Labour Party, though they were responsible for its extension, both directly through their own emphasis on party unity and indirectly through the reaction thus produced in other more loosely knit party groups on local authorities.

Although elected on a party ticket, councillors may then act as individuals in decisions over the whole range of council policy. But it is common for Labour groups at least to adopt 'standing orders' in their 'loose' or 'strict' interpretations.[38] In London the 'strict' interpretation during thirty years of Labour domination of the county council led to a highly centralized system of party control of council committees from which the opposition was excluded;[39] in Manchester a much more flexible approach to group coherence, in all parties, has been yielding to an increasingly 'strict' interpretation of standing orders by the majority Labour group.[40] Heclo found that

> none of the freshmen Labour councillors considered voting against the whip, and most said that if they disagreed on a matter of conscience they would abstain. Labour Party leaders seemed to accept this procedure.[41]

Majority party structure may find expression in sub-committees of major statutory committees, where important decisions can be taken away from public and minority party gaze but can benefit from council officers' advice. The opposition may capture small, usually unimportant formal groups such as boards of governors and use them to influence decision making; this can often be effectively dealt with by the grouping of boards for different schools, thus reducing the deployment of majority party manpower necessary to retain control.

Within the education committee, the chairman, as in other local government committees, has considerable influence. Apart from his powers as a chairman, he is increasingly called on to fill the role of a minister, watching the day-to-day developments within his department, and reporting back to the committee on his actions between meetings.[42] His relationship with the chief education officer can be very important:

> Policy really depends on an inter-relation between the Officers and the Chairmen of Committees. A strong Officer can run a Committee, but a strong Chairman can offer creative resistance.[43]

The chairman will again be equated with a minister in his responsibility for education policy when he reports to his council on his committee's work, and if he is the nominee of the majority party group he will be regularly answerable to the party caucus.[44]

The combination of committee and education officer would leave the balance of power on most matters firmly with the education officer, were it not for the party political structure in many local authorities, which substitutes for the statutory policy-making process this private parallel process within the majority party group.

One role tending, in a limited way, to counter the democratic centralism of local party government is that of the co-opted member. As in central educational government, the role of outside educationists has been in part institutionalized. The practice of co-opting educationists to local education committees was made compulsory under the 1944 Act, for both counties and county boroughs, and divisional executives. Before 1944:

Co-opted members frequently were selected from the clergy, the teaching staff, the medical profession, college or university faculties in the area, and from among those who through organisations had shown an interest in public education.[45]

However, by 1948 co-option was accepted only in name by about one-sixth of the education committees, since it was permitted from within the council. Most education committees do practise co-option of between 10 and 48 per cent of their members, mixing individuals and representatives of groups. But the system of co-option may vary significantly between authorities, in the extent, for example, of its integration of the teaching staff into the policy-making process. In Stockport it was found that one NUT representative was the only co-opted teacher between 1945 and 1954. In Bolton the different stages of education – primary, secondary and further – are specifically represented through election by teachers. Elections of teacher representatives were also first held in Southport, where there has been resistance to the idea by the education committee, but the co-opted members were not those at the top of the poll.[46]

The supposed effect of the co-opted members is to help to secure continuity of policy 'as well as bring to the deliberations of the committee much accumulated experience'.[47] On party political issues the co-opted members may opt out or take a position and run the risk of identification with one political view. Co-option can of course be used to increase the proportion of sympathizers with the majority political view.

Consultative procedures

The ministry's report in 1951 distinguished four types of consultation developed since the 1944 Education Act. First, there were the central advisory councils which had wide terms of reference, but were not intended to 'concern themselves with Administration'. Secondly, two national advisory councils were set up on specific subjects, education for industry and commerce and the training and supply of teachers; these formed part of 'a comprehensive system of advisory bodies caring for the whole country'. Thirdly, the minister made financial grants to some outside organizations of value to its policy formation, such as the National Foundation for Educational Research. Fourthly, and perhaps most important, 'the Minister maintains close relations with the main associations of local education authorities, teachers and other responsible bodies, and, in regard to important questions of policy, seeks their advice by correspondence or discussion'.

One of the major formations of interest groups in education has been that of the religious denominations. They demonstrated their concern, if not their power, in their attempts to influence the thinking of the president of the Board of Education prior to the drawing up of the education bill. They remain important parties to the provision of education through their financial stake and partial administrative control of the various forms of voluntary schools which they originated. The Church of England is still a formidable source of education, and the Roman Catholics make up for what they lack in overall numbers by the coherence of their pressure and the relative concentration of its sources in certain areas such as the north-west.

While the tendency has been towards conformity of organization of maintained schools, the basis of organization of voluntary schools is more complex. They are classified according to the nature and extent of the financial support received from the Ministry of Education or the local education authority. While 'controlled' schools are almost completely run by the local education authority, the board of governors or managers containing a minority of 'foundation' governors or managers selected by the sponsoring body, in 'aided schools' the preponderance of power is with the sponsoring body, and a sizeable financial burden is consequently placed upon it.

A most important group of schools appropriately mentioned here, though by no means necessarily denominational in character, and explicable historically if not educationally, are the direct grant schools. Limited in number, hovering between independence and assimilation with the statutory system, varying among themselves in size, facilities and achievements almost as much as state schools, yet all preserving some prestige, the direct grant schools receive financial aid from the Ministry of Education in return for the allocation of a proportion of places to pupils from the state primary system. The local education authority may also support these schools by taking up a further proportion of places in them, and paying the fees. Independent though these schools really are of the local education authority, they had to be included in the development plan drawn up under the 1944 Education Act, and their existence as selective schools has implications for any secondary reorganization plans.

Far more important than the denominations (although the limitations on their power is one of the subjects this book seeks to explore) are the groups of teachers who may have representation directly or indirectly on local education committees, on official national consultative bodies and on working committees at all levels. There is no doubt that teachers, through their official organizations such as the NUT, the NAS and the Joint Four secondary associations, are consulted formally or informally on many aspects of policy. Their reactions to decisions, and the anticipation by government of their reactions to decisions, have been of increasing importance during this century. Similarly the associations of local authorities, especially the AEC, see themselves playing a vital role in the policy process.

Most of these groups have an 'interest' in education but few of them would not want also to be characterized as promoters of the 'cause' of education. Some groups have only a specialist interest or limited base for recruitment, the IAHM or the NAS being examples. Others attempt to be all-embracing, such as the NUT or the NEF. This last organization, precariously but persistently poised on the fringe of the educational world, exemplifies the purely promotional group; the ASE, with its considerable influence on curricular change, is another. Most school subjects have their specialist association, some more effective than others in reaching a wide public. Of course, some small associations are as interested in spreading influence downwards and outwards through the teaching profession as in concentrating pressure on central government or local education authorities.

Size is a major variable in educational groupings, affecting the scope of activities, the degree of influence, and the extent of concern with internal management of consensus: it is perhaps linked particularly with style of pressure. For the groups with access to government the appropriate (in the sense of long-run effectiveness) style of bargaining or persuasion is very different from that of the 'outsider' groups. Again, different leaders, especially as they gain a personal foothold in government, may well give a distinctive pattern to the activities of the groups they represent. Other groups may conduct an internal dialogue with only the most general intentions of directly influencing people outside the group.

In talking about the influence of interest groups in education, it would be an over-simplification to apply the same criterion of success or failure to all. With limited evidence for the diffusion of ideas it may be impossible to show conclusively that organizations like the NEF have had any significant impact on policy-making, but it is as difficult to show the opposite. The role of the NUT may be easier to explain in this sense, because of its wholesale engagement in the machinery of government.

The struggle for power between the administrative, political and interest groups outlined does not, of course, proceed in a vacuum, either of more widely based structures of power or of concomitant consensus on legitimate claims and procedures for satisfying such claims.

Experiences of the controversy associated with the passing of the 1902 Education Act had united many politicians, who were otherwise divided, in the conviction that dislocation of educational progress through the disputes of the religious denominations should be avoided at almost any cost. It was this historical perspective that led Churchill, in 1942, to try to persuade R. A. Butler not to sponsor a new Education Act. The reverse of the coin was the widely held belief that a substitution of party political dispute for denominational quarelling would be intolerable. No doubt this view tended to find most support among those who were happy with the *status quo*, but it was nevertheless more widely based than that. Among Labour leaders nationally, and often locally, it was compatible with their general political positions, since there was little or no party political basis for dispute over the ends that development of the state educational system was supposed to serve; the pace of change might be disputed hotly but the nature of change rarely. From the administrative viewpoint there was everything to be gained by steadiness of progress, and the radical redistribution of power between central and local government under the 1944 Education Act needed to be clothed in an ethic of partnership which reflected in part make-believe and in part the realities of smooth operation of the Act.

'Partnership' can serve to mask disputes between the locality and the ministry; 'steady progress' rules out-of-bounds national conflict on the goals of education. 'Consensus' avoids the question of goals. How should politicians in parties, and out of them, react to this situation: should they strain the partnership in their direction or break it, subtly redirect educational progress or question it openly, emphasize different aspects of the consensus or seek through open conflict to redefine it? These were the tactical questions supporters of comprehensive schools had to answer in their quest for a more radical refashioning of secondary education than the contemporary consensus envisaged.

Chapter Two

T HE background to policy-making in education

Some of the main lines of activity and development in English education need to be sketched in if the more detailed description of the activities of the politically and administratively active are to have any meaning. This sketch must necessarily include something of the history of education in England before the 1944 Education Act, since precedent and custom play so large a part in the formulation of current policy.

Development of state education has been slow; while other countries, including Scotland, were developing state systems, England was still only subsidizing a system run independently by the various religious denominations.[1] Nor have successful educational innovators ever sought to overturn the system developed on precedent:

> Educational revolutionaries have been few, and their audiences small. If the position taken by the pioneers discussed in this book are closely examined it will be seen that their anxiety was in nearly all cases to overcome the effects of a mere time-lag between common practice and a very moderate degree of progressiveness in the current world of ideas.[2]

One educational administrator expressed satisfaction with the conduct of education by post-war governments in the following slightly ambiguous words:

> It says much for our political system that at no time was there any violent breach of policy, but rather that a steady progress was maintained.[3]

The wholesale reorganization of secondary education into comprehensive schools is, in principle, just such a 'violent breach of policy'.

Educational policy-making has been plagued in the past by the conflicting interests of the various religious denominations, catholic and protestant, established and nonconformist. Whether they acted through parties or directly on the government, religious pressure groups set a pattern for educational policy-making which is still with us today. Though religious controversy is no longer very important, teachers, administrators and academics, both as groups and as individuals, are closely involved in policy compromises; the value attributed to consensus and continuity is a response to the bitter conflicts of the past.

Whether as cause or effect of English educational history, education has rarely been thought of as a unity; in the nineteenth century it was openly divided along class lines:

The subject of education may be comprised under three heads:
1. The education of the poor in primary schools;
2. The education of the middle classes in grammar schools and commercial schools;
3. The education of the higher classes and of the clergy at the university.[4]

The state system of education, begun in 1870 as a supplement to the subsidized but inadequate church schools, has developed from 'the education of the poor in primary schools' to a system embracing all aspects and levels of education, while in return it has been permeated by the educational and social philosophies of the middle-class 'grammar schools and commercial schools'.

In 1868, when the Liberal government came into office, a number of its members and most of its supporters believed that one of its most pressing tasks was to introduce a national system of elementary education.[5] The ideal of a powerful group, the middle-class nonconformists, may have been a universal, compulsory, non-sectarian national system, but within the government there were powerful sympathizers (including Gladstone) with the voluntary church schools.[6] The bill introduced by W. E. Forster, vice-president of the council, on 17 February 1870 delineated a new system based on voluntary schools, which were to be given a year to remedy deficiencies of provision before the state, acting through elected school boards, could intervene to provide non-denominational elementary schools. The new schools, financed from central government grants and from the local rates, formed a solid base for the educational system of the twentieth century. Though local boards might vary in area from a rural parish to an urban borough, the enthusiasm of the big towns, London,

Manchester and Birmingham, led to the development of evening schools and higher day schools, technically going beyond their brief as providers of elementary education. The partial eclipse of the voluntary schools was bitterly resented by many Conservatives, and the 'Cockerton judgement' of 1900 gave the Conservative government an opportunity to reform state education and its administration.[7]

> The general body of Liberals in the House in the Bill not only a gratuitous affront to the School Boards, but an attack on the education of the working classes, and more especially on the popular higher grade schools. They felt, too, that much of the driving force behind the Government in this unnecessarily wide measure came from the Church and its fears for the voluntary schools.[8]

The 1902 Education Act abolished the boards and established the major local authority, the source of most educational finance, as the proper authority for organizing all state elementary and secondary education, except for a range of smaller local authorities (known as Part III authorities) which were allowed to organize elementary education in their areas.[9] Whatever the motive behind the Conservative government's policy of reorganizing educational administration, the major features of the system they instituted remain in force today, and educational development as a whole was not impeded.

Under the 1902 Act, the church schools, now known as non-provided schools, were for the first time explicitly subsidized out of the rates.[10] Control of them was apportioned between the sponsoring denomination and the local education authority, representatives of both being on the boards of managers. The buildings were almost wholly a church responsibility. Thus, it was the church schools which had most difficulty in undertaking educational development which involved the provision of new buildings.

It was not until 1936 that a system of subsidy for the new church schools was agreed;[11] little was actually built before the outbreak of war.

The elementary schools which the local education authorities took over were normally limited to children under sixteen, but a policy of experiment and variety in the elementary schools' curriculum had the powerful backing of Robert Morant, permanent secretary of the Board of Education.

As a result of the 1902 Act, many of the higher grade schools and pupil-teacher centres were taken over by the local education authorities and turned into secondary schools. However, Morant's policy[12] for secondary education was based on providing for the minority of secondary school children who went on to university. In the context of the 1904 regulations for secondary schools, whatever tradition the higher grade schools had built for themselves was to be crushed by the rigid application of the values of the private sector of education:

> Where two languages other than English are taken, and Latin is not one of them, the Board will require to be satisfied that the omission of Latin is for the advantage of the school.[13]

The placing of both elementary and secondary education under their control forced the local education authorities to consider the relations between them. In 1907 the regulations for secondary schools outlined a grant of £5 per head for each pupil between the ages of twelve and eighteen, but only on the condition that 25 per cent of admissions were of non-fee-paying pupils from public elementary schools. As demand for these places grew, so the qualifying examination became more competitive. Nevertheless, the education system was now organized as a ladder, recognizing the right in principle of any child, however poor, to as much education as he could benefit by. Between 1913 and 1927 the number of scholarships held rose from 60,000 to 143,000 per year.

In 1911, as part of the London system of elementary education, a number of 'central schools' were established. These schools were intended for the abler child who did not go to secondary schools; others were opened in Manchester, but they never became very numerous. They received official recognition in the 1918 Education Act; admissions were usually made on the basis of results of entrance examinations for secondary schools. Secondary technical education, although it was not favoured while Morant was at the Board of Education, slowly developed in the form of junior day technical classes and later junior technical schools, which aimed at artisan or domestic occupations. The normal entrance age was thirteen, and the pupils, fee-paying or on scholarships, were drawn from elementary schools. Between the wars, the number of pupils in these schools more than doubled to 27,901.[14]

In 1926, the consultative committee to the Board of Education published *The education of the adolescent* (the Hadow Report), the first government report to suggest the integration of the elementary and secondary systems, and the division of the system according to the age of the child – primary education before the age of eleven and secondary education afterwards:

Educational organisation is likely to be effective as it is based on the actual facts of the development of children and young persons. By the time that the age of eleven or twelve has been reached children have given some indication of differences in interest and abilities sufficient to make it possible and desirable to cater for them by means of schools of varying types, but which have, nevertheless, a broader common foundation.

Thus the state education system which had been designed to segregate children according to their socioeconomic class was now to be adapted so as to segregate them according to their various interests and abilities. The report envisaged a bipartite system of secondary education, with the central schools and senior elementary schools as secondary modern schools on an equal footing with the secondary grammar schools. There was no enlarged or modified role for the technical school. The essential precondition for the implementation of this plan was the reorganization of all-age elementary schools. By 1938, 'reorganization' was an essential part of the creed of all educational reformers, though with the financial difficulties of the early 1930s, not a great deal had been achieved; while only 28·3 per cent of provided schools were still unreorganized, the proportions of unreorganized Church of England and Roman Catholic schools were much greater (54·3 per cent and 55·2 per cent respectively).[15]

A setback in the development of a full free system of secondary education occurred after the financial crisis of 1931, when the Free Place scholarship system was abolished and replaced by a new Special Place scholarship system. Under this, the parents of children who were successful in the selection examination paid fees on a graded scale according to their income.

It was in 1938 that the consultative committee, under the chairmanship of Sir Will Spens (master of Corpus Christi College, Cambridge), reported on secondary education, this time 'with special reference to grammar schools and technical high schools'. The Spens committee modified the earlier Hadow plan for secondary education by adopting a tripartite model, in which technical high schools would play an important part:

It is becoming more and more evident that a single liberal or general education for all is impracticable, and that varying forms of both general and quasi-vocational education have to be evolved in order to meet the needs of boys and girls differing widely in intellectual and emotional capacity.[16]

The committee maintained that all secondary education was, in purpose, 'technical', and that 'technical education', in the more limited sense of separate secondary technical schools as they had developed in England, was as much a part of secondary education as that provided in the grammar school:

> Secondary education, therefore, as inclusive of technical, may be described as education conducted in view of the special life that has to be lived with the express purpose of fitting a person to live it.[17]

The picture of the psychological development of the child which the committee drew was based much more closely than that of the Hadow Report on the contemporary theories of psychologists, especially Cyril Burt; at the same time it was quite cautious in drawing conclusions from these theories:

> Certain qualitative changes in the child's personality, particularly the apparent emergence of specific aptitudes and interests, become noticeable after the age of eleven, though these may be attributable more to temperamental and environmental causes than to any spontaneous ripening of fresh capacities.[18]

> We were informed that, with a few exceptions, it is possible at a very early age to predict with some degree of accuracy the ultimate level of a child's intellectual power, but this is true only of general intelligence and does not hold good in respect of specific aptitudes or interests . . .[19]

The committee accepted contemporary findings of the development and variation of intelligence, and tried to reconcile them with its proposed system of secondary education:

> In general, minor differences, which were hardly noticeable in the Infant School, will be distinctly observable in the Primary Schools, and by the age of eleven will have increased so much that it will no longer be sufficient to sort out different children into different classes. Different children, by the age of eleven, if justice is to be done to their varying capacities, require types of education varying in certain important respects.[20]

Any action on the consultative committee's report had to be deferred on the outbreak of war, just as the proposed raising of the school-leaving age to fifteen in September 1939 had to be abandoned.[21] At the time plans were beginning to be formulated for educational reconstruction after the war, one other important report, with its own philosophy of secondary education, was published. The Norwood Report (1943)[22] is the least defensible in the light of subsequent experience and research; it is the least intellectually profound, but it is also probably the nearest in tone and bias to the prevailing theory of education among many establishment administrators.[23] Quite explicitly they saw the problem in terms of practicability of administration and justified their conclusions in terms of established practices:

> School organisation and class instruction must assume that individuals have enough in common as regards capacities and interests to justify certain rough groupings. ... Our point is that rough groupings, whatever may be their ground, have in fact established themselves in general educational experience, and the recognition of such groupings in educational practice has been justified both during the period of education and in the after careers of the pupils.[24]

Much educational research since the war has set out to challenge this point of view.

The Norwood Report defined three types of mind and proposed three types of schools: the pupil who was to go to the grammar school was 'interested in learning for its own sake';[25] the technical school would take pupils 'whose interests and abilities lay markedly in the field of applied science or applied art';[26] while the third and much larger group would consist of those who deal 'more easily with concrete things than with ideas'.[27] The justification for these three types of mind was not the explicit product of objective enquiry, though there were psychologists working on theories that intelligence was a function of qualitatively different abilities, verbal or spatial; it was simply 'the experience accumulated during the development of secondary education in this country', quoted above. The partial justification of the *status quo* produced a predictable reaction from the most radical reformers, but this theme in the committee's report nevertheless seems to be the inspiration behind the 1944 Education Act.

The academic study of psychology has expanded greatly during the twentieth century, especially in the sub-discipline of educational psychology. Researches in educational psychology recorded for the period 1935–51 are almost treble the number recorded for the period 1918–34, despite the retarding effect of the war years. In other fields of educational research (theory, history, methods) the increase in the second half of this period was only about two-thirds.[28] Research within educational psychology has been uneven too: some university departments, such as Birmingham under C. W. Valentine, expanded rapidly in this field, while others neglected it.[29] There was also recognition among administrators of the growing importance of educational psychology. As early as 1913 the LCC appointed a psychologist to its staff; Cyril Burt, one of the outstanding figures in this field, held the post from 1922. A government pamphlet on the use of psychological tests was published in 1924.[30] The reformers of examinations, among others, drew their intellectual sustenance from the psychologists' research:

> Indeed, all the reports which have been mentioned (Hadow, Spens, Norwood) bear evidence, whether in the text or in the appendices, to the importance which the educationalists were attaching to the work of the psychologists; there is a kind of psychological background to them all, and that is something new in educational literature.[31]

The expansion of educational psychology in university departments of education almost swamped research in other fields of education; one observer notes that there was an 'apparent absence of studies devoted to the assessment of aims and values in contemporary educational thought'.[32] The assumptions of the psychologists were hardly open to question, except among themselves, until after the war. One of their most powerful weapons was the appearance of 'objectivity' and 'science' which the emphasis on measurement, the use of statistics and the sometimes esoteric vocabulary gave to their research. One educationist with a profound belief in this 'scientific' approach was nevertheless acutely aware that 'the real danger is in the use of a statistical tool by the untutored and the unskilled'.[33] Resistance to the psychologists was found mainly among practising teachers of whom some 'profess to have more faith in their own intuitive judgement than in the rigorous analysis of the statisticians'.[34] Some academics were wary of the increasing emphasis on psychology in teacher training:

> Anyone examining the papers set to teachers in training cannot fail to be impressed by the preponderance of questions dealing with psychological rather than educational questions; the interwar literature on the subject tells the same tale; indeed, the dividing line between the two tended to be progressively obliterated, and the theory of education to be lost in a theory of psychology.[35]

The emphasis on psychology, the emphasis on 'measurement', and the needs of educational administrators, produced a vast literature and research on tests of intelligence. In the process of adaptation from their original purpose as aids in a sociological survey of the nation's manpower, via their use as aids to teachers and school doctors in detecting the mentally deficient, to their widespread employment after the war as the basis of selection for secondary education, intelligence tests came to be widely regarded as the key to socially objective selection. The psychologists (or at least many of them) claimed that intelligence was innate, fixed and general.[36] Thus schooling and domestic and social background had little effect on it, or on the measures of it provided by the tests. The disparity between a child with high intelligence and a child with low intelligence became more marked as they grew older, and by eleven or twelve it was thought that separate schools would be necessary.[37] An important task then was to refine and multiply tests of intelligence. No fewer than 118 of the 775 theses presented at British universities for higher degrees in education during the period 1918–43 were on intelligence tests.[38] Though Godfrey Thomson was one of the leading experts on 'intelligence', he tried to reconcile his findings as a psychologist with his democratic ideal of social solidarity and his belief in the system of the American high school for all pupils of secondary school age.[39] However, twenty years later as professor of education at the University of Edinburgh, he was in charge of Moray House, the source of millions[40] of copies of intelligence tests used in post-war secondary selection. In this way educational psychologists came to have something of a vested interest in the perpetuation of the concept of general, fixed, innate intelligence. If intelligence was not fixed or innate, but subject to social environment and remedial teaching techniques, then a considerable part of their work might be jettisoned, and their prestige as 'scientists' would suffer.

Although educational psychologists remained ostensibly 'unattached intellectuals',[41] they cooperated on many occasions with local authorities in introducing intelligence tests into selection procedure, and their work generally had far-reaching implications for the organization and content of education. Some psychologists explored the implications themselves:

> Now suppose that a child's education will really be determined by his capacity and promise; suppose further that entry into any profession or occupation whatever will be the reward of merit and not the result of family influence or school of origin; then will any occupation or position or responsibility be equally available to every pupil?

> The correct answer would seem to be 'no', particularly in a free society, since not so many 'duds' would get through in that case. Again, the limiting factors are the upper limits of intellectual capacity coupled with temperamental traits. Even in a democracy, or rather because of a democracy, allocation of young people to different vocational levels will depend, in the long run, on their capacities. Therefore, in so far as secondary school curricula are connected with vocational preparation, each adolescent in a free society will get the training most appropriate to his high potential vocational capacity.[42]

Some psychologists were working on the theory that aptitudes for different types of education and adult occupation were innate and were discernible in the child by means of special tests. The Norwood Report, with different premises and a different set of facts, also encouraged the belief that specialized secondary schools could be filled with neatly labelled eleven- and twelve-year-olds. Just as the administrators selected what suited them from the findings of the psychologists, so did the general public. J. C. Flugel found that the 'layman' agreed with the psychologists in thinking that 'tests are better than examinations for measuring intelligence'; but, on the other hand, he parted company with the psychologists in being 'ignorant or neglectful of the evidence pointing to the inheritability of intelligence', and 'inadequately informed concerning the relative constancy of the IQ'.[43]

Psychologists themselves were often quick to point out that they had been misinterpreted. Burt quickly demolished the psychological arguments of the Norwood Report and other unwarranted conclusions by administrators and politicians:

> In the present stage of knowledge, psychological reasons for specialisation are probably less important than non-psychological. ... Local Authorities should therefore be allowed the utmost freedom to experiment with different modes of school organisation and school allocation, according to the requirements of their own particular districts.[44]

Other educationists took their cue from Burt's critiques of official and semi-official policy. But the prevailing belief in the child's rights in education, in the ordering of education as much to suit his immediate needs as his future career, encouraged unconcern with the social and occupational implications of the education system. M. L. Jacks commented:

[It is held that] one school is 'better' than another because it offers its pupils better opportunities of getting on in life; whether it does so or not is an arguable point, but even if the claim is substantiated the school will be no better than another for the pupil who because of his temperament or intellectual capacity is unable to avail himself of his opportunities; and if it leads him to an occupation or a way of life for which he is unfitted, it will be an immeasurably worse school.[45]

On the whole, the academics, administrators, educationists and politicians all found little fault with the organizational outline of the state education system, other than the administrative division between elementary and secondary education; once this artificial barrier had been removed and more generous finance provided, the framework would suffice for the provision of an education attuned to post-war needs. Burt had already produced evidence which purported to show that

wide inequality of personal income is largely, though not entirely, an indirect effect of the wide inequality of innate intelligence.[46]

Nevertheless, as the artificial consensus among politicians necessary to the passing of the 1944 Education Act began to crack, critical psychologists were also heard. The anticipated development of aptitude testing never achieved the same success as intelligence testing. There were claims that the evidence showed the environment considerably affected the ability to answer intelligence tests, and the usefulness of these tests themselves was questioned:

All that has been shown in fact is that they measure the ability to answer intelligence test questions.[47]

C. M. Fleming, a social psychologist, suggested possible lines of attack on the post-war secondary education system when she claimed

If there is any reason to doubt the early fixity of the intelligence quotient, the abruptness of other changes during adolescence, the clear delimitations of specific aptitudes, and the absolute necessity for class instruction, the foundations of much of the present structure of educational organisation will have been shaken.[48]

By the end of 1940 questions of educational reform were beginning to be discussed widely. A joint letter from religious leaders had been published in *The Times* under the title 'Foundations of peace'.[49] As might be expected, it asserted the need for the Christian religion as the basis of education, but in its specific proposals for reform it antagonized the teachers and others by reviving all the earlier controversies over religious control of the schools.[50]

The coalition government seems to have had no plans for rapid major changes in the education system; indeed, much of the general enthusiasm for reform was based on the suspicion that the government might go back on its pledge to end the suspension of the 1936 Education Act after the war.[51] However, discussions of reform went forward at religious and educational conferences in 1941 and 1942, and as a result of various pressures in 1942 a 'Green Book' of draft proposals was issued by the Board of Education to selected interest groups as a basis for detailed private negotiations.[52]

> Had the representatives of the teachers and the administrators taken their cue from the philosopher the story of the reform movement would have been very different and a good deal happier. Regrettably they took it from the politicians. They did indeed accept from the philosopher (as did the politicians) the general principle of 'equality of opportunity', but instead of courageously analysing its implications and attempting to give expression to these in concrete proposals, they were content to accept as a basis for discussion the modest programme of remedial measures which the Board of Education put before them.[53]

This strategy, or lack of it, was unaffected by the minority movements in favour of more radical reform which appeared at group conferences in 1942 and 1943.

The inter-war period was pre-eminently the period for progressive ideas in education; but this did not reflect simply a dominance of educational cranks. It was part of the widespread urge for reform characteristic of the left but also strong among the younger generation of Conservative politicians. The post-war Labour government's legislation in the economic field, the implementation of much of Beveridge's plan for social insurance, and the post-war revivification of Conservative Party policy, were all anticipated in spirit by the 1944 Education Act. While the political left was still not clear about its views on the form of 'secondary education for all', the NUT, predictably, and the AMA, less so, were strongly in favour of the institution of multilateral schools.[54] Approached from another angle, the existing post-primary system also came under attack because of the competitive entry system. External examination in general 'caused a great deal of ill-feeling' between the NUT and the local authorities represented by the AEC.[55] The Spens Report, with its implicit acceptance of a bipartite or tripartite system, and consequently 'selection', was also the subject of official attack in the NAS.[56]

Nevertheless, the questioning of the established education system that is indicated seems small beside the record of debate generated by the war, by the disruption of the service, and by the draft proposals put forward by the Board of Education. The consideration of these proposals was nothing if not thorough: the NUT appointed five panels to consider the various aspects of the board's proposals. Few educational groups did not publish their own proposals or reactions, and this was despite the intense activity involved in maintaining a skeleton education service during the war:

> Consideration has been given to questions of war-time nurseries, the supply of milk to school-children, agricultural education, clothing and footwear for necessitous children, the purchase tax on school requisites, school holidays and the liberation of children for potato-planting and harvesting, to mention no other, and in all these matters representations have been made to the Board of Education and other Ministries.[57]

Support for the multilateral school was redoubled rather than dissipated by the experience of war. The IAAM produced a report[58] in 1942 favouring the combined school, and the following motion was put to the annual conference that year by its executive:

> The Association reaffirms its belief that secondary education should be given in multilateral schools catering for the need of all pupils in properly equipped and well staffed departments of many kinds.[59]

The only opposition, though a prophetic one, was on grounds of size. In its comments on the white paper on educational reconstruction, the association's leaders more pointedly asserted that:

> Many of the difficulties resulting from this new conception of secondary education can only be resolved by the general support of the idea of the combined school and its adoption to a much greater degree than is officially envisaged.[60]

Among the educational 'promotion' organizations, the NEF was adopting a similar view. The commission set up to examine secondary education after the war, and the summer conference of the English section in 1943, both came to the conclusion that the 'multilateral principle' was the one to follow. A potential source of conflict lay in the different emphasis which the commission put on 'various types of secondary education' in 'different departments of the same school'[61] and the conference on the school 'which need not be larger than many existing secondary schools'.[62]

A more cautious approach can be seen in the welcome the 1943 NUT conference gave to 'substantial experiments' with respect to multilateral schools and the place they might occupy in the future of post-primary education.[63] Caution in undertaking experimentation may be seen in the CCA's reaction to the Norwood Report's call for maximum flexibility in the age of transfer to secondary education: the CCA's advisory sub-committee thought any variation from the eleven plus should be 'wholly exceptional'. They did advise a continuous review of a child's allocation between eleven and thirteen, but in this they showed implicitly their basic acceptance of a tripartite system.[64]

Though the secondary associations formulated their policies separately, they also cooperated as far as possible in the drawing-up of a common set of proposals by the Joint Four committee. Here the solid commitment of the IAAM and AMA produced only the more cautious statement that:

> The social and educational opportunities presented by 'multilateral schools' are of great importance, and full advantage should be taken of the post-war building and re-building opportunities to establish a number of experimental multilateral schools; though it is recognised that such schools do not present the only solution to many of the problems associated with the secondary stage.[65]

And the Joint Four's reply to the government's draft proposals for education make no mention of multilaterals; it is more concerned to oppose the suggestion 'that all grammar schools should remain as at present until all other types of post-primary schools have been dealt with'.[66]

There was rather more scepticism of the multilateral school at the assistant mistresses' conference of 1943, when an attempt to include it in a composite motion listing essential items in the education bill was defeated by 102 votes to 71.[67] Nevertheless, it remains true that this was the period of greatest enthusiasm among groups for the multilateral school. Is it possible to dismiss this support as the result of the disorientation of war, or the euphoria engendered by theoretical reconstruction? To put into perspective the later criticisms of the multilateral or comprehensive concept, it is certainly necessary to remember this short-lived but widespread enthusiasm.

The education bill was introduced into the House of Commons on 16 December 1943, and its main principles met with general approval. Criticisms were either softened by the prevailing general enthusiasm for educational reform, or overridden by the government. The Act received the Royal Assent on 4 August 1944, and educationists began to prepare for the vast problems of implementing it in the aftermath of war.

The 1944 Education Act covered all levels of state education and the independent schools, but its most important sections (of those which were implemented) refer to the state system of secondary education.

Secondary education was henceforth to refer to education beyond the age of eleven, and the local education authorities had the duty, not just the power, as previously, to provide it efficiently. The Act spells out in some detail the meaning of efficiency in this context:

> ... the schools available for an area shall not be deemed to be sufficient unless they are sufficient in number, character, and equipment to afford for all pupils opportunities for education offering such variety of instruction and training as may be desirable in view of their different ages, abilities, and aptitudes, and of the different periods for which they may be expected to remain at school.[68]

As soon as the Act came into force, the local education authorities were to begin to prepare long-term plans for the development of the education system in their area for submission to the new minister, who could approve or reject them or ask for modifications.[69] This long-term scrutiny of the local education authorities' efficiency was to be complemented by day-to-day observation through the inspectorate, and through the sifting of individual proposals which had to be ratified by the ministry.

The Act also provided for the raising of the minimum school-leaving age.[70] This had previously been arranged, under the 1936 Education Act, for September 1939, but the war had forced a postponement. Under the 1944 Education Act the age was to be raised automatically to fifteen in 1945, but the minister could, and did, defer the change until 1947. No date was fixed by the Act for implementing the undertaking to raise the minimum school-leaving age to sixteen.

The history of English education reflects the history of social and economic class divisions; the initial development on the voluntary principle and the subsequent piecemeal additions and reforms by the state have ensured that at no time has educational policy run far ahead of quite generally accepted needs. At no time has there been a thorough revaluation of the education system as a whole or a unified central direction of policy.

Contrasting images of the 'ladder' and the 'broad highway' of education are a reflection of the 'élitist' preconceptions of English educationists. The process of development which culminated in the 1944 Education Act is a process of modification of the system of selection, of élite recruitment. Those who have looked at secondary education as having immediate value for the child have not succeeded in eradicating this élite conception from its position as the basis of English education, rather than just a necessary part of it. In particular, the dominating values in education have been those of administrators. The period of maximum compatibility between administrators and educationists came with the 1944 Education Act, when the theories and findings of educational psychologists were both used and misused in support of the modified education system then at the planning stage. Without technically becoming 'bureaucratic intellectuals', the psychologists nevertheless filled this role through their commitment to the development of intelligence tests and through the intellectual justification with which they provided the educational policy-makers. The value of the 1944 Education Act lay in its embodiment of a consensus, especially among religious denominations, that had been fought for during two years of private negotiations; it was the justification of the policy of 'continuity' followed by both Labour and Conservative presidents of the Board of Education between the wars. The Act was inadequate in relation to the expectations of the contemporary education public, in that consensus was achieved at the expense of educational vision and innovation. Its promise of transformation was illusory: the great strides taken by education in this country since the war are not attributable so much to the educational provisions of the Act, but to the increasing importance of education in the economic and political life of the country, of which the 1944 Education Act is but a symbol.

This account of education before 1944, and some of the values inherent in it and in educational policy-making, emphasizes those aspects and values which are most important for a consideration of the direction and effectiveness of educational pressure-group policy. The groups, too, have simplified educational values along these lines in the course of extreme pressure, and have sometimes seen the comprehensive school as an uncompromising threat to them or as the promise of deliverance from them.

The educational policy-maker clearly does not operate in a policy vacuum: to some extent he creates or sustains his own constraints on policy options, but to a greater extent he is constrained by previous policies, standards of public provision and events outside his effective control. The commitment of British governments during this century to the provision of free primary and secondary education, compulsory for those between the ages of five and (from 1947) fifteen, presents the policy-maker with a clearly defined area of concern, and also puts his plans for development (or retrenchment) at the mercy of variations in the total eligible child population. If his aims involve the bringing into service of new institutions, new facilities and new equipment, he is limited in his initiatives. The radical may urge him to speed up the rate of replacement, but even the most radical need some time to replace bricks and mortar. If educational policy is to achieve its aim through change in the curriculum or in teaching technique, then the existing stock of teachers may prove a hindrance in many different ways.

This much is clear to any educational administrator, though it can often be forgotten in enthusiasm for reform or in appraisal of the effectiveness of policy-makers. In the case of English secondary education since the 1944 Education Act these constraints have operated both to promote and to retard the aims of policy-makers.

Between 1938 and 1947 the total number of pupils on the register of maintained and assisted primary and secondary schools in England and Wales diminished by about half a million. This was the direct consequence of the fall in the birth rate for much of the inter-war period. But it was clear that the rise in the birth rate since 1941, and especially the sudden large increase in 1946 and 1947, would pose acute problems of educational provision, first at primary level in the early 1950s and then at the end of the decade in the secondary schools. Thus at the end of 1950, of 952 new schools under construction, 738 were primary schools and only 48 of these were replacements of existing premises. Of the 214 secondary schools under construction only 13 were replacements. The scope for new institutional arrangements in secondary education was thus largely constrained by the nature and location of the existing stock of schools.

The most pressing problem for the ministry and for local authorities was the housing and staffing of the extra classes resulting from the statutory raising of the minimum school-leaving age. During 1948 secondary schools had to cope with nearly 400,000 more pupils remaining in full-time education. Voluntary staying on at school beyond the minimum leaving age was also on the increase, and despite the problems of accommodation and staffing it posed, the ministry was concerned to encourage the trend.[71]

The pressure on places in infant schools and in junior schools continued throughout most of the 1950s. In 1958 the total number of primary school pupils declined by 55,000 marking the first reduction in pressure on junior schools since 1949.[72] Although secondary school population was still increasing as a result of the earlier rise in the birth rate, the government saw the opportunity for a substantial improvement in secondary education provision in the period up to 1964.[73] Sixth forms had nearly doubled in size and the number of pupils staying on beyond the age of fifteen had risen from 187,000 in 1948 to 290,000 in 1958. During the following decade the proportion of pupils free to leave school who chose to remain continued to increase dramatically as is shown in the table below.[74]

| Year (January) | Percentage of age-group in maintained schools | | |
	Age 15	Age 16	Age 17
1959	29·2	14·6	7·0
1964	51·3	19·0	9·8
1969	61·6	27·9	14·5

Source: Department of Education and Science and former Ministry of Education, annual reports for appropriate years.

But by the middle of the 1960s the rise in the birth rate at the end of the previous decade was again causing problems in the provision of sufficient primary school places. In 1964 most of the £200 million school-building programme for 1965–8 had been decided. Most of the new primary places planned were to meet the basic needs of an expanding school population, as were about half of the secondary school places.

The school population has consistently increased throughout the postwar period and is likely to continue to do so into the foreseeable future. The constraints that this has placed on policy-making have not prevented (in some cases they have encouraged) substantial changes in the nature of the education provided. Institutionally the changes are clear though their significance can be exaggerated. The next table indicates the deviation from the institutional pattern suggested immediately after the war. Separate technical schools and their ethos have tended to be absorbed either into the selective system or into comprehensive schools. Nearly a quarter

Percentage of all secondary school pupils in different types of secondary schools in England and Wales

Year (January)	Modern	Technical	Grammar	Comprehensive
1951	58·5	3·8	26·0	negligible
1961	53·8	3·1	22·1	4·5
1969	40·0	1·7	19·4	23·8

Note: Percentages do not total 100 because of pupils in other types of public secondary school or in assisted and independent sectors of education.
Source: Social trends, HMSO, 1970, table 77.

of secondary school pupils were in comprehensive schools by 1969 compared with 4·5 per cent only eight years earlier.

If fluctuations in the birth rate made 'roofs over heads' the most pressing demand on policy-makers, it was in the field of educational building that the 1944 Education Act could clearly be seen to imply new and considerable demands on financial resources. The replacement of bombed schools, the raising of the school-leaving age, the abolition of all-age schools, and parity of esteem between secondary schools of different types, would all have been costly and adventurous policies even if Britain had not had to recover from the effects of war in other equally costly ways.

The virtual cessation of educational building during the war prevented immediate visible progress until preparatory planning at national and local level was under way. In 1946 building was restricted to 'a miscellany varying from war damage repair, temporary building for the school meals service, the adaptation of buildings for use as emergency training colleges for teachers and small contracts for the relief of overcrowding, to the first small instalment of building for raising the compulsory school age'.[75] Very soon the ministry had to establish priorities, dropping plans for an expansion of nursery schools, adult education centres and youth clubs. Even with the emphasis on an emergency programme centrally organized to cope with the raising of the school-leaving age, only 42 per cent of the rooms required by September 1947 were completed.[76]

The demands of the immediate post-war period as well as the new definitions of central government's role in education led to a more extensive and positive participation in educational building by the ministry. Problems of materials supply, and of escalating costs, stimulated a concerted effort to standardize building. At the same time the actual nature of building was largely determined by unavoidable priorities. Whereas between the wars attention was concentrated on building senior elementary schools to provide for Hadow reorganization and the raising of the school-leaving age, some three-quarters of the new schools brought into use between 1945 and 1950 were for infant and junior children. A drive to reorganize rural all-age schools was launched in 1954, and in 1958 a five-year programme of educational building worth £300 million had as its main aim the final elimination of such schools. While primary school improvements were not to be wholly neglected the government was 'satisfied that the most urgent task is to provide secondary schools in which a sound and varied secondary education can be offered to children of secondary school age'.[77] Priorities were to change again to provision of primary school places in the second half of the next decade. In 1963, of a total of 260,000 school places started, 142,000 were for secondary school pupils; by 1966, the larger total of 306,000 contained only 96,500 secondary places.[78]

While parity of esteem meant equally equipped buildings it also meant staff of equal capacity and range. Immediately after the war the demand was for more teachers, especially men teachers. By 1948 the number of men teachers in maintained and assisted primary and secondary schools had nearly doubled, largely as a result of the work of the emergency training colleges. Salary scales for teachers were unified in an attempt to create equality between former elementary schools and the grammar schools. In 1949 only 14 per cent of teachers in secondary modern schools were graduates, while in technical schools the proportion was 45 per cent, and in grammar schools 78 per cent. Ten years later the situation had not changed significantly, nor had it done so by 1969, except that the comprehensive schools cutting across the traditional boundaries had on average 45 per cent graduate staff, compared with an average for all maintained primary and secondary schools of 30 per cent.[79]

The officially recognized problem of parity of esteem can be, and has been, variously tackled. However, the particular concern of this study is the radical proposal for institutional change at secondary school level and its promotion and partial implementation since 1944.

Chapter Three

DEFINING secondary education: the Labour government 1945–51

In the general election of 1945, Labour had gained a large majority. Though new legislation was envisaged to put through a variety of social and economic reforms the party had been developing since its inception, in the field of education the passing of the 1944 Education Act meant that it was administration – the leadership of the local authorities, the preparation and ratification of development plans, building programmes, teacher training, the supply of materials – which was to demonstrate the nature and quality of a Labour education policy. The importance of education was acknowledged by a seat in the cabinet for the minister. Prime Minister Attlee saw Chuter Ede, who had seconded R. A. Butler during the preparation and passing of the 1944 Education Act, as the ideal choice for minister of education. But Chuter Ede was made home secretary, and Ellen Wilkinson appointed minister of education.[1] It is difficult to tell what the attitude of Chuter Ede was to comprehensive schools at that time. During the debate on the education bill he had not shown any preference; later he denied that a tripartite system was implied by the Act and in the 1950s he came out as a supporter of the comprehensive schools.[2] It seems probable that, like so many of his colleagues who went through a similar period of readjustment of attitude, he was not at first very firmly committed either for or against comprehensive schools.

Miss Wilkinson had a reputation as a radical, though Attlee seems to have given her the education post on the grounds that she was a woman.[3] The *New Statesman* commented that:

> Ellen Wilkinson, always an enthusiast for educational reform, will have plenty of informed supporters.[4]

It was with the planning of secondary education that the new minister had to face her first outright criticism from members of the Labour Party both in the House of Commons and in the local authorities.

The electoral swing to the left nationally was reflected locally in increased representation of the Labour Party in most local education authorities, and control in some counties and a large number of county boroughs. In the localities, education was a much more important area of policy, and the chance of an active clash between local and national bodies more likely. The statutory requirement for long-term development plans in education to be drawn up by the local education authorities and submitted to the minister for approval supplied the framework for dispute.

The significant point about local authority plans for the development of secondary education after the war was that they represented considerable deviation from the model handed down from the Ministry of Education and the adaptation of educational principles to local situations. The acceptance of a system of segregation arose not from a belief in the quasi-psychology of the Norwood Report but from the exigencies of the existing educational systems, in terms of sites, buildings and staff. Even then, variety and experiment are the keynote of most of the plans. While only two county authorities and three county borough authorities intended to set up only comprehensive schools, nine and eleven respectively were planning at least one such school. While over half the county borough authorities were planning to provide secondary education only in separate grammar, technical and modern schools, no more than a quarter of counties had similar intentions.[5] Varieties of the tripartite system in the form of bilateral schools were common. Most authorities displayed a combination of intimate knowledge of their local problems and scepticism for general solutions:

> It is dangerous at this stage for educationists to mesmerise themselves with educational statistics and for education authorities to lay down hard and fast rules as to the character and type of this or that secondary school. After all that has been said and written in recent years with regard to types of school and types of child, it can only be said now that because of the unpredictability of human material and the limitations of educational truth, whatever types of secondary school are decided upon by the East Riding Education Committee, they will inevitably make mistakes. Time and experience gained while the new secondary schools are sorting themselves into shape,

rather than current educational fashions, will enable these inevitable mistakes to be put right.[6]

Though the advocacy of a complete system of comprehensive or multilateral schools was by no means the prerogative of Labour-controlled local councils, in cases where there was a political motivation behind the plan, publicity and controversy were considerable.

There was an undoubted political impetus behind Middlesex's plans for a system of comprehensive schools. The educational development sub-committee of Middlesex education committee had considered certain proposals as early as November 1945, but it was after the first post-war county council elections, which put Labour in power and changed the composition of the education committee, that the principle of multilateralism was adopted.[7]

The distinctive feature of the Middlesex plan was the size of the comprehensive schools proposed. The long-term intentions of the committee were to provide secondary schools of only four-, five- or six-form entry, half the size of London's proposed comprehensives, and quite out of line with the Ministry of Education's suggested minimum size for non-selective secondary schools. In the short term, as an earnest of intention, it was planned to start some comprehensives by grouping existing schools, by small alterations, or simply by making entrance to suitable grammar schools non-selective.[8]

A conference on the plan was held at the Guildhall,[9] at which members of the education committee and of divisional executives were present with county and local education officers. Teachers' associations at local and national level were also represented. As the discussion proceeded it became apparent that the majority of the divisional executives broadly approved the council's plans. But there were some queries on precisely the question of the size of the proposed schools and the consequences of this for the development of academic sixth forms. The chairman of the education committee was prepared to concede on details but not on the basic principles. The schools chosen as the prototype comprehensives were, indeed, slightly larger than those envisaged in the plan as ideal, but still much smaller than the ministry's requirements.[10]

The county's teachers appear to have been divided from the start on the value of the experiment with comprehensives: the supporters had their main strength within the local organizations of the NUT, while opponents were to be found in the secondary associations. During this period the Middlesex teachers' association consistently submitted motions for debate by the NUT annual conference, pledging support for the comprehensive schools; some of the most vocal supporters of the comprehensive school at national level came from the Middlesex association and it had also a very active group of Communist and left-wing Socialist members.[11] In September 1948 the association held its own conference for teachers on the comprehensive school, and in the same year the NUT education committee agreed that the association should keep adequate records concerning the development of comprehensive schools in their area.[12] On the other hand there was an early statement of opposition to the plan by the Middlesex technical association, claiming that there was a strong tradition of technical school education in Middlesex which should be fostered, not abolished.[13]

The Central Joint Four worked with the Middlesex Joint Four in mounting opposition to the plan,[14] which in its initial stage involved the abolition of Ashford grammar school as a selective school. Three hundred people attended the meeting addressed by the general secretary of the AMA[15] and the local Joint Four organized a meeting at which Professor Kandel, an opponent of comprehensive schools from America, spoke. One MP claimed at this meeting 'that the 1944 Act imposed impossible tasks. . . . We ought first to have completed reorganisation'.[16] The head and staff of Ashford grammar school wrote to the local Press suggesting that only one experimental school should be set up, while the existing tripartite system should be developed.

Nevertheless, in February 1948 the Middlesex secondary education sub-committee urged the establishment of some comprehensive schools the following September by the short-term methods already outlined,[17] and the county council gave its approval to the whole education development plan.[18] Opposition centred on the proposal to merge Ashford grammar school with another secondary school 'about a mile away'.[19] The headmaster of the school, among others, received notice to quit, his first formal intimation of the proposed changes.[20] It was in this context that the general secretary of the AMA said that his immediate concern was to ensure that everything possible should be done to protect the legitimate professional interests of members of staff of Ashford grammar school. Taking the lead now in protesting against the plan was the Middlesex secondary schools' association, which comprised a number of grammar school old pupils' associations. With considerable expertise, presumably supplied through sympathetic teachers' organizations, this association organized publicity for its campaign. It arranged a protest meeting for parents, which was advertised in the local Press and on posters; 10,000 handbills were distributed. A hostile audience of 500–600 heard Mrs Forbes, the chairman of the education committee and the chief education officer defend the proposals, while Kenneth Lindsay MP and a local teacher spoke against them. Only 25 people voted against a motion at the end of the meeting to be sent to the Ministry of Education:

> We citizens of South-West Middlesex hereby protest against the introduction of comprehensive schools in this area as submitted to you by the Middlesex County Council, and we hereby invoke sections 10, 11, 68 and 76 of the Education Act 1944.[21]

Documentary evidence and arguments were sent with this motion on behalf of the 10,000 affiliated members of the constituent societies of parents, old pupils and teaching staffs of the Middlesex secondary schools' association. The evidence was 'lacking in new ideas'[22] and was totally opposed to comprehensives but it was the first protest to be pressed to ministerial level.

The south-west Middlesex divisional executive had also asked the county council for reconsideration of the plan[23] and any alteration to the status of Ashford grammar school was postponed for a year. Two other experimental comprehensives were opened, however: Mellow Lane and Mount Grace.[24]

The county council was still Labour-controlled when the Ministry of Education sent back its development plan for reconsideration on the expected ground of the small size of the comprehensive schools proposed.[25] While considering its reply the education committee consulted the ministry as to whether it should allow children in the catchment area of the newly-established comprehensives to take the eleven-plus examination for entrance to selective schools in other areas. The ministry was of the opinion that the children should not take the examination but the immediate protests of parents notified of this ruling led the education committee to disregard the ministry's advice.[26]

In the county council elections of May 1949 Labour lost control of the council and the new Conservative majority immediately went ahead with the revision of the development plan along bilateral lines.[27] Despite the protests of some of the divisional executives who maintained their support for the comprehensive school and refused to cooperate, the county education committee went ahead in the knowledge of strong support from parents.[28] The final blow to earlier plans for comprehensives was struck by the parents again, when it was found that every one of the children in the catchment area of one of the comprehensive schools who had been selected for an academic stream had preferred to go to a selective school. The county education committee felt that there was no alternative for the school but to revert to a secondary modern.[29]

As hopes began to be translated into plans, and later into actuality, a distinctive theme in discussion among education groups was the role of 'experiments'. The wholesale commitment of several organizations was modified to a support for 'experiments' with multilateral schools, apparently in an attempt to avoid a hard line either way. But this was not the only use to which the convenient formula was put: the IAHM reported the plans of the Foundation for Educational Research to cooperate with some local authorities on conducting 'experimental' secondary schools of all types including a multilateral school.[30] For the headmistresses, 'experiment' involved the establishment of different types of multilateral school, in a broad attack on the problems of selection in the new secondary education.[31] The London teachers' association was able to reconcile its support for the London School Plan to 'convert the whole of the post-primary system of London into multilateral units' with the definition 'large-scale experiments'.[32] More cautious, and more typical, was the view of the secretary of the AEC that

> there would be virtue in careful experiment in a multilateral school where the area made such experiment opportune; it would be most unwise to embark on a general policy of multilateral schools.[33]

It was this last interpretation of 'experiment' which gave rise in time in some quarters to an emphasis not on the careful observation of multilateral schools at work, but on the limitations on innovation beyond which experiments became established policy. Some suggested that a wholesale system of multilaterals contravened the 1944 Education Act, whereas one 'experimental' school would not. In 1947, the IAHM issued a special statement expressing their new fears. They had hesitated

> to make any formal pronouncement on the multilateral school as it had hoped that some schools of this type would be begun as an experiment. Now that so many LEAs propose to adopt the multilateral school as the only form of secondary school, it seems necessary for the Association to express an opinion.

They concluded:

> It seems to us strange that a form of education too little understood for profitable consideration and discussion by adult educationists

seems likely to become for the majority of our adolescent population the only kind of secondary education available to them, a kind so unfamiliar that parents, teachers and pupils alike who have had experience of the older and more differentiated types of secondary school show no eagerness at all to welcome it.[34]

By 1949, the headmasters were firmly opposed to 'further experiments' in the comprehensive school system.[35] It is noticeable that 'multilateral' and 'experiments' had become synonymous by this time; but a special report on the secondary school prepared by the NAS, advocating the common school, turns the arguments upside down by saying:

> Children have been classified at 11 for many years. There is surely no need for experiment with separate grammar schools.[36]

It was, however, experiments with and investigations into classification and 'selection' that were again to dominate educational discussions as they had done in the 1930s. Official thinking and the majority of plans by LEAs involved some sort of selection process, and the reactions of educational organizations were in terms of support for different criteria, as much as of general support or opposition. As early as 1945, the NUT agreed to set up a consultative committee 'to prepare a report on the methods of placing children in the different types of post-primary schools',[37] and the early plans of the NFER, to whose policy all the partners in education contributed, were for:

> major research, which will provide, it is to be hoped, a satisfactory answer to the question of the validity of the 11 +.[38]

Opposition to the whole concept of selection was voiced however by one president of the NUT:

> The division of secondary schools into three types suggests that children are also divided into three types ... the experience of most teachers fails to discover that this trichotomy actually exists in nature. It appears to be founded not on psychological insight but upon administrative convenience.[39]

Criticism of the selection process was by no means confined to outright opponents. To the headmasters in the IAHM, at least at first, or at least for some of them, the danger was that 'the intelligence test might be the determining factor'.[40] Discussing the Surrey development plan, the editor of the *AMA Journal* commented:

the plan is based on the assumption that it is impossible to select children for different types of education at the age of eleven. This assumption is strongly contested.[41]

The nature of the danger in concentrating on intelligence tests as elaborated by the president of the IAHM illuminates a conception of grammar school education soon to be superseded; he feared

the probable elimination of the boy who was not good academically, but who had character, loyalty and other virtues which made him and his kind the backbone of the grammar school. He did not go as far as to agree that the grammar schools might be filled with 'smart Alecs', but believed that, on balance, the grammar school would lose.[42]

The newer conception of the grammar school contrasted an egalitarian education system with the alternative that

a country which was fighting for its existence should insist on finding and training the best brains only, and retain thereby a high academic standard for the universities.[43]

Teachers in grammar schools had to make up their minds, through their associations, as to which conception of grammar school education would preserve most fully the values they believed in. The late 1940s was the period when these teachers felt most under attack, not only from the supporters of multilaterals, but from the local authorities applying the new 'common code' for secondary schools, from the 'common salary' scale, and from central government. In reply to internal criticism that the IAHM was not having any influence on educational policy, the secretary stated:

Every meeting that is constituted by the Ministry is now packed (before it starts) against the sort of view we represent.[44]

Within the NUT, the grammar school teachers found an

apparent lack of sense of responsibility shown by the NUT towards the Higher Education Sections, and requested immediate and energetic action to protect the interests of the grammar schools.[45]

In 1946, the IAHM published a memorandum, *The threat to the grammar schools*, which provoked the comment from the secretary of the AEC:

This pamphlet seems to us not to be concerned with the standard of education of the half million boys and girls in grammar schools. It is concerned with the dignity and privileges of the Headmasters of such schools.[46]

This separation of the grammar school teachers was recurrent. It split the NUT executive over the question of an internal examination available to all secondary schools in place of the School Certificate. It appeared in the assertion by headmasters that 'there is only one of the three projected branches, namely our own, which is in any considerable sense capable of secondary education';[47] and that of the president of the AMA, that 'they accepted the well aired parities, but parity of attainment lay beyond the wit of the most hardened bureaucrat'.[48] The one strand of grammar school education described at the 1946 conference of the IAAM as 'educating for life', which allowed the schools to educate 'children of many types differing both in social background and in aptitude and ability', was giving way to the other strand, fulfilling 'the claims of the ablest and the best'.[49]

Despite the radicalism of the 1944 Education Act, and of the wartime educational discussions, among the grammar school teachers, as among other sections of the profession, there lay a deeply rooted conservatism. With reference not to secondary reorganization but to innovation in examinations and teacher supply, it was said that headmasters are cautious in their attitude to new schemes of education: 'They look to the past for guidance in planning the future, they would rather develop what has been proved to be good than break down and start afresh'.[50]

Time and again the London School Plan is the touchstone of criticism of wholesale change; it tended to produce the most conservative reaction. The heads of the pre-war London secondary schools publicized their complete opposition to the plan, their 'constructive suggestions' being limited to welcoming the raising of the prestige and amenities of new schools for the less academic pupils:

> All that can be said at this stage is that any arrangements which disturb the autonomy and individuality of schools, whatever their type or size, is calculated to bring difficulties and disadvantages outweighing whatever advantages may be expected to accrue.[51]

The *AMA Journal* echoed the government policy that 'past experience suggests that schools with a limited and well-defined aim are the most likely to succeed', while still regretting the difficulties that this put in the way of establishing multilateral schools.[52]

The explanation of this conservatism was the belated realization that 'changing the name did not change very much'.[53] The most effective conservative argument concerned the size of multilateral or comprehensive schools: the two models were found in the London School Plan, and in the ministry's requirements for a secondary school capable of supporting and producing a sixth form. It was impossible for most people to imagine any sense of community remaining in a school of more than 2,000 pupils, and teachers' imaginations ran riot in anticipation of regimentation and factory organization.[54]

It was only at the 1945 Conservative Party conference that preparations and policy for a general election were seriously envisaged, and then education was not to be a major topic for either party. Parliamentary candidates were 'more often content with pious expressions',[55] even more the Conservatives than Labour candidates. The Conservative Party conferences did not provide a focus for educational discussion. Even if they had, it is doubtful whether they would have done more than acquiesce in policy established elsewhere, as was the case with the major topics they did discuss.[56]

This absence of conference discussion may be due as much to the nature of educational development as seen by Conservatives as to any lack of interest:

> The practical objectives of any statesman, whatever his political persuasion, for the next fifteen years, will be to live up to the successive targets which are set by Mr Butler's Act, not the least valuable feature of which is that it has placed the general framework of our educational system beyond the range of party politics.[57]

As yet no clear party educational philosophy was discernible, though a future Conservative minister of education was already claiming that 'sharing of power on the basis of merit, and merit alone, was true Conservative democracy'.[58]

The Conservative Political Centre in its programme of 'The two-way movement of ideas' did not turn to education until 1949 when, that September, a pamphlet, *About education* by Hugh Linstead, was distributed to discussion groups throughout the country. Linstead gave no backing to the Norwood tripartite philosophy; he claimed that:

> an ordinary parent ... knows that every child cannot be fitted into one of three groups – 'intellectual', 'commercial', and 'technical' for which secondary schools are now organised;

but he was perhaps over-sanguine in his belief that the same parent is realistic enough to see that you must limit the types of secondary schools and he will accept the division of schools into 'grammar', 'modern', and 'technical' as the best that can be done in practice.[59]

Linstead goes on to attack 'education factories', directing the attention of the discussion groups to what he considers 'a fundamental problem where Conservatives and Socialists are miles apart. The question can be most simply put in the form, "What are we to do with our brilliant children?"'[60]

Nevertheless, Linstead had earlier claimed that Conservatives were not opposed to multilaterals as such. 'Experience has shown that the advantages of the multilateral system can be secured in schools of the size of the traditional secondary school'.[61] Butler was also prepared to accept the multilateral as part o the English educational tradition,[62] and another Conservative educationist went so far as to say:

I think that ideally there should be only multilateral schools. I fully subscribe to the view that there should be separate schools to go on with, but I feel that the modern school will only be a mongrel.[63]

The main objection at this time was to the size of the schools proposed by such local authorities as the LCC and to the application of the principle so that 'a school was unable to retain a life of its own'.[64]

There was also an undefined but articulate opposition to the comprehensive school within the Conservative parliamentary ranks. Commander Galbraith, in the context of the advocacy of 'omnibus schools' by the Central Advisory Council for Scotland, considered that they were, 'in existing circumstances, nothing less than a menace'.[65] For the neutrals or the waverers it soon became easy to concentrate on opposition to the 'clumsy doctrinaire application of the principle by Socialists'[66] or to declare:

While everybody will watch this experiment with great interest, we are all Conservatives, not only in our politics, but also in our outlook, and it will therefore have to prove itself to the hilt before it is adopted and extended.[67]

Continuity had been the watchword of educational policy-makers, Labour or Conservative, in the pre-war years.[68] The 1944 Education Act was the product of a coalition government, of a left-wing Conservative minister and a Labour parliamentary secretary, now in the Labour cabinet. Miss Wilkinson did not see herself as changing the direction of education policy but as speeding it forward on the already agreed lines. Nor, as it turned out, was she quite the radical the *New Statesman* had predicted. She herself was a working-class product of the state education system and she made her position clear soon after her appointment, at a meeting in London. It was not her intention

> ... to destroy the grammar schools. They were the pioneers of secondary education and were in fact the only schools which had closed the gap between the Act and the fact. It would be folly to injure them.
>
> The most urgent need in the field of new development was an adequate number of modern secondary schools because more than half the children of secondary school age would attend these schools.[69]

This conservative attitude might have passed unnoticed if critics had not been able to focus on a government pamphlet, *The nation's schools*, which had been written before Miss Wilkinson became minister but which had been on sale since. This pamphlet was much more definite in its support for a tripartite system and the minister was forced to find a face-saving foundation for its withdrawal. But in addressing the conference of the AEC she appeared to defy her critics and adopt for the first time a distinctly hostile attitude to comprehensive schools:

> People have said that by talking in terms of three types of schools we are promulgating a wrong social philosophy. I do not agree. By abolishing fees in maintained schools we have ensured that entry to these schools shall be on the basis of merit ...
>
> I cannot agree with those people who say that by setting up distinction of brains between people you are only producing another kind of distinction. I am sorry if people feel like that, but I am glad to think that we are not all born the same. ... I hope the LEAs who propose to start such (multilateral) schools will think out thoroughly the practical problems involved.[70]

The Labour Party's main statement of school education policy[71] was, whether deliberately or not, vague about the detailed structure of a reformed education system. It might be argued that the authors themselves did not recognize the ambiguity of Labour education policy. At least one of those intimately involved was quite sure before Labour came to power in 1945 that it meant the common secondary school. Attacking the minister of education, who held office for the short period between the break-up of the wartime coalition and Labour's accession to power, W. G. Cove said:

> I thought I was helping to put on the Statute Book – and we did help – an Act which would give an extended secondary education, commonly called a grammar school education. If that class approach is not to rule in this country then it is quite clear and definite that we have to get the progressive forces – the Labour Party – in power on that side of the House. It is true, as I have said before, that the National Government put that Bill on to the Statute Book and made it an Act. It is equally true – I say it with every confidence and conviction – that the real implementation of that Act – that is, giving it a substance and reality, making it a progressive instrument, an instrument of social equality – will depend on Labour coming to power . . .[72]

The issue on that occasion was again the pamphlet *The nation's schools*. In the same debate, Chuter Ede, the former parliamentary secretary to the Board of Education, argued that if the facilities for secondary education according to age, ability and aptitude were there,

> I am not very much concerned as to the exact proportion that may be provided in separate schools, because I do not believe the separate schools will long survive.[73]

In the Parliament elected in 1945, W. G. Cove and R. Morley were the only members supported by the NUT. Cove held the post of parliamentary secretary in the NUT and Morley was the immediate past-president. Both were open supporters of the common school, but it was Cove who led the attack on the minister, Ellen Wilkinson, for her secondary education policy.

By the time of the 1946 party conference 'the hard facts' were not enough to convince delegates that the minister was pursuing an educational policy 'in accordance with Socialist Principles'. Despite her claims that

> if the teachers get the same pay, if the holidays are the same and, if as far as possible, the buildings are as good in each case, then you get in practice the parity for which the teachers are quite rightly asking,[74]

the attack centred on the tripartite philosophy and the call for a reduction in overall provision of grammar school places contained in the ministry pamphlet *The nation's schools*. W. G. Cove, on behalf of the National Association of Labour Teachers, proposed a motion which condemned the pamphlet and, by implication, the minister; replying to the debate for the National Executive Committee, Henry Clay announced that the pamphlet was out of print and would not be reprinted, but when Ellen Wilkinson made it clear that, despite this concession, she was not repudiating the pamphlet, Cove forced a vote and his critical motion was carried.[75] The controversy over *The nation's schools* was a symbol rather than a cause of the growing estrangement between the minister and her more radical supporters.

In the Commons debate on education in July 1946, Cove moved that the minister's salary be reduced as a token of dissatisfaction, and claimed that deep disappointment was felt in the educational world at her performance.[76] Morley dissociated the NUT from Cove's attack on this occasion and assured the minister of its support. When Cove went on to ask:

> Does she or does she not subscribe to the policy enunciated in the education policy of the Labour Party over a number of years?[77]

and called on the minister to repudiate *The nation's schools*, he got no support from the house. The chairman of the Labour Party's education group of MPs deplored the exaggerated and vituperative remarks made by the Honourable Member for Aberavon,[78] and the parliamentary secretary, in summing up, was able to expand on the government's educational philosophy without interruption:

> There are differences in intelligence among children as well as among adults. There are distinctions of mind and these distinctions are imposed by nature . . ..[79]

The strongest backing for the common school among Labour MPs came in the debate on Scottish education,[80] when supporters could point to the favourable findings of the Central Advisory Council for Scotland, but there was no response from the front bench.

George Tomlinson, the second minister of education in Labour's governments between 1945 and 1951, had spent his political life involved in educational government at local level. Though his appointment aroused criticism, as he had only had an elementary education himself, the critics did not include the local authorities' organizations, the teachers, or the AEC, of which he had been president before the war. Attlee called him 'an ordinary man, and a very useful man';[81] he was certainly no revolutionary, but during his period of office, many of the administrative bottlenecks in the development of the education system were sorted out. To be minister of education had been Tomlinson's 'secret ambition'; he described his policy as 'an extension of the old school tie'[82] and

> was glad of the opportunity of carrying a step further a vow I had made as a youth deprived of the opportunity of a secondary education through poverty, that no handicaps of a similar kind should be allowed to stand in the way of any young person, if any action of mine could prevent it.[83]

He accepted wholeheartedly the educational features of the British system, not even wanting to get rid of the public schools; he maintained an open and sympathetic mind on comprehensive experiments;[84] such a minister, given Tomlinson's personal qualities, found acceptance everywhere. It was difficult for critics to fault his attitude to the development of comprehensives without attacking the basis of English educational government, 'a partnership between central and local government'. Even when he was accused of discouraging experiments in Middlesex, an MP from the area claimed that he had, on the contrary, given every encouragement.[85] Tomlinson was typical of those members of the Labour Party who owed loyalty to the school system they had participated in developing before the war, an implicitly tripartite system; he was at the same time typical of educationists who refused to view education as a party political matter. In his view comprehensive schools were planned and founded under his ministry, but the initiative came from local authorities, not from the minister, nor through the minister from the supporters of comprehensive schools on the backbenches of the House of Commons.

A change of minister and a new account of secondary education published by the ministry[86] did nothing to abate Cove's zeal for questioning government policy. At this point in the 1945 Parliament he seemed to be almost alone in his advocacy of the 'common school'. The new minister went out of his way, in the 1947 debate on the education vote, to emphasize 'that it is no part of our policy to reduce in any way the status or standing of the grammar school'.[87] It may have been a result of the initiation and implementation of development plans including comprehensive schools in London and Middlesex, and the corresponding growth in favourable pressure from the Labour local authorities involved; or it may simply have been a response to the growing criticisms of their plans from the Conservative benches; but in the second half of the period of Labour government more voices were heard calling for comprehensive schools or questioning the minister about his attitude to them. R. Morley asked the minister about

> what steps his Ministry are taking to encourage the formation of comprehensive schools seeing that that is part of the programme of the Labour Party and the TUC.[88]

Tomlinson's reply, that he did not press any form of secondary organization on the LEAs, led to a series of questions from Piratin, W. G. Cove and Alice Bacon. When questioned by Conservative members hostile to particular plans for comprehensives the minister began to appear more enthusiastic about them. Nevertheless during the 1950 Parliament, while supporting comprehensives himself, Fred Peart felt forced to admit that there was 'considerable hostility in the educational world and that hostility is not confined to party divisions'.[89]

The most significant aspect of parliamentary pressure for comprehensive schools at this time is its relative insignificance; no more than half a dozen Labour MPs came out in support of comprehensive schools throughout the first Labour government. This cannot be explained as a lack of interest in education, nor wholly as dissociation from W. G. Cove's savage attacks on Ellen Wilkinson. It must at least indicate a different scale of educational priorities in the minds of Labour backbenchers, a scale more in line with that of the minister; but it may hide considerable opposition to the comprehensive school, an opposition which could find its intellectual and political justification among the academic educationists, and the vast majority of Labour local authorities. Even so the supporters of comprehensives could look to Labour Party conferences for support when they claimed that 'we shall never let this issue die; we shall always raise it'.[90]

Chapter Four

Bringing politics into education: the survival of the comprehensive school idea in the early 1950s

The Co-operative Party annual congress debated education in April 1947, with speakers both for and against the multilateral schools. In a motion claiming that Tory local authorities were sabotaging the 1944 Education Act, the congress also voted in favour of the multilateral school.[1] A slightly milder but still critical education motion was put before the Labour Party conference in 1947:[2] this drew attention to the social bias in the tripartite system. No speaker openly opposed the motion though a variety of opinions were heard. Alice Bacon for the NEC admitted her belief in multilateral schools, but would not commit the party to making it compulsory for local authorities to introduce them – her advice was that Labour controlled authorities should go ahead themselves.[3]

Something of the unity of the official party leadership and the Labour government can be seen in the publication by the party, later in 1947, of a pamphlet by the parliamentary private secretary to the Ministry of Education, and the assistant secretary in the Labour Research Department, called *Advance in education*; this pamphlet damns with faint praise the comprehensive school and spends its time in describing, justifying and legitimizing the Ministry of Education policy for secondary schools:

> The great majority of children will have to be selected for different secondary courses between 11 and 12 years of age, irrespective of whether such courses are provided in different schools or in a single school.[4]

The Labour conference in 1948 was still concerned with the same educational topic. Two motions, one calling for the affirmation of 'the principle of the common secondary school' and the other for freedom to develop grammar school and technical school courses without any central limitation on institutional arrangements, were accepted by the executive. In proposing the second motion the delegate for the NALT said:

> All of us who are Labour members of local authorities do wish to try to implement Party policy and to develop comprehensive schools. The only way in which we can do it at the moment is by broadening the curriculum of the grammar school or of the modern school.[5]

This was accurate as a prophecy of the way secondary education was to develop in the next ten years, even if Labour local authorities can hardly be seen as solely responsible! Interest in secondary reorganization may have been beginning to flag; the physical state of schools produced a much more vigorous debate.[6]

Labour believes in Britain, published in 1949, strays but a short distance from government policy in saying that 'in the development of secondary education comprehensive schools will be encouraged wherever possible'; and at the 1949 conference only one delegate, Fred Peart, spoke on education, drawing attention to this statement as a potential 'excuse for inaction on the part of local authorities who are responsible for educational development'. Peart admitted that 'in this field even some of our own Labour authorities are backward in their approach to secondary education'.[7]

It was true that few local authorities, even among those which were Labour controlled, were convinced of the viability of the comprehensive school. In a period of stringent economy local authorities often agreed that

> Separate grammar, technical, and modern schools correspond with the organisation of post-primary education before 1944 into secondary, technical, and senior schools and therefore this form of organisation is easier and more economical for LEAs who had already organised the schooling for those over 11 in accordance with the recommendation of the Hadow Report.[8]

Labour local authorities were also acutely aware of the function of the grammar school in creating opportunities for some working-class children and were sometimes content to plan future developments round this one stable element. The supposed enormous size of the comprehensive school was an obstacle to its acceptance by many local authorities, both because of the practical difficulty of finding an adequate site and because of antipathy to 'factory schools'.

While the research from which the arguments above are culled was not designed to expose political bias in planning secondary education, the author, J. Thompson, nevertheless concludes:

> This study shows that most Labour-controlled LEAs are not whole-heartedly supporting a policy of comprehensive schools. The four County Boroughs which have most of their pupils in comprehensive schools are Coventry, Oldham, Reading and Southend. Of these the first three were Labour-controlled when the development plans were made, while Southend was not. The four Counties with most of the secondary school places in comprehensive schools are Caernarvonshire, Cardigan, Westmorland and the West Riding, and the first three were not Labour-controlled, while the West Riding was.[9]

Nevertheless, the considerable feeling in favour of comprehensive schools, expressed through mass votes at Labour Party conferences and through individuals in the House of Commons, began to produce reaction from the official party machine in anticipation of the 1950 general election – or as a result of the exhaustion of the Labour government's stock of policies worked out before the war – and as the need for fresh initiatives in education as in other areas of policy became apparent. The NALT had assumed leadership of the comprehensive school lobby[10] and in 1950 sent a delegation to the Labour Party NEC. This led to a meeting between the NEC home policy committee and the minister of education to discuss his policy on comprehensive schools.[11] Though electoral defeat precluded any practical effect on government policy as a result of this meeting, at the 1950 party conference the executive supported a motion calling on the government to implement a 'comprehensive' policy.[12] During the debate the NALT offered its services to any LEA wanting information about comprehensives.[13] The Labour Party Research Department had produced a research paper on multilateral schools as early as 1947;[14] now the NEC set up a sub-committee to report on comprehensives. The Fabian Society was also preparing for increased policy-making activity.[15] While some of the strongest supporters of comprehensive schools were members of the Fabian Society, there would nevertheless be sympathy for the views outlined in a report to the Fabian Society by J. Thomson:

> There are opinions in the Labour Party which do not wish to see the special heritage of our day grammar schools destroyed or reduced to

meet the immediate needs of this epoch. A policy of comprehensive schools might widen the gap between 'secondary' and 'public'. An aristocracy of learning amongst the adolescent is not necessarily, they believe, incompatible with an egalitarian age. To hold this view does not involve a lot of vague thinking about 'leaders of the people'. It does involve however a sincere belief in the values of scholarship as an end in themselves.[16]

As opposed to this analysis of Labour thinking, a Fabian approach to the problem can be seen in the author's conclusion:

It is imperative however in the next ten years that carefully devised research should be made into the results of the separate and comprehensive schooling . . . until there is solid evidence on which to build long-term secondary education policy.[17]

She was nevertheless aware that

a majority view in the Labour Party has for some time been in favour of all secondary school pupils being educated together in 'comprehensive' schools.[18]

The Fabian executive was also agreed that it was right for it to take a closer interest in the society's research programme because.

the historical Fabian function inside the Labour Movement has once again become particularly necessary.[19]

A year later, after the 1950 general election, it was aware of a movement in the Labour Party away from administrative and 'social engineering' problems towards reconsideration of principles or more basic features of democratic socialist policy.[20]

However, preparations for the 1950 general election, by way of pamphlets and manifestos, show little signs of any change of policy, only of conflicting pressures within the party. The 1949 pamphlet *Labour believes in Britain* has been mentioned already. The 1950 pamphlet *Let us win through together* makes no mention of comprehensives, while *Labour and the new society* (published in the same year) assumes the 'meritocracy' principle, whereby through the education system the distribution of intellectual ability is positively correlated with the distribution of economic and political rewards, and calls for the raising of the state school standards to compete with the 'independent' schools.

The 1951 election manifesto was debated at the party conference in

October of that year, but no mention was made of education. The sub-committee appointed earlier by the NEC had produced a report, published in June 1951 as *A policy for secondary education*. This questioned the tripartite system, especially the eleven-plus selection, and attempted to set out a plan for a successful comprehensive school. It was the first attempt to take the debate within the Labour Party beyond the realm of egalitarian theory. Thus while education policy for presentation to the electorate appears to have been temporarily frozen, within the Labour movement preparations were being made for influencing policy within an opposition party, reassessing its achievements, its failures and its prospects. After Labour's 1951 defeat the Fabian Society was encouraged and supported financially by the party in undertaking 'a general review of Labour's work in Government in four major fields', one of which was education.[21]

As the cold war intensified there was a growing fear among Conservatives of the infiltration of the teaching profession by Communists. Though an editorial in the Conservative teachers' journal as late as June 1948 could claim that 'cases where the teacher had used his or her dominant place in the classroom for the furtherance of political views are practically non-existent',[22] one of the constitutional aims of the Conservative teachers' association was to 'discourage any improper political activity in the schools', and R. A. Butler drew attention to this objective when he addressed the first post-war conference of the association:

> The Association could form a vital breakwater in helping to stem the threatening tide of Communism. Every effort should be made to counter attempts to capture the children in the schools.[23]

A recruitment leaflet issued by the association in 1949 concentrated on this function in 'the scholastic world'.[24] Lord Woolton pointed more shrewdly to the role of Communists in teachers' organizations,[25] and in 1949 the association's central committee reported that

> Branches have done their best – with success in many cases – to prevent the election of Communists to positions of importance in the various teachers' organisations.[26]

The Conservative teachers had also taken a hostile interest in multi-lateral schools since the reformation of their association after the war. Their function of supplying information to the Conservative education group in the House of Commons may have contributed to the later

hardening of views on comprehensive experiments. At their 1948 conference, multilaterals were condemned, despite Butler's statement that he
did not 'mind at all the principle of multilaterals'.[27] The subject was again
discussed at the 1949 conference when multilateral schools were said to be
'contrary to the highest principles of education' and their size was once
more held against them. Linking the two themes of anti-Communism and
opposition to the setting up of comprehensive schools, one speaker
claimed that 'they come more from the East than from America'.[28]

In summary, then, the Conservative teachers' association seems to have
provided a solid bulwark against comprehensives, despite the more fluid
attitude of the parliamentary party.

The Conservative Party *Statement of policy* published in 1949 reflected
this hostility, but kept the door open for experiments:

> We regard with suspicion the tendency to create enormous and
> unwieldy multilateral schools. Under certain circumstances varia-
> tions of the multilateral idea may well be adopted.[29]

More positive support on the other hand was given to the grammar
schools, and especially to the maintenance of the standards of the sixth
form.

In their reaction to some aspects of the existing systems, particularly
selection for secondary education, the Conservative teachers were more
critical, condemning intelligence tests at their 1951 conference. An article
in the association's journal called for wider criteria for selection, including
'perseverance' and 'persistence', to eliminate 'smart Alecs' lacking
stamina and character.[30] At the Conservative central council annual meeting in 1951 the association's central advisory committee also proposed a
motion acknowledging the deterioration of education standards of attainment and attributing this to over-emphasis on 'self-expression' rather
than 'examination' as a measure of ability, industry and character.

Concern over the defects of transfer and selection were expressed also
by the leaders of the Conservative Party. Sir Anthony Eden suggested
that this was a suitable subject for the Central Advisory Council for
Education,[31] and in 1951 Florence Horsbrugh gave an indication of her
awareness of the problem of selection in explaining that one of the
arguments for the comprehensive school was that it would eliminate the
examination at eleven. She went on:

> That is the only reason I have seen advanced, but nevertheless we
> still have to divide the children by some examination at some time

into different streams if they are to advance in accordance with their ability. I think it is wrong to suggest that the only way to find a better system than the choice at 11 of seeing what sort of education the children should have is by placing them under these mass factory arrangements. I am quite certain that some keen educationists think that it is the best thing to do, and I can see that experiments have to be made, but I urge the Minister to use his influence to see that these experiments are not on a very large scale. We are just starting the new scheme after the 1944 Act. We have the tripartite scheme. Cannot we try that out and see whether it succeeds?[32]

If her actions in office were to be eminently satisfactory to the Conservative teachers and to Conservative opinion generally, nevertheless the language in which her policy was stated was pragmatic rather than doctrinaire, capable of coexistence alongside the language of politically uncommitted groups of teachers and educationists.

A common group reaction to the nascent party political conflict over secondary reorganization was to adopt some sort of neutral pose. This could be linked with support for experimentation or with some other group value such as local freedom. Even the left-wing president of the NUT referred, in 1944, simply to a 'synthesis of all that is best in our senior, grammar and technical schools',[33] and the extensive campaign of the union to consolidate the advances of the 1944 Education Act make no play with multilaterals.

Most striking, perhaps, is the decision of the AEC in 1948 that the organization of secondary education should be wholly a matter for each local education authority. While individually local education authorities could not avoid a decision, as a body they could and did. When Alderman Hyman proposed on behalf of the West Riding education committee that the AEC should declare itself of the 'opinion that the multilateral (comprehensive) secondary school is to be preferred educationally', he was heckled by other delegates to the annual conference. The executive moved as an amendment

> that this association welcomes experiments in the organisation of secondary education and urges the Ministry of Education that each local education authority be left full autonomy in its determination of its scheme for the organisation of secondary schools in its area.[34]

With this decision supported by an overwhelming majority, the AEC precluded itself as a body from any part in public discussion of the substantive issue.

This official neutrality did not prevent the secretary of the association, Sir William Alexander, from expressing his views on the subject. Though he asserted his impartiality, he agreed with Professor Kandel[35] in preferring 'functional schools', each having a definite aim.[36] As secretary, Sir William wrote a column each week throughout the period in the association's journal, and was thus able to transmit his views to an alert and widespread audience of administrators and councillors.

The CCA had difficulty in asserting a suitably neutral or 'open-minded' attitude. Its education committee twice referred back the report of the advisory sub-committee on education reconstruction because it strongly opposed multilaterals.[37]

The advisory sub-committee of the CCA had accepted one argument for the multilateral – the necessity for all-purpose schools in sparsely populated areas. This was the general solution for rural areas, according to the Welsh secondary schools association;[38] and multilateralism even found favour with the IAHM and the governors of a small county grammar school, when the alternative was closure and the substitution of a secondary modern.[39]

There were those who soon saw the secondary modern school as a sham, others who refused to think in terms of school organization. Few educational groups were trying to think any longer in terms of 'educational or social principles'; they were now concerned with the practicalities of development plans. The NEF alone seemed to foresee the character and terms of the debate yet to come, when they planned their future activities:

> Each group should set itself certain tasks of research ... NEF groups could undertake certain aspects of sociological study in their own communities. These aspects might refer to the nutriment of children in houses and in school; the housing situation and its effects on the hygienic habits and health of school children; the meaning of home life and its part in the upbringing of children; the nature and condition of employment which the young people enter on leaving school; the nature of and opportunities for the leisure activities of children ...[40]

The sociological approach was to inform the fellowship's concern with the principles which underlie reorganization, as it was soon to provide some of the main arguments against the tripartite system for a wider group of educationists.

The leaders of the NUT seem to have been divided from the start on the question of secondary organization. Support for the comprehensive school is linked with political sympathies in some cases, but neutrality or opposition not necessarily so. In 1946 the president was a Labour MP, Ralph Morley, and he was much more direct in attacking the tripartite system; in advocating the neighbourhood school he suggested that on this 'a Labour Government might be able to give a lead to local education authorities'.[41] The retiring president, however, was concerned that 'we should concentrate effort on building up'.[42] Other leading members of the union criticized the conception of the secondary modern, one comparing it unfavourably with grammar and technical schools which offered 'opportunities to reach the highest levels of education'.[43] The chairman of the 1947 higher education conference claimed however that teachers

> were not so much concerned with academic discussions of types of school as with finding how the needs of the boys and girls could be met in a practical way.[44]

In its internal reorganization consequent on the re-casting of the post-primary education system, the NUT planned a system of sectional committees which would parallel educational tripartitism; for the Christmas conferences which reflected in their sectional organization the sub-divisions of the state education system, the secondary modern teachers were invited to join the former higher education section in a common secondary teachers' conference.[45]

This reorganization did not prevent the higher education conference of 1946 from vehemently criticizing the executive for its 'lack of sense of responsibility' towards the grammar schools, nor a split appearing in the executive between the grammar school teachers and others over secondary examinations.

Nevertheless the history of the setting up of two consultative committees by the NUT is one of relative unanimity among the different organs of the union. In 1946, the higher education conference called for an investigation into secondary selection, and the education committee supported them before the executive, which also agreed with the idea. A year later the special committee on secondary grammar, training college and university education asked the executive to set up a consultative committee on 'the organisation of the secondary stage of education, with special reference to the curriculum'.[46] This too was agreed, though the final terms of reference omitted any mention of the organization of secondary education,[47] and the committee was forced, in its report, merely to record and then ignore the conflict of views on this subject so relevant to their discussions.

Leadership disputes in 1948 were ostensibly over procedure, but concealed deeper divisions. It was felt that members of the executive could not oppose policies at conferences which they had not opposed at executive meetings. Members under attack here were Communists, whose strength had grown in the union both during and after the war.[48] Their main strength seems to have been in London, in the London teachers' association, and in Middlesex, especially in the Middlesex secondary association. This latter association had doubled its membership in the decade of the 1940s, and was a staunch supporter of comprehensive schools. The Middlesex teachers held their own conference on the comprehensive school in 1948, and in the same year undertook to keep records, with the help of headquarters, concerning the development of comprehensive schools in their area.[49]

The London teachers' association, far from opposing the LCC's plans for comprehensives, wanted to make sure that it was consulted at every stage in 'the institution of large-scale experiments in multilateral schools'.[50] The 1945 conference which adopted this policy saw some opposition during 'a protracted and somewhat heated discussion', but only two delegates voted against. By 1947, the association was critical of the LCC's policy because its first 'common secondary schools were not fully comprehensive in that they excluded the grammar schools'. They also called for a more active prosecution by the NUT of its policy of support for multilateral experiments.[51]

A small but steady flow of motions were submitted each year for the annual conference agenda, supporting with varying degrees of enthusiasm the comprehensive or multilateral school, but none were successful in the ballot. The opportunity for a debate came only in 1948, when the executive put forward a long motion listing the impediments to parity of esteem in secondary schools. An amendment was moved to include as one of these impediments 'a tripartite system of education at the secondary stage'. Opposition came from the floor and the executive, though a delegate from the London teachers' association supported. On a vote the amendment was lost and the unchanged motion carried.[52]

The supporters of comprehensives were at first more successful at the Christmas sectional meetings. At the higher education conference in 1947, a motion calling for the 'common secondary school' was approved by a narrow majority, despite opposition from an executive spokesman. The debate was largely in political terms; speeches called for 'the mobilisation of the progressive forces of the country', and argued that

> if they could not get the common school set up while a Labour Government was in office there would be little hope under another government.[53]

The following year, a reaffirmation of support was proposed by the left-wing ex-president, but this time an amendment calling for careful experiments and thorough enquiry before general adoption of the comprehensive school was successfully moved.[54]

At the 1950 Christmas conference, separate meetings for grammar and secondary modern teachers were held. The latter did not produce any call for comprehensives, but at the grammar school teachers' meeting a discussion on selection led to a motion proposing the comprehensive school as the answer to selection problems. This was defeated, but the subject came up again at a joint session, on school organization. An attempt was made to obtain a declaration in favour of comprehensive schools as 'the only satisfactory organisation for secondary education', but the discussion was allowed to continue until it was too late for the resolution to be put.[55]

Within the NUT support for the comprehensive school was not widespread; most of the leadership were quite prepared to avoid the subject unless pressed, and attempts to spur them into action were concentrated in one small section of the union, the grammar school teachers' conference. Secondary modern teachers showed no inclination to support their colleagues, and the one appearance of the issue at the annual conference involved a decisive defeat for the advocates of comprehensive schools.

After a short success, even the support of the grammar school teachers evaporated, and the political driving force behind the comprehensive school lobby was diminished when, in 1949, the Communists in office in the union were defeated after an internal union quarrel.[56]

The history of support within the NUT's rival, the NAS, follows a similar pattern, though on a shorter time scale. The 1945 conference shows that the NAS was very much divided on the issue of the 'all-purpose' school; no definite decision was taken. By 1946, a special report on the secondary school was ready, which was strongly opposed to tripartite or 'campus' secondary schools, and in favour of a 'common school'. The report was not adopted by the annual conference, after a motion to refer it back had been proposed and then withdrawn, and the report was not heard of again.[57] This time it had been the leadership which had retained their enthusiasm for the multilateral after the mass of members had become more cautious. It was only in the NEF that leadership and members remained in step together in support of a re-cast secondary system. In such a small organization there was no rigid distinction to be made between these two categories, but it is evident from the reports of conference and study groups that there was sustained support on all sides and at all levels.[58] The evangelical spirit of the members of the fellowship is perhaps further evidence and an explanation of the unanimity:

> Members who have a habit of going to holiday conferences think of them as a means of intellectual stimulus and a renewal of friendly associations. But they also give an opportunity for the kind of fellow-ship which maintains our educational morale and enables us to con-tinue to bear witness to progressive ideas and ideals in places where they are not merely unwelcome but may be actively resented.[59]

A group of teachers produced a pamphlet on the comprehensive school in 1950 which, though it was not official NEF policy, based its judgements 'upon the educational criteria upon which the NEF takes its stand'.[60]

At this stage the policies of the four secondary associations on secon-dary education were still in flux, and it is possible to detect distinct differences of emphasis and approach between them, if not within them, given that two of the associations, the headmistresses' and the head-masters', were smaller even than the NEF. Support for multilateralism, undogmatic and individualistic, has already been noted in the AHMI in 1945; the IAAM also felt

> somewhat less restricted by the academic branches of the much older (boys') grammar schools, and equally faithful to the principle of educating for life . . .[61]

A long discussion at their conference in 1946 led to a large majority for a motion reaffirming support for the 'combined school' and opposing long-term tripartism. There was opposition to very large multilaterals in 1947 but it failed to arouse much support among conference delegates.[62] Enthusiasm had waned still further by 1948 when selection procedures were being discussed; a lone articulate supporter of the comprehensive school as the answer to selection problems was ruled out of order by the chair.[63]

The formation and character of opinion within the AMA was more complex. Before the war the association had been one of the first to support 'multilateralism'; in 1945, a motion proposed by the Bristol branch recommending other branches to urge on their LEAs 'that the multilateral principle should be applied wherever possible' was defeated after a long debate.[64] The president that year strongly opposed multi-laterals and the general secretary, A. W. S. Hutchings, had been a signatory to the Norwood Report. He was forced to defend this report at the 1947 conference, when the Ministry of Education was attacked for its acceptance of the theory of child types; the criticism was voiced by the London branch, the seconder of the motion being a Communist, but the conference rejected it after Hutchings had spoken several times.[65]

Hutchings was very active in defence of grammar schools threatened by comprehensive plans; he spoke in Middlesex on the theme of the danger to grammar school education, and in Northampton in favour of tripartism. The association's journal, in its editorials, had earlier reiterated the conference's support for multilateral experiments, but by 1947 it was arguing that selection for different types of education at the age of eleven was perfectly possible.[66]

Perhaps the only group which maintained a consistent attitude, one towards which the other secondary associations rapidly moved, was the IAHM:

> Whatever the eventual future, for years to come we shall be predominantly an association of Heads of the Secondary Schools of the old-style. The numbers of such an association may be small, compared with those of similar bodies, but its influence is not small, if exerted in cooperation.[67]

From the first, there was virtually unanimous opposition to the comprehensive school; the few supporters of the comprehensive school had their natural home in other organizations. This unanimity may have given the IAHM the advantage in the deliberations of the Joint Four; they may have been helped too by the institution of a policy committee to represent the association on the Joint Four committee, and to meet just before the meeting of the Central Joint Four.[68] It was through this organization that a common policy began to be formed and active opposition to be organized. It was the central committee which took the initiative in opposing the West Riding's development plan for a large number of multilateral schools; a letter was sent to the local Joint Four asking what action had been taken or was contemplated, and offering 'the help and advice of the Central Committee'.[69]

Despite the pressure on both Labour and Conservative parties from outright supporters and opponents of comprehensive schools, education did not figure largely in the elections of 1950 and 1951, and secondary reorganization was not an issue. The appeal by the Joint Four to the party leaders prior to the 1951 election does not mention any threat of comprehensives, though it does call for a Royal Commission on Grammar Schools.[70]

The NUT gave its support to a quota of four Conservative teacher candidates, but none of these were elected. In fact only five teachers were successful Conservative candidates in the 1951 election, and only one of these had been a schoolteacher.[71] So far the aim of the Conservative teachers' association of providing parliamentary candidates from their ranks had not been realized. That education was less important in the eyes of a Conservative government was indicated by the initial exclusion of the minister, Florence Horsbrugh, from Churchill's first post-war cabinet, in 1951. Not until September 1953 was a cabinet seat found for her. She had, in opposition, indicated the main lines of her policy on secondary organization.[72] In 1952, in speaking both to the Conservative teachers' association conference and the party conference, she refused, despite hostility, to condemn comprehensives completely. She was content to say that

> the comprehensive school must be regarded as an experiment and should not yet be responsible for secondary education in any one area.[73]

When opening a comprehensive school in Anglesey, she said that no more similar schools were likely to be built in the near future; 'priority was being given to schools in the new towns'.[74] Yet she was able to tell a questioner in the House of Commons in 1954 that 32 out of 36 proposals for comprehensive schools had been approved, and 25 of these had been included in approved building programmes.[75] On the other hand she explained that in her conception of comprehensive experiments it was desirable that the schools should be constructed so that they could be reorganized later as separate secondary schools.[76] Nor was she willing to do more than consider the proposals put up to her by local authorities; she was not 'willing to press local education authorities to experiment with this form of secondary school in cases where they do not suggest it themselves'.[77] From these statements it can be seen that Miss Horsbrugh was not a party to the uncritical acceptance of the tripartite system, nor an outright opponent of comprehensives. Whatever the role she played in particular disputes with individual local authorities, her general policy was a contrast to that advocated by the Conservative teachers' association at the party conference. Her successor, David Eccles, was to claim that he too would consider proposals for comprehensive schools 'on their merits'.[78]

While Labour remained the government, the distribution of power over educational policy within the Labour Party remained predominantly hierarchical; the situation in education corresponded with the picture drawn by R. T. McKenzie, of a party led from above, with its centre of gravity in Parliament.[79] Despite the votes of the party conferences, despite the sporadic protests from the Labour backbenchers, the Labour government had remained committed to a policy of neutrality on secondary reorganization; at most the comprehensive school supporters could claim to have succeeded in stilling overt government criticisms of comprehensive school plans. Even though it was the NEC which prepared for the general elections of 1950 and 1951, there was still no sign of any commitment to a particular form of secondary organization.

The defeat of the Labour government in 1951 shifted the centre of gravity of the party back towards the extra-parliamentary organization. Despite the evidence that the parliamentary leadership was still dominant and the NEC safely in its pocket, Saul Rose points out that 'what is sometimes lost sight of is that it is not very extraordinary that the majority of Conference supports the NEC most of the time'.[80] It is rather the incidence of successful opposition to NEC and leadership policy that is important for a fair analysis of the distribution of power in the Labour Party; the history of the comprehensive school policy provides an important example.

A policy for secondary education, published by the Labour Party in 1951, was hesitant and sketchy, open to attack on numerous points; but the main burden of its content was an expression of belief in comprehensive secondary education, rather than a detailed exposition of how such a system might work.

Other organizations within the party were now placing their support behind research. The London Labour Party published a pamphlet on the London School Plan by Margaret Cole.[81] She also contributed the education section to the *New Fabian essays*, stating 'unequivocally' that

> I do not believe that any socialist can call any education system socialist or even democratic which does not bring children together in a common school life, whatever their parents' income or previous history.[82]

But she warned

> that the question of segregation or non-segregation is ultimately a question of principle, on which compromise is not possible. But we are far from the ultimate stage, and it is certain that compromise, in the sense of several co-existing systems, will remain for a considerable time to come.[83]

The implication of this was that comprehensives were only one of several possible ways of achieving common secondary education.

It was among the intellectual Fabians that scepticism of any move to abolish the grammar schools had been found. They were certainly more cautious in their advocacy of comprehensives, and gave considerable attention to the problem of the public schools as well, another aspect of segregation. Their caution may have been partly due to their understanding of the time scale of the development of Labour policy:

> The old programmes which had been so successfully implemented had worked as well as they had done only because there lay behind them not only a great deal of thinking and planning at the centre, but also a long process of diffusion through all levels of the working-class movement. . . . This process would have to be repeated before real success could be expected again.[84]

The Labour teachers were more impatient; their secondary education policy had been clear since the end of the war:

> After lengthy discussion of the principles and problems involved, the Association reaffirmed its belief that the establishment of comprehensive schools as a general policy is an essential prerequisite of a social democracy.[85]

The association presented its views by offering information on comprehensive schools to any party group. They organized a conference for London constituency Labour parties in 1953, addressed by the leaders of the LCC education committee.[86]

At the party conference in 1952 Wilfred Fienburgh moved a resolution outlining a new Labour programme, and calling for 'radical education reforms . . . to ensure the fullest possible opportunity for all'. He made no mention of what this might entail; another MP on behalf of the NALT specified the lines of development in detail:

> I hope too that we shall end the tragedy of selecting finally at 11 plus the destiny of our children; that we shall create new secondary

modern schools for those children who are yet deprived of secondary education, that we will make it easier to transfer children at any age to any type of school from another; and above all that we shall really begin to establish comprehensive secondary education.[87]

This eclectic and evolutionary approach gave way later in the conference to a more dogmatic advocacy of the comprehensive school, perhaps as its supporters became increasingly aware that the whole Labour movement was not as yet behind the policy:

This Conference is convinced that the present tripartite system of secondary education is by all standards unsatisfactory and calls upon local education authorities to implement the declared Labour Party policy of the comprehensive school.[88]

Other speakers also pointed to the apparent apathy of those with the power to act:

The position with regard to comprehensive schools is a most peculiar one. Everybody is in favour of it, but with very few exceptions nobody is doing anything about it.[89]

Alice Bacon, for the executive, was even more despondent:

I must admit that I am becoming a little pessimistic about the prospect of getting our policy put into operation. Nearly all of us believe in the principle, but as time goes on and as we develop our educational system along existing lines it will become more and more difficult to change from those existing lines to a policy of comprehensive schools.[90]

Nevertheless she announced that the executive would set up a social services sub-committee of the policy committee to make a thorough review of the education services. She ended by calling on all delegates to go home and put Labour's policy into operation.

The vulnerability of Labour's position on secondary organization, in view of the mixture of neutrality and hostility expressed by other educational groups, encouraged attempts to turn accusations of the intrusion of party politics into education against the Conservatives. Miss Bacon tried to make out a case that the Conservative minister, Florence Horsbrugh, was doing precisely that in explaining her cautious policy on secondary experiments at the party conference rather than through official channels to the local authorities.[91] Apart from trying to blame the

Conservatives for introducing the party political element, the other tactic, more successful in the long run, was to concentrate on the inadequacies of the eleven plus. Here the Press could be counted on for more sympathetic treatment, and the intentions of the makers of the Education Act adduced in support. Chuter Ede told the North of England education conference that

> The foremost thought in the minds of those who had drafted the White Paper in 1943 had been the elimination of the competitive examination at the age of 11.[92]

The Labour Party secretary told the Joint Four:

> We are convinced that the whole policy of examination and selection at the age of 11 is against the interests of all children.[93]

Hugh Gaitskell claimed that

> in our English educational system we still decide too definitely the future of a child at the early age of 11.[94]

Labour MPs tried to widen the debate by calling on the minister to set up a departmental committee to investigate 'the varieties and problems of selection at 11 plus'.[95] The minister always parried these attempts. Electoral propaganda concentrated increasingly on the pledge to abolish selection. Once again it is difficult to know whether the party was responding to a genuine disquiet among the electorate, or whether it created this disquiet. It would seem that Labour's emphasis on this aspect of secondary education did increasingly evoke a sympathetic response from the electorate as a result of both experience of the selection process and the alternatives operated by some local authorities.

But as yet, in 1953, Labour's policy was still amorphous. While the commitment grew stronger, the form of its expression had still to be articulated, modified and consolidated.

The education section of *Challenge to Britain*[96] involved the complete reorganization of secondary education along comprehensive lines. But it envisaged a transfer of pupils at the school-leaving age of fifteen to more specialized secondary institutions. This means of escape from the problem of buildings, though it was not stated as such, proved unacceptable to MPs, to Labour teachers and to the party conference. The Fabian Society neatly side-stepped any responsibility for the idea in its annual report:

It would not be unfair to claim that much of what is most realistic in the Labour Party's 'Challenge to Britain' is a result of opinion created by the Society's publications.[97]

Ralph Morley MP thought that the education proposals were far from realistic:

The Executive in drawing up this policy does not seem to have consulted any organised body of teachers or any individuals experienced in educational politics or administration.[98]

Michael Stewart considered that

the proposals for reorganising secondary education are startling. Apart from their defects, which are serious, they are presented with a wholly incorrect emphasis.[99]

Since both of these MPs were members of the NALT it seems unlikely that the association had played any large part in the drawing up of the education proposals. This is confirmed by the reaction of the NALT conference in June 1953. This conference felt that the proposal to institute schools for the age-group eleven to fifteen followed by high schools for the fifteen- to eighteen-year-olds

would lessen numbers remaining at school beyond 15, and make the raising of the school-leaving age to 16 more difficult. The proposals were 'a retrogressive step' and the Association reaffirmed its belief in the all-through comprehensive school and dissociated itself from the proposals for secondary education put forward by the Labour Executive.[100]

Though there was almost unanimous agreement here, there was some disagreement over what action to take. The alternatives were to make their disapproval immediately public or to press forward with discussions within the Labour Party, after further explanations from the NEC. In the event both courses were followed: the association put its views on record and carried the dispute forward to the Labour Party conference that October.

Challenge to Britain covered many other topics apart from education, so it was essential that the conference should be able to debate and accept or reject it section by section rather than as a whole. But from the start it was admitted that it was education that had 'aroused more interest in the country as a whole than any other section of our document'.[101]

The first move was an attempt to commit the party to an 'immediate abolition of the private schools';[102] this is relevant in the evolution of policy on comprehensive schools in that it reveals one recurring element of dissension in the Labour Party as to what constituted the next step in promoting educational equality. The completely different perspective in which the two main facets of Labour education policy were viewed may be gauged by the proposer's claim that their integration in the state system would mean that 'the undoubted advantages of the so-called public schools [would] be available to children whose ability deserves them'.[103] This argument got some support in Hugh Gaitskell's speech from the floor.[104]

But the main topic for discussion was the plan for comprehensive schools for children from eleven to fifteen years old. The NALT proposed a complete amendment to the education section which would retain the commitment to comprehensive schools, but with the insistence on immediate reorganization with existing buildings, and subject to some choice of the form of reorganization at the local level. To wait for the building of new comprehensives, said the proposer, would take between fifty and one hundred years.[105]

Another amendment from a constituency party wanted to shift the emphasis away from comprehensive schools. It was said that educational shortages and the unacceptability of destroying the grammar schools made only a policy of experiments with comprehensives viable. The proposer claimed that the intellectual standards of the brightest children would suffer in comprehensive schools. One speaker called the comprehensive school 'an obsession',[106] but others spoke in favour of the Labour teachers' amendment, as did Alice Bacon, replying to the debate for the executive. She countered the arguments of those who wanted to concentrate on abolishing the public schools by claiming:

> Mr and Mrs Brown, the ordinary parents of this country, do not feel aggrieved because their Tommy goes to a Council School while little Lord Pantalduke goes to Eton; but what does grieve them is that Jimmy Jones over the road has a scholarship to the Grammar School while their Tommy has to stay in the modern school.[107]

In summing up she emphasized that the essential point in their policy was the abolition of selection:

> We do not propose to give the local authorities the choice as to whether or not they will get rid of selection at 11. What we propose to

do is to give the local authorities the choice of how they will get rid of selection at 11, and this can be done in a variety of ways.[108]

Hostile reaction to the education section of *Challenge to Britain* was not restricted to educationists within the Labour Party; and the revision of the section undertaken at the annual conference did little or nothing to modify these reactions.

Conservative attitudes to comprehensives were to be articulated publicly and formally only in reaction to Labour's increasing commitment to them,[109] which had culminated in the publication of *Challenge to Britain*. In 1952 the Conservative Party conference made a clear choice in favour of tripartism. The chairman of the Conservative teachers' association proposed the motion that

> This Conference believes in the value of separate grammar, technical and secondary modern schools and deplores any attempt to replace the system by comprehensive schools.

The motion made no qualification about experiments or evolutionary developments, and appeared to regard the secondary system as basically fixed for all time. Only one delegate voted against it.[110]

It was predictable that the following year there was unanimous support for a motion congratulating the government on its educational policy and expressing the

> conviction that Socialist policies for destroying the grammar schools and undermining the position of the independent schools would result in a reduction of educational opportunities for all children.[111]

The Conservative teachers' conference also concentrated its attack on the education proposals contained in the Labour Party policy statement *Challenge to Britain*. They claimed that the individual character of grammar and technical schools would be destroyed and 'the best use of those brains on which the country depends for its future' would be prevented. One speaker from a secondary modern school claimed that most of his pupils 'deserved to be there'; only a Conservative MP, I. J. Pitman, spoke up for comprehensive schools as possibly the only solution in rural areas.[112]

But the controversy over secondary reorganization still did not feature strongly in Conservative education policy propaganda, except at election time. The accounts of early Conservative educational achievements concentrate on the increased levels of expenditure and the great number of schools being provided after 1951. Even in a 1956 Conservative Research Department pamphlet, *Socialist arguments examined*, there is no mention of Labour's comprehensive schools policy. To some extent this can be explained by a Conservative reluctance to make education a party political matter; it corresponds to the earlier low priority given to education at party conferences, and the relative inexperience of the organized party in local government. Throughout this period the Conservative teachers' association was the backbone of support for tripartism and opposition to the 'triumph of mediocrity'.

Though there was some disenchantment with the minister over the teachers' superannuation proposals in 1954,[113] she was congratulated for her action in forbidding the closure of Eltham Hill grammar school to make way for a comprehensive school and was encouraged to take similar steps again.[114]

Apart from their conferences, the Conservative teachers expressed their views on secondary education through reports which they prepared for the Conservative parliamentary education committee and the minister. In 1952, the national advisory committee set up an *ad hoc* committee to consider 'comprehensive schools and the examination at 11 + and suitable alternatives'.[115] Their report accepted criticism of the eleven plus as valid, but could see no alternative to some sort of selection: 'the quicker brain, the greater ability, cannot be given its opportunity if it is grouped with children of all grades of intelligence'.[116] Having countered the arguments in favour of the comprehensive school, they gave their support to the development of the technical school.

Almost immediately, preparation of another report on *The future of secondary education* was under way, at the request of the Conservative parliamentary education committee. The terms of reference were

> to investigate and report upon the forms of secondary education contemplated in the Education Act, 1944, their organisation and administration, and the best method of selection of pupils therefrom in accordance with their age, ability and aptitude.[117]

The committee appointed to prepare the report spent twelve months considering reports and memoranda from area committees and branches, and taking oral evidence from 'important witnesses' (though these came from different educational institutions they did not include anyone from a comprehensive school).[118]

There was early agreement that 'some form of examination' was necessary, and the committee worked in the knowledge that the association was already committed to tripartism; it concluded that

> Generally the Association supports the three-fold division of secondary education and advocates selection tests . . . allied with machinery for transfer.[119]

Twenty per cent of places should be in grammar schools, 10 per cent in secondary technical schools.

> There should be enough grammar school places for all children whose parents desire it for them, and who show reasonable promise of profiting by all that is implied in this type of education, in addition to the small proportion who will qualify for entrance to a university.[120]

While government policy remained consistent regardless of the party in power, groups within both parties were taking up more militant positions for and against the comprehensive school. The fierce defence of the tripartite system by the Conservative teachers was echoed much more widely in the Conservative Party and beyond. However the Conservative teachers can hardly have been said to have originated opposition, while teachers within the Labour movement and others committed to radical educational change can claim to have kept the case for the comprehensive school alive, despite the Labour government's opposition, and to have achieved a precarious ascendancy during the first year after Labour's fall from national power.

Chapter Five

A TIME to experiment: the development of secondary education under the Conservatives

The leaders of the NAS were quick to investigate the success of comprehensive schools and the feeling about them among their membership. It was claimed that 'the Education Committee had laid before members through articles and memoranda in the *New Schoolmaster* some of the undeniable advantages of comprehensive schools and some of the obvious disadvantages'.[1] The London branch produced its own report in 1954 declaring that 'until a truly comprehensive school has been operating for at least 10 years, teachers will continue to doubt the wisdom of the change'.[2] Motions were put before the annual conference each year, sometimes by branches, sometimes by the executive, advising caution while not closing the door on eventual acceptance of the comprehensive school. An attempt was made in 1953 to commit the association to 'disapproval of comprehensive schools', but the executive intervened and no motion was put to conference.[3] A year later the executive's own motion had to yield to the noncommittal one:

> This Conference is of the opinion that sufficient evidence is not yet available to justify the widespread establishment of comprehensive schools in the secondary stage of education in this country.

This was passed unanimously.[4]

The AMA was still subject to cross-currents of opinion on the comprehensive school at all levels in 1951. A motion deploring 'the possibility of the displacement of the grammar schools by comprehensive schools as a general principle' encountered opposition from those who wished to insert the phrase 'until proved successful'. However, the general secretary spoke once again on the side of the grammar school, and the motion was passed unamended by a large majority.[5] By the end of that year the education sub-committee of the AMA had managed to compile a short report on comprehensive schools from among its few members already working in them. The evidence thus gathered indicated no great advantage in the comprehensive, nor even any guiding principles; rather that the highly charged disagreement among teachers generally could be paralleled within the staff room of some of the schools already established. The executive discussed the report at length but eventually agreed with its sub-committee's observations that there was not sufficient evidence for a considered judgement of them, and what there was strengthened the view that enough 'experiments' were already in progress.[6]

There was outright support for the more 'academic' grammar school among the leaders of the IAAM, just as there was also some scepticism about the final validity of either the 'egalitarian' or 'elitist' educational philosophies:

> This tension, which has increased ever since 1943, is between two opposed but equally dangerous theories, either of which finds few sponsors among English educationists. On the one hand the segregation of the intellectually most gifted children, to their detriment and that of others ... on the other hand, equally harmful is the indiscriminate herding together of children of very varying ability, as in the non-selective American Comprehensive high schools.[7]

In its concern to stabilize the system of secondary education, the IAAM urged the minister 'to set up a Royal Commission to enquire into the nature, scope and function of each form of secondary education'. Faced with the political impracticality of this proposal the association continued the search for 'some common mind on general administrative policy with a maximum amount of flexibility and room for experimental arrangements'.[8] The association studied in detail the various plans for secondary education that were put forward, but felt forced to admit its inability to formulate its own conception of what the secondary education system should be.[9]

The IAAM, like the NUT, maintained a persistent interest in selection processes during the 1950s. At its 1954 conference:

> The questions of selection at 11 plus were once again discussed at length. Speakers from the Essex branch urged a full investigation of the methods used by the LEAs in selection for different forms of secondary education, and the discussion revealed considerable

anxiety, both in respect of local variations and the effects on the work in primary schools and consequential problems for the secondary schools . . .[10]

The insufficient use of two-way transfer was criticized in 1956, though it was a recurrent suspicion that selection problems would not be eliminated within a comprehensive school.[11]

In 1949, the report of the *ad hoc* consultative committee of the NUT on transfer from primary to secondary education was published. Like the NUT's other consultative committee, they did not consider it within their terms of reference to question 'the organisation of secondary education', or the choice of eleven as the age of transfer; but they were outspoken in declaring where the sympathies of some members lay:

> As practising teachers and educationists, some of us hold strong views on these questions, and it must not be assumed that because we attempt to propound solutions for some of the problems that will arise in the course of the administration of a particular plan of organisation of secondary education, we could either act as a Committee or as individuals approve that plan or organisation without qualifications.[12]

The secondary teachers' joint sessions at the national sectional meetings of the NUT in January 1952 roundly condemned selection at eleven, and the grammar school teachers' meeting expressed their disapproval of the weight given to intelligence tests. R. S. Fisher, of the grammar schools committee, feared that such tests might be used to cut down the sum total of grammar school education, and the meeting agreed that the union should undertake an enquiry into the 'scientific validity and educational usefulness of intelligence tests in selection'.

At the 1953 grammar school teachers' conference of the NUT there was another call for an enquiry into transfer to secondary education, and for a more flexible transfer system among secondary schools.

Selection procedure continued to draw the attention of the NUT education committee. In 1951 it asked the executive to circulate to secretaries of local and county associations an appropriate letter asking that an examination or selection board, with adequate teacher representation, should be set up in the area of their LEA.[13] The grammar schools' committee, responding to the demands of the grammar school teachers' sectional meeting of January 1952, had appointed a panel which decided to determine whether there was a prima facie case for doubting the predictive value of intelligence tests used in selection for grammar school courses. Questionnaires were sent to a sample of schools, and during 1953 the panel proposed a memorandum condemning as educationally unsound the widespread practice of making intelligence tests the major factor in selection.[14] The grammar schools committee adopted this and submitted it to the education committee; but the latter did not find the memorandum suitable for publication, neither did the committee think it wise to make a policy statement on this subject at that time. The grammar schools committee sent a deputation to the education committee which then agreed that the document should be presented for discussion at the national sectional meeting in 1954–5; but it had to be made clear that the memorandum was not union policy.[15] The NUT executive was strongly divided as to the value of intelligence tests; some members stressed their objectivity, while others took the same line as the grammar schools' memorandum. Either way there were regrets later that the NUT had not taken a more definite stand earlier in the controversy over these tests.

The sectional meeting, where this subject was eventually discussed,[16] called for an official statement by the executive on the role of intelligence tests in selection; it asked the grammar schools committee to revise its memorandum so as to include more reference to evidence collected by the committee which cast doubts on the validity of the theory and practice of intelligence testing. The grammar school teachers realized the need to convince the executive. The memorandum was revised several times in committee before a draft was circulated for comment to local associations and the final memorandum published as a discussion document in 1959.[17]

During the 1950s, selection procedures were the dominant educational issue within the union and outside; as one president put it:

> Even more than discussion on salary policy, tests and examinations, especially the one used at 11, have caused more argument, leading to downright friction and ill-will, than anything I have met.[18]

Transfer among secondary schools, selection for technical schools, and relations between junior schools and grammar schools, were all discussed at the 1956 sectional meetings; the partial success of teachers' efforts for marginal reforms in selection and transfer brought its own problems, as expressed in the complaint at the annual conference that:

> There are many of us here who work in secondary modern schools who have been reduced to despair by having these very children upon whom we might build our fifth and sixth forms taken from us to do specialist courses elsewhere.[19]

This was a reaction which was to grow stronger as the freedom of second-ary modern schools to develop upwards was encouraged; it was a reaction which was sympathetically viewed within the IAHM, though emphasis was also put on the need for genuine transfer facilities.

The IAHM had first formalized their opposition to the comprehensive school in 1949. In 1952, they reaffirmed their opposition at their annual conference after the withdrawal of a noncommittal motion which had stated that 'the comprehensive school system is an experiment which must be approached without prejudice or haste'.[20] They found themselves committed consequentially to a defence of the tripartite system, of selec-tion and of transfer. These latter aspects of the secondary system were discussed by a large group at the 1954 annual meeting, and it was felt that:

> It was important that this [widespread use of transfer] should be known by the public, because there is evidence at the present time of a certain lack of confidence in the selection procedures for secondary education. Further . . . the comprehensive case needs an answer, and in ready and easy and natural transfer between secondary schools lies the answer to one of the arguments of the comprehensive school.[21]

Occasionally it was admitted that there was a case for the comprehen-sive school; in 1954, the main speaker in a discussion on the organization of secondary education said that:

> The comprehensive school is probably the best way of providing education in rural areas, and has been a success in such areas as Scotland . . .

Some headmasters thought that there was real inequality in the present system: 'If we don't accept comprehensive schools, we must find another solution.'[22] The annual report in 1958 warned that it would be fatal 'for members to assume the role of educational backwoodsmen'. Nevertheless, on the whole the IAHM consistently opposed and denigrated the com-prehensive idea, while reluctantly allowing a case for experiment. Leading headmasters made their position clear: Eric James of Manchester gram-mar school proposed the reaffirmation of opposition to comprehensives in 1952; in 1956 Dr Birley of Eton claimed that 'the comprehensive school . . . was a real danger to education'.[23] The president of the association spoke of 'false egalitarianism' and the heresy of 'grammar school educa-tion for all'.[24] It seems undeniable that the IAHM misrepresented the reality of the comprehensive school, though not perhaps the arguments of some of its most vocal supporters.

The annual conference, rather than more elaborate surveys or investigations, gives headmistresses in the AHMI the opportunity to view developments in education in a wider perspective than that of their own school. The subject of the 1954 conference was 'Current trends in educational planning'; participants welcomed experiments and the assessment of the advantages and disadvantages of different types of secondary school. One speaker concluded 'that we must accept confusion a little longer', and 'to deny the principle of growth is the last thing we must do'.[25] No play was made at all with the Labour Party's commitment to comprehensives. 'When the experiment seems the outcome of political ideology or mistaken economic expediency we can welcome it less warmly' was, however, the warning given in 1957 by the president of the association.[26]

But the warning was given in the context of the assertion that 'it is right that local education authorities should experiment with comprehensive, co-educational, bilateral [and] single-sex schools'. There was still no emphasis on the professional consequences of comprehensive education: perhaps this was because some of the most publicized and successful comprehensive schools by this time were run by headmistresses, as at Kidbrooke and Woodberry Down.

More positive support was coming from the NEF. Despite the fellowship's feeling that its ideals were generally under attack, and despite a drop in finances and membership, it was active in discussing and publicizing the comprehensive school at its conferences and through its publications. Local groups in London and elsewhere were, on its own account, observing and helping, not uncritically, the development of comprehensives.[27]

Considerable publicity also came through the AEC journal, *Education*, especially through the comments of the association secretary. He put forward his own plan for comprehensives alongside selective schools for the extremely bright and the extremely backward.[28] Nevertheless the official policy of the association remained: '. . . we do not believe that this is properly a matter for determination at central government level';[29] and the association was careful to distinguish between the particular case of the refusal of the minister to allow the closure of a London grammar school as part of the LCC's plan for comprehensive schools, and the general principle of local automony which it felt was being infringed in that same case.[30] In a later similar instance of ministerial veto, this time of

Manchester's plan for comprehensive schools, the AEC's educational advisory committee argued, despite the Manchester education authority's request for support, that they were satisfied the general principle of considering local circumstances had not been infringed, and that therefore no action on their part was necessary.[31]

The Labour Party's commitment to secondary reorganization on comprehensive lines in 1953 was a new external development which had repercussions within teacher groups. It is doubtful whether the particular nature of the comprehensive schools proposed, which was almost immediately changed, had any differential effect on the reaction of teacher groups. The most restrained reaction was the comment of the IAAM that:

> It is always easier for the party political groups and others to outline a ready-made scheme than it is for those in the schools.[32]

Later the IAAM was to reaffirm its sense of the distinction between 'plans founded on educational ideas' and 'those emanating from party political philosophy'.[33]

But in 1954, motions on secondary education submitted for the agenda ballot at the NUT conference showed a distinct change from the previous years; only one, from north-west London, implied approval of comprehensives in its call for the abolition of the eleven-plus examination in areas where such schools existed, while eleven associations wanted the NUT to oppose further comprehensive experiments, at least until the existing ones were proved satisfactory.[34]

When *Challenge to Britain* was published the AMA decided that its public reaction should be through the Joint Four, to which it sent the opinions expressed at its education sub-committee's meeting.[35] Internally the executive took the lead in deploring the building of large numbers of comprehensives, and 'vigorously opposing the destruction of well established competent grammar schools to make way for comprehensive schools'.[36] Only token opposition to this line was put up from the floor at the annual conference, or to the condemnation of the original Labour plan for comprehensives for the age-group eleven to fifteen.[37]

As part of its contribution to a proposed Joint Four statement on comprehensive schools the education sub-committee was trying, during 1954, to collect information on comprehensive schools, but was finding this difficult.[38] The IAHM's opposition focused on the newly adopted policies of the Labour Party. From then on it became necessary to engage in the defence of grammar schools publicly. The need to think through a complete case may be what encouraged the IAHM to make plainer their agreement with a policy of limited experiment. Their policy was now unanimously accepted as 'opposition to the provision of secondary education exclusively in comprehensive schools'.[39] A new emphasis was put on the desirability of variety in secondary education. It was the sense of crisis they felt at the 'threat to the grammar schools' that led them to hold their first Press conference.[40]

The IAHM predictably went furthest in producing its own leaflet in reply to Labour's new education policy, which was sent, through members, to all MPs and to the delegates attending the 1953 Labour Party conference. At this stage, before conference revision of *Challenge to Britain*, they could expect sympathy even from committed comprehensive school supporters for their claim that 'the proposal we oppose does not even provide comprehensive schools but only a cheap travesty of them'.[41] The annual meeting of the Headmasters' Conference came out in full support of the IAHM leaflet.

A leading article in the NUT newspaper also picked holes in Labour's policy for secondary education.[42] On the other hand, Sir William Alexander of the AEC was more conciliatory, playing down the revolutionary overtones of the proposals, and the problems of keeping children at school beyond the minimum school-leaving age.[43] While the AMA remained absolutely opposed to 'a wholesale changeover to comprehensive schools',[44] the assistant mistresses were readier to admit the existence of a problem in secondary education, though they were just as opposed to a general national solution rather than a particular local one:

> What we seem to need is some more common mind or general administrative policy with a maximum amount of flexibility and room for experimental arrangements. Can we find a way to reduce the wide variations in administrative arrangements for Grammar School education and yet avoid a 'plan' in secondary education, which however conceived might well pose for teachers an even greater number of perhaps more serious problems than now?[45]

The Joint Four advised members to help in the campaign against Labour policy 'by putting forward the Grammar School point of view at local meetings'.[46] At national level it approached the Labour Party's NEC with a request for consultation during the redrafting of the policy after its virtual rejection by conference. However, they were informed that 'as the Executive were tied by the decisions of the Margate Conference they felt any consultation would be impracticable'. The Joint Four then deferred further action until the revised policy should be published.[47]

The initiative was also taken within the Labour Party to involve educationists in the revision of educational policy. The Fabian Society organized a conference with the title 'What is wrong with Labour's education policy?'[48] and invited representatives from the main teachers' organizations and the AEC. The IAHM and the NUT were among those who accepted, while the AEC education committee felt that it was 'inappropriate that the Association should accept'.[49]

During the three-day conference Alice Bacon put forward the party's policy; Eric James spoke on the case for the independent schools; W. A. Claydon, the author of the IAHM leaflet opposing *Challenge to Britain*, gave the view of the maintained grammar school; and Miss M. Green, headmistress of Kidbrooke comprehensive school, spoke on this type of school.[50]

The three main points disputed were the proposed abolition of selection for secondary education at eleven plus; the imposition of a universal system of comprehensive secondary schools; and the nature and timing of measures for bringing independent schools within the state system.[51] One result of the meeting was that the IAHM resolved to hold 'an informal dinner of a few headmasters and three or four members of the Education Committee of the Labour Party'.[52] At the same time the IAHM made another attempt to bring the Labour Party's policy on secondary education into line with their own views. When Division XII (the north-west) organized a weekend houseparty for Labour leaders, including Hugh Gaitskell, Alice Bacon and Michael Stewart,[53] education administrators and inspectors were also present. Though some agreement seems to have emerged,

> there was no glossing over the serious anxiety which Labour's education policy particularly on comprehensive schools is causing many grammar school heads.[54]

However

> all present were impressed by the way Mr Gaitskell, after the outspoken discussions, found a measure of common ground for the differing points of view.[55]

The public debate still continued despite such private manoeuvres. The Joint Four went ahead with its plans for a statement on secondary education, agreeing: 'that it should be a positive statement of policy and not merely an answer to the Labour Party's proposals'.[56]

All four secondary associations contributed to the policy expounded in

1955 and in 1959 in reply to proposals to institute a comprehensive system. But these two documents[57] come nearest to the views of the IAHM, paying lip-service to the need for change, while defending with considerable logical and rhetorical power the established grammar schools.[58] The acceptance of 'growth', the recognition that 'the grammar school had not yet found its proper role', give way to unrelenting criticism of every secondary innovation that might alter the institutional character of the grammar school, its intake, its age range and its change of courses. With the opening of the 1955 general election campaign the Joint Four sent out a letter to all political parties containing a 'plea to preserve and develop schools which have proved their value'. Of the comprehensive school the letter said:

> Let the comprehensive school show by experiment whether it can increase equality of advantages and solve the problem of early selection, while yet avoiding the two main dangers of excessive size, the swamping of the individual and the loss of high scholarship.[59]

The NUT's regular questionnaire to parliamentary candidates concentrated on the freedom of local education authorities to determine their own secondary school provision, and avoided the substantive issue itself.

After 1955 the campaigning by opponents of the comprehensive school seems to have excluded access to Labour leaders at the national level. While Labour education policy remained openly in flux even within the party, non-political educational organizations were able to intervene. But later they were restricted to activity during general elections or at the local level. By 1959 the Joint Four general election statement was ostensibly more conciliatory, but in substance it put forward exactly the same united opposition to any threat to existing grammar schools. While more emphasis was put on consultation with teachers and there was recognition that:

> questions of policy in education must finally be decided by the elected representatives of the people

the preservation of 'what is best in our educational heritage' was still, by implication, preservation of the grammar school.

Among academic educationists, after 1944, the psychologists were more wary than before of dogmatic claims for their predictive and diagnostic tests of ability. Some grammar school headmasters had reacted strongly to the admission of what they termed 'smart Alecs' to their schools under the new selection system. There were critics too of the predictive accuracy of the intelligence tests, and one important psychologist, in an attempt to reply, seemed to overturn the political basis of the 'scientific' and 'objective' approach to education:

> It is true that most verbal intelligence tests measure what we call the 'G' factor only to the extent of about 40% and that they involve nearly as great an amount of verbal education ability. Undoubtedly therefore, IQs are somewhat affected by upbringing and education. But since success in the secondary school also requires high linguistic ability, our predictions at 11+ would actually be less accurate if we used purer non-verbal tests of 'g' or if we could devise any tests that were entirely free from environmental influences.[60]

Another psychologist described the state of thought in educational psychology in the following terms:

> Until recently, the idea of 'late developers', particularly in intellectual development, had not gained support among psychologists, but accumulative case-study work, and results in different fields – physical, temperamental and intellectual – indicate more clearly that each individual has his own particular pattern in respect to growth and maturation, and furthermore, that maturation is a complex matter, depending on many variables, each making a variant contribution to a general maturation.[61]

This new scepticism about the usefulness of intelligence tests was in part due to the work of psychologists themselves, but during the 1950s the scope of educational research was modified by the increased interest in sociology. Before the war most social analyses in English education had been undertaken by royal commissions or advisory committees, though there had been some development of educational sociology in other countries, notably America and Germany.[62] In England political commitment seemed to inspire the post-war research, at least in the choice of problems to be investigated,[63] as well as the desire to counteract the domination of educational psychologists. In a more general way, Floud and Halsey see this increased interest as the result of education's new 'strategic place as a central determinant of the economic, political, social and cultural character of society'.[64] The principal contribution of the sociologists has been and remains 'to refine and extend the notion of social environment',[65] in response to the psychologists' concentration on inherent characteristics. Sir Fred Clarke, director of the Institute of Education of the University of London, interpreted and disseminated the ideas of Karl Mannheim, both predicting and stimulating the development of educational sociology. At the London School of Economics, the large-scale study of social mobility, under D. V. Glass,[66] led directly to the publication of *Social class and educational opportunity*,[67] a study of the relationship between educational and social selection. In numerous articles sociologists drew the conclusions that

> despite the changes introduced into secondary education by the Education Act of 1944, it remains the case that a boy has a greater chance of entering a grammar school if he comes from a middle-class rather than a working-class home. . . . It would seem . . . that some of the factors which were known to reduce the chances of entry to a grammar school as the holder of a free or special place still continue to exercise their effect.[68]

In 1959 Halsey carried the fight into the psychologists' camp, with a statistical demonstration that the chances of high intelligence being positively correlated with high socioeconomic class were minimal in the context of English social history. Sociological evidence of the inefficiency of the secondary education system was also mounting in government reports: it is seen at its most thorough in the Crowther Report.[69]

These developments in the academic field coincided with some disquiet among the public and in the Press about the eleven-plus selection mechanism. The incidence of coaching in intelligence tests, the 'late developers', and the emotional disturbance experienced by some children before and during the selection process, were all newsworthy topics. As the number of comprehensive schools slowly grew, especially in London, more evidence became available relevant to the claim that such schools avoided the anomalies and disadvantages of the tripartite system.

By the late 1950s it was acknowledged by many teachers, administrators and politicians that the secondary system needed some modification. Local education authorities had not been slow to react to the protests concerning the dominance of the intelligence test in selection procedures, but few had abandoned the eleven plus. In London, in spite of the complex nature of the secondary education provision, the LCC had, on its own account, gone some way towards satisfying the demand for education in specific schools by instituting a system of parental choice at entry to secondary education.[70] In Leicestershire, a solution had been found without an extensive building programme. Again, there were developments of examination courses within secondary modern schools in an attempt to minimize the sensed and real deprivation of children who failed to gain entry to the grammar school, and to recognize the achievements of some of these schools:[71] the success of secondary modern school pupils in such examinations was often seen as another indication of the inaccuracies of the selection procedure. The Central Advisory Council for Education (England) reported in 1963[72] that the number of pupils voluntarily staying on after the minimum school-leaving age had doubled since 1958, and soon afterwards plans were announced for the raising of the school-leaving age to sixteen in 1970.

An increasing number of local education authorities found their answer in comprehensive schools, the number of which had risen to 175 in 1963, spread over 23 counties and 16 county boroughs. Another 66 schools were classified by the ministry as bilateral or multilateral. This compares with nearly 4,000 secondary modern, over 1,000 secondary grammar and 200 secondary technical schools in 1963.[73]

Three basic alternatives were before the education committees of local authorities: they could decide to retain the tripartite system virtually unchanged in form; they could agree to a gradual alteration and development towards a comprehensive school system as finance and existing buildings permitted; or finally they could decide upon a radical reorientation of secondary education in their area along comprehensive lines, adapting the existing buildings as best they could. The initiative for change in local education authorities came from a number of sources not all overtly political. The plans which received most publicity during the 1950s were those which brought local education authorities directly into conflict with the Ministry of Education.

In Coventry the external situation provided the opportunity for a policy of comprehensive schools based on the merits of the case.[74]

> Though there were two maintained girls' grammar schools in Coventry before the war, secondary education for boys was limited to 38 places per year at the independent grammar schools Bablake and King Henry VIII. After the war, then, given this complete inadequacy, the devastation of the city by bombing, the imaginative attitude to re-building generally, and a sympathetic Labour majority on the City Council, Coventry was able to include large scale experiments with multilateral schools in its Education Development Plan 1946.[75]

There was no group opposition by the minority Progressive Party nor from the teachers' organizations. The 1953 plan included two Roman Catholic comprehensive schools and one Church of England comprehensive school. It was the chief education officer who had objected to the tripartite system. And it was a combination of local and national education officials who cooperated in the planning and establishment of the first comprehensive schools. There were

> numerous occasions when Ministry and County officials met to consider the many problems which had to be overcome if the new form of secondary education was to be launched successfully. Caludon Castle was the first of the Coventry projects, and in this wrangle discussions began in 1948 and continued at frequent intervals throughout 1949 and 1950.[76]

The original plan for this school was completely transformed during discussions, but its 'comprehensiveness' was in no way diminished. The ministry's development group took part in the planning of two further comprehensives in Coventry.

Great pains were also taken to create a favourable public opinion of these schools. Meetings of parents at which governors and headteachers of each school explained the purpose of the school were held for some years.

It was only in the later 1950s, when the development of the plan involved the future of the existing girls' grammar schools, that parent and party groups made the issue controversial. In its first phase the pace was made by the minister of education, speaking locally, and claiming that:

> I will not have grammar schools destroyed to support a political theory ... I believe parents should have a choice ... If you have only one or two comprehensives there will still be a choice, but as soon as you get what the Labour Party desires, which is all comprehensive schools, there will be no choice ...[77]

Later the old girls' associations of the two grammar schools were to make a much stronger protest leading to a debate in the city council on the issue.

If this was, until 1955, a case of discussion on the merits of the case, it was so in a context of administrative professionalism tempered by local political commitment.

The inspiration behind the West Riding development plan was at first solely that of the chief education officer. He gathered together from leading educationists what he knew would be opinions antagonistic to the tripartite system and presented them to his education committee with the comment:

> It is clear from these expressions of expert opinion that the authority
> would be unwise to assume that secondary schools can reasonably be
> divided into three main types . . . or that children can be allocated to
> them according to their aptitudes.[78]

His recommendation that the authority should continue to build wherever
possible 'community schools large enough to take all types of children in
the area' was completely supported by the committee.[79]

The decision reached at this stage, to some extent as in Coventry by
discussions on the merits of the case, was soon to give way to politically
authoritative determination of policy, when a year later the chairman of
the education committee ordered the preparation of a second plan, even
more strongly committed to multilaterals.

In other areas the role of the chief education officer – rather than that
of politicians or of professional groups – in the development of comprehensives was to remain important for a long while.

Croydon provides the most well-known example of a policy initiated by
a chief education officer.[80] Here political allegiance played a small part in
the generation of an acknowledged problem, the scarcity of places in the
borough's maintained grammar schools. The council accepted a Labour
minority motion calling upon the education committee to prepare plans
for dealing with the shortage. The new chief education officer, with the
assistance of the borough's chief inspector, took this opportunity to put
forward his own plan for a junior college, an amalgamation of the sixth
forms of maintained grammar schools. It was probably the premature
publication of the plan, before even the *ad hoc* sub-committee on the
subject had considered it, that prevented its implementation. Teachers'
organizations were not all hostile – there was tentative support from the
non-selective schools – but the chief education officer had no time to
marshal groups firmly in support of the plan. The strategy of opposition
groups was to challenge the legitimacy of his semi-authoritative policy.
The adverse report of an outside educational consultant, brought in at his
request, helped this challenge.

In the case of the Leicestershire experiment in 1957, the originator of
the idea was again acknowledged to be the director of education, S. C.
Mason, who took advantage, whether consciously or not, of a low level of
political and group commitment.[81] Even the Conservative organizations in
the area had given mild approval to the comprehensive school.[82]
Irrespective of its educational advantages and disadvantages, the political
viability of the Leicestershire experiment lay in the possibility of its

immediate implementation, and of its combination of attractions for all interested parties. For the secondary modern school teacher there was the fillip of work with the whole ability range, for the grammar school teacher the more restricted age range. Mason claimed that 'it would be unreal to believe that the public would become used to the idea of selection and accept it' and 'unless some satisfactory alternative is devised local education authorities will be relentlessly drawn to adopt the large scale comprehensive schools'.[83] Mason's plan had the advantage for parents and others that it combined abolition of the eleven plus with the retention of the existing school system. The tactics of publication, timing and implementation of the experiment rendered impotent any organized opposition.[84] While the heads directly involved in the change had been consulted before publication, the heads of the feeder primary schools only heard of the plan from the newspapers, and the representatives of the NUT were informed on the same day that the news was released to the Press. Tactics which failed to work in other cases worked for the Leicestershire authority and its director of education because of the necessary time lag in organizational reactions to what was an unexpected innovation: attitudes built upon support or opposition to all-through large comprehensive schools or to the abolition of existing grammar schools were largely irrelevant to the situation. Planning the new schools was a matter of curriculum, and here the teachers were given complete freedom, but were by implication committed to the success of the experiment from the start.[85]

The Leicestershire director of education in effect struck a preemptive bargain with other interested groups; this timing combined with the authority deriving from the director's office were the essential ingredients of success.

The crucial position of the chief education officer could also be used to block the implementation of comprehensive schools. The Liverpool chief education officer made his position clear when he addressed the National Association of Head Teachers of Secondary Technical Schools: 'in this gathering there are probably none of us prepared to accept the comprehensive school as the answer'.[86] Later he reported to his education committee that it was impossible to provide comprehensive schools without depleting existing schools; and though the report was rejected by his committee, the impasse remained.

The London School Plan was approved shortly before the defeat of the Labour Party in the 1951 general election, and the replacement of George Tomlinson as minister of education by Miss Florence Horsbrugh. Her sympathies were very definitely with the grammar schools, though she maintained a policy of experiments with comprehensives. Also before the change of political control at the ministry, the plans of the first purpose-build comprehensive school had been approved. Kidbrooke, for 2,000 girls, had been included in the 1950 building programme, but then deferred to 1951; the ministry was kept informed and the legal procedures for notification of a new school observed.[87]

The new school was controversial in that it involved the closure of several older secondary schools, including a girls' grammar school, Eltham Hill. A meeting of 121 parents of girls at the grammar school opposed the transfer of pupils to the new comprehensive, and the opposition was reported to the education committee.[88] When a further meeting of parents was arranged, the LCC education committee moved quickly to interpose their own meeting for parents of children at Eltham Hill, at which its officials tried to convince the audience of the advantages of the change.[89] The parents were initially extremely hostile, in agreement with the lady who said 'It's an experiment and I won't have my daughter experimented on',[90] but became more sympathetic as the LCC's officers explained. Nevertheless, at the independent meeting on 4 March 1953, a resolution of protest was passed without dissent by the 200 parents attending. It was decided to ask every parent to sign a petition to the minister.[91]

The LCC education committee countered with further meetings of parents of children at the other schools affected by the opening of Kidbrooke. Though one of these was very poorly attended[92] the meeting at Charlton secondary school for girls, a non-selective school, had a very different atmosphere and result. The headmistress from the chair spoke strongly in favour of the change, and a motion, again unanimous, stated that:

> We, as parents, welcome the opportunity of sending our children to the Kidbrooke Comprehensive Secondary to be opened in September 1954, and hope that this great experiment will receive the full support of all those concerned, so that it may be a complete success.[93]

It was then that the minister entered the controversy, after requiring the LCC to publish notices of its intentions to discontinue the schools involved in the Kidbrooke reorganization. She had already intimated to the Joint Four (when they urged her, on behalf of the London Joint Four, to oppose any considerable development of comprehensive schools in

London) that she would 'consider very carefully the individual merits of each new proposal that may be submitted to her'.[94] Later in the year she addressed the Conservative women's conference in London, explaining her position with regard to London's comprehensives and telling them that:

> in considering the plans of local authorities to close schools, or to alter them out of recognition, she had to consider the views of the local residents.[95]

It was in this context that the petition of parents and friends of Eltham Hill was sent to the minister. Answers to the objections were submitted by the LCC chief education officer and a plea was made by the LCC:

> Surely, if the people who ask for such experiments are sincere in their statements, they will not interfere with the first of these post-war schools to be specifically built for the purpose and put into operation.

Despite this the minister refused to sanction the closure of Eltham Hill, though allowing the closure of the other schools involved. A deputation from the LCC and from the AEC produced no response.[96]

The Labour controlled Manchester local education authority drew up their educational development plan in 1947 without coming to a decision about the best organization of secondary education. They claimed that their plan had been 'drawn up as a response to the requirements of Order 28 and has no other objective'.[97] In other words, it supplied the statistical information the ministry wanted. The tripartite system which was implicit in some of the informational requirements of Circular 28 was already suspect in the eyes of the Manchester education committee.

> This is debatable ground . . . child psychology does not lend it much support . . . it is reasonable to assume that the task of separating children at the age of 11 or indeed at the age of 13 on these lines will prove impracticable.[98]

Manchester's plan assumed, but did not advocate, a system of secondary grammar, technical and modern schools, and on that basis described an immediate five-year programme of building rather than a sketch of long-term needs. Expansion of selective secondary education included the provision of a new grammar school and a new technical school at Wythenshawe, a large council housing development in the southernmost part of the city.

One school at Wythenshawe, Yew Tree, a combination of an old selective central school and a senior elementary on the same site, was to serve as an experiment in multilateralism.

This programme to cover the years 1948–53 was never finally approved as the Manchester development plan by the minister, and in 1953 another development plan for education, drawn up while the council was controlled by the Conservative Party, was submitted and this 'attempts to look forward for a period of about twenty years'.[99] Not only long term in outlook, it embraced the principle of tripartism.[100] Plans for secondary education were to be based on the proportions of 70 per cent of secondary school children in secondary modern schools and 15 per cent each in the secondary grammar and secondary technical schools. Yew Tree, the multilateral, was to become a secondary modern, while a new county grammar school and a county technical school (the latter in two halves, one for boys and one for girls) were to be built at Wythenshawe to complete the secondary provision.

Dissatisfaction with the principle as well as the premises of Yew Tree was expressed by HMIs in their report in 1953, and the education committee set in hand enquiries into various possibilities of adapting the school as a grammar/technical or secondary modern school.[101] The headmaster of the school, who was consulted in detail, was in favour of the school becoming fully selective,[102] but the memorandum put before the secondary education sub-committee is clearly in favour of making Yew Tree a completely non-selective secondary modern.

No change had taken place, however, when on 14 June 1954 the secondary education sub-committee, now under Labour control, asked the chief education officer to prepare a report on possible locations for an experimental comprehensive school.[103] The chief education officer's report, while putting many difficulties in the committee's way, came up, not surprisingly, with the single suggestion of Yew Tree, and the general purposes sub-committee in turn requested a report on this possibility and on the further possibilities of adapting the proposed West Wythenshawe secondary technical schools or of a site in Moston.[104] After visits to the Wythenshawe school by the committee, to existing comprehensive schools in London and Coventry, and further reports on the possibilities in Manchester, on 21 March 1955 the secondary education sub-committee resolved decisively in favour of establishing comprehensive schools at Yew Tree, at West Wythenshawe and at Poundswick, the proposed Wythenshawe grammar school. Detailed plans were prepared and the education committee approved them by a majority vote, the division being on party lines. Alderman Miss Mary Kingsmill Jones, for the Conservatives, opposed the plan for three comprehensives and suggested an experimental one instead. She drew attention to the recently devised development plan to which the minister had given his approval only the previous month.[105]

This division along party lines was followed at the city council meeting when the plan was approved by 80 votes to 51. No Labour voice was raised against it, and no Conservative was in favour. Even the Conservative deputy chairman of the education committee opposed the proposal.[106] It was nevertheless immediately forwarded to the ministry for consideration, and protests from outside the council began to be heard.[107] It was soon agreed that the parents of children passing the eleven plus would be allowed to choose between the Wythenshawe comprehensive and the established Manchester grammar schools.[108] An attempt to publicize the advantages of the comprehensive school was made in a letter to the *Manchester Evening News* from the secretary of the Wythenshawe Labour Party.[109] The letter contained a report of an interview with the chairman of the education committee, Councillor Pariser, and Lady Shena Simon: its tone and content could only have helped the case for comprehensive reorganization.

The proposal sent to the Ministry of Education explained that it was essential to bring the partially built schools into operation as comprehensives that September.[110] Under the 1944 Education Act, a change in the designation of existing or proposed schools required the minister's approval. First, notices of the changes must be published, then two months must be allowed for any objection to be sent to the minister before he can ask for the LEA's comments on the objections and subsequently assess the case for the change. Given that the proposal was not submitted to the minister until 7 April 1955, and notices of the change not published until 14 May 1955, the education committee were asking a lot of the minister to give his decision in time for the opening of the Autumn term in September 1955. They nevertheless went ahead with their plans for Wythenshawe's secondary education. The committee as a whole could plead ignorance of the situation, since it was not informed of a letter from a ministry official to the chief education officer[111] stating that an official decision could not be reached before July, and that therefore it would not be a practical proposition to open the schools concerned as comprehensive schools in September.[112]

The education committee spent July in approving comments on the various objections to the plan for submission to the minister. Councillor

Kathleen Ollerenshaw, a co-opted member (later to become Conservative spokesman on education), protested against the committee's proposed reply to the criticisms of the Wythenshawe residents. She claimed that parents of 118 out of 119 children who had passed the eleven plus had demanded places in established grammar schools. Her amendment to the committee's comments was defeated by only 8 votes to 7, with several abstentions.[113]

On 1 September a letter was received from the ministry stating that the minister did not approve of the proposals for comprehensive schools. The chairman of the education committee commented:

> This decision has been received only four days prior to the opening of the two comprehensive schools. In these circumstances it would be impossible for the Education Committee to open these schools in any way other than in the way they planned to do so. They will open as comprehensive schools on Monday.[114]

In the discussions which led up to the confrontation between the minister and the local education authority, teachers and parents seem to have played little part. Apart from 'voting with their feet' in the way Mrs Ollerenshaw had suggested, no articulation of grievance appears to have occurred. The teachers too, though more deliberately, appear to have left the decisions to the politicians.[115] Any intervention on their part would inevitably be stigmatized as support for one party or another. The minister's decision did produce some 'grass roots' activity: a Wythenshawe community association meeting with about ninety people present supported Manchester's attempt to get the decision reversed. A young schoolmaster proposed the motion, and references to the inadequacy of the eleven plus produced applause from a group of teachers present.[116]

The education committee prepared to send a deputation to the minister in an attempt to get him to reverse his decision. However, once again the party political nature of the conflict became apparent, when Alderman Miss Kingsmill Jones, a Conservative, refused to join the deputation as she was not to be allowed to put anything but the committee's majority view to the minister.[117]

On 4 October the deputation spent nearly two hours with the minister in 'off the record' discussion, and left convinced that the minister had considered the proposal seriously and was personally responsible for the decision. The only comfort they were given was his repeated assurance that he was prepared to approve experiments with comprehensive schools where the conditions were favourable.[118]

The Manchester education committee now had to consider how it was going to turn the comprehensive schools at Poundswick and West Wythenshawe, which had opened in September, back into a grammar and secondary modern, and two secondary technical schools respectively. Since only the internal organization of Yew Tree had been altered the minister's ban did not directly affect its future, which merely remained 'uncertain'. The education committee eventually decided in favour of building up Yew Tree as a nine-form entry comprehensive, its only remaining chance for an experiment in comprehensive education.[119]

The surprising element here is the ability of the leading Labour members of the education committee to push through their plans, despite strong Conservative opposition and despite the apparent lack of support in some sections of the Labour group on the council,[120] without arousing to active opposition any other educational groups in the area. The final decision was once again 'hierarchical', involving an authoritative intervention from the ministry presumably prompted by the Manchester Conservatives and by the formal protests of local residents; at most, the teachers' organizations might be said to have largely withheld themselves from 'the system of activity being concerted towards the adoption of the proposal'.[121]

It would seem clear that in the first few years of Conservative government there was no dogmatic opposition to experimentation with comprehensive schools; there was however a definite commitment to the preservation and extension of the grammar schools. Such effective support as there was for comprehensive schools usually came from Labour-controlled local education authorities and thus the debate brought party political considerations to the forefront. Nevertheless, the minister could assume wide support among the electorate for a cautious policy.

Chapter Six

BRINGING education into politics: Labour takes the initiative

After the initial reaction to Labour's proposals for secondary education in 1953, Conservative Party conferences concentrated on other educational topics. In 1954, the importance of adequate teachers' salaries in ensuring a successful education was stressed; in 1955 there was a call for the expansion of technical education 'especially at the secondary stage', which was supported by an overwhelming majority.

The party's approach to education in the 1955 general election reflected the traditional non-partisan conception of educational policy and an awareness of the possibilities of making electoral ammunition out of Labour's radicalism:

> Our manifesto confirms our intention to reduce the size of classes, to reorganise all-age schools in town as well as country, to replace slum schools and greatly to expand technical education. All this any Minister would wish to do with maximum speed and vigour. But how can a Labour Minister succeed? He will have to instruct local authorities to scrap their development plans and draw up new plans for turning their secondary schools into comprehensives.[1]

The Times noticed that the shift of emphasis to secondary school building 'made Labour's long-held policy of comprehensive secondary education immediately relevant for the first time' in the 1955 election. The questionnaire which the NUT sent out to parliamentary candidates also reflected the importance of the controversy. It asked whether it was thought that local authorities should be free to develop secondary education 'in the manner they consider most appropriate to the needs of the area'. While *The Schoolmaster* reported that most candidates agreed with the proposition, some, from both parties, replied negatively, suspecting that their answer might assist or impede the provision of comprehensive schools.[2] However, the Conservatives' election policy was quite clear that they would 'not permit the grammar schools to be swallowed up in comprehensive schools'.[3] The *Campaign guide* presented a picture of a flexible tripartite system, and pointed out that nearly all the comprehensive schools under construction in mid-1954 had been included in approved building programmes during the period of Conservative government. It was only the provision of secondary education solely in comprehensive schools which a Conservative minister would stand firmly against. 'Parents must have a choice; they may not wish experiments made on their children's school life.'[4]

The same election made clear that Labour's leadership was still not fully committed to the idea of complete secondary reorganization, despite the trend of the earlier debate. For the first time comprehensive schools were a material issue, and Labour's leaders and candidates were always on the defensive. While 53 per cent of Labour's parliamentary candidates mentioned the abolition of the eleven plus in their campaign addresses, only 28 per cent went on to refer to comprehensives.[5] The national manifesto was similarly cautious in saying that to realize 'the fulfilment of the Education Act 1944, we shall encourage comprehensive secondary schooling'.[6] Herbert Morrison was more frank:

> I don't want to argue that the comprehensive school should be the universal means of higher education of a secondary character. I do believe that the comprehensive school has got a part to play. I don't say that the comprehensive school should wipe the other schools out of existence.[7]

Spokesmen in the House of Commons and the House of Lords watered down the party's official policy to almost the same extent.[8]

It would seem possible after Labour's electoral defeat in 1955, despite the immediate reaffirmation by the NALT of their belief in comprehensives, that this controversial policy might have been shelved. In one sense it was; a policy revision over three years was begun, and educational policy was relegated to the last year of this programme,[9] thus effectively curtailing conference discussion, and encouraging private negotiations. But the policy that was to emerge in 1958 was even more firmly committed to comprehensive schools; the remaining area of educational controversy was the future of the public schools. While for some left-wingers radical reform in both the state and independent education sectors was equally necessary, for other Labour leaders they were alternatives:

> We are afraid to tackle the public schools to which the wealthy people send their sons, but at the same time are ready to throw overboard the grammar schools, which are for many working-class boys the stepping-stone to the universities and a useful career – I would rather abandon Eton, Winchester, Harrow and all the rest of them than sacrifice the advantage of the grammar school.[10]

The general election seemed to have settled the issue of secondary organization nationally for some time. The Conservative Party conference of 1956 debated the more esoteric subject of tax relief on school fees as an incentive to parents to reduce overcrowding in state schools by sending their children to independent schools. The proposal was opposed by the minister and defeated, but in 1957 the subject of secondary organization came up again with the motion

> That this Conference, believing in the true educational value of separate grammar, technical and secondary modern schools, deplores any attempts to displace this tripartite system by the extensive construction of comprehensive schools.[11]

One speaker opposed the motion strongly, and it was agreed to focus disapproval on politically motivated 'attempts', whereupon the motion was passed by an 'overwhelming majority'.[12]

The Conservative government was able to rely on the majority of educational groups for general support for its policy on one aspect or another. Even in 1963 the secretary of the AEC gave warm approval to the minister's view that there must be variety and that no regional system of comprehensives could be applied nationally. The NUT could find common cause with the government in securing 'more adequate provision of all forms of secondary education';[13] what was for the government a policy in line with English educational tradition was also a convenient formula for the avoidance of controversy in the NUT. The Joint Four echoed another aspect of government policy in its declaration 'let the comprehensive school by experiment show whether it can increase equality of advantage and solve the problems of early selection'.[14]

The government could also look beyond the organized groups to the unorganized but interested parties among the electorate, the parents. Miss Horsbrugh told her Labour questioners on selection procedures 'from what I have heard of the opinions of parents, what they dislike more is the idea of their children going into comprehensive schools'.[15] Perhaps they could at least rely, at first, on the apathy or ignorance of the electorate. Despite the amount that both Conservative and Labour candidates had to say on education in one constituency in the 1955 election, knowledge of party policy by voters was very low on the matter of comprehensive schools.[16] But later, although some Conservatives might claim 'that teachers as a whole were against the idea of vast conglomerations', and that the public would not tolerate the abolition of the grammar schools, other politically uncommitted educationists were beginning to claim that 'the parents, whom ultimately the politicians must obey, are not going to accept segregation much longer'.[17]

It remains questionable whether the government's policy was the result of the pressures of organized and, even more critically, unorganized but acknowledged groups, or whether it was the government who exercised the influence, dominating and directing into uncontroversial channels the conflicting pressures of teachers, educationists and parents. On the whole it would seem that the role of the groups was simply to express dissatisfaction with the secondary education system. So long as the government was able to provide educational policies in terms of relative priorities, of eclectic innovation and of the traditional norms of educational development, it retained the capacity to satisfy the organized party's demand for retention of the grammar schools.

The Conservative teachers' association played an active part in the politics of the NUT, as did the Labour teachers. More importantly, successive ministers of education came to the conferences of teacher groups and put forward their policies on secondary organization. Sir David Eccles got a warm reception when he told the IAAM that:

> to settle the pattern you have got to choose between justice and equality, because you cannot have both principles at once. Those who support the comprehensive school prefer equality. Her Majesty's Government prefer justice, and my colleagues and I will never agree to the assassination of the grammar schools.[18]

Geoffrey Lloyd got a more mixed reception at the 1958 AEC conference when he claimed that a Labour government would impose comprehensives on all areas despite local differences.[19] But other ministers of education succeeded in adapting their message more suitably to their audience. At the NUT conference in 1955, Eccles concentrated on the government's positive plans for support for all secondary education institutions, grammar, technical and modern, and even for experiments in comprehensive education.[20] Sir Edward Boyle, echoing the assumptions of the tripartite system about the validity of different types of secondary education, felt able to tell the conference of the National Association of Head Teachers of Secondary Technical Schools that 'technical education was peculiarly able to induce that precision and accuracy both of thought and execution without which one could get nowhere'.

The Labour Party set up a study group to prepare a new educational policy statement for 1958. Within this group the comprehensive school policy seems to have produced no dissension. It was its suggested policy of leaving the public schools to their own fate that took the longest to work out, and which exposed conflicts of view on the NEC.[21] Though the NEC managed to shelve its differences,[22] there was some dissension at the 1958 annual conference. A move to repudiate the policy on public schools received such support from the trade unions as well as constituency parties that it was lost by only 500,000 votes.[23] By contrast there was a majority of nearly 4,000,000 for the policy document as a whole with its plan for comprehensive schools.[24]

Learning to live, Labour's new statement of education policy, was not just the product of discussion within the Labour Party. As well as the breadth of representation among the members of the study group, the consultations they had with the parliamentary education committee and an 'exchange of views' with the TUC education sub-committee,[25] a weekend conference was held to which some forty outside educationists, including chief education officers, were invited.[26] The group also had the benefit of the publication, by organizations and individuals, of accounts of the activities and success of the existing comprehensive schools.

The arguments of *Learning to live* were an attempt to secure a wider backing for the comprehensive school than that among committed Socialists. It claimed that 'the Government must seek to organise education so that the sum total of talent in the community is fully developed',[27] and that 'there is far more ability in our people than was dreamt of before the war'.[28] It was similarly conciliatory in its definition of 'comprehensive':

> This name is particularly used if the school caters, as do the grammar schools today, for children from the age of 11 to 18. However, as will be shown, the establishment of schools of this kind is not the only way in which children can be provided, in the secondary stage, with the opportunity for real choice. A system of secondary education which succeeds, by any of a variety of means, in providing this opportunity, is described as a 'comprehensive system'.[29]

By emphasizing as far as possible the flexibility of their own approach, the Labour Party tried to put the onus on the defenders of the tripartite system to show that it could be equally flexible in supplying the educational needs of the individual child. What made news in the comprehensive school was the academic success of a greater proportion of children; what made news in the tripartite system was nearly always the exclusion of a child from some particular type of education.

Learning to live remained ambiguous as to the terms of reform under a Labour government and its method, but in many respects it took a more assured and aggressive attitude towards its opponents.

Hugh Gaitskell was in tune with the earliest exponents of comprehensive schools and perhaps with the interested public when he commented:

> It would be nearer the truth to describe our proposals as 'a grammar school education for all' . . . Our aim is greatly to widen the opportunities to receive what is now called a grammar school education, and we also want to see grammar school standards in the sense of higher quality education extended far more generally.[30]

Educationists were more likely to sympathize with the introductory remarks of the chairman of the study group which prepared *Learning to live*:

> Our proposals are based upon a survey of the existing system of secondary education, our realisation that it contains certain fundamental defects, that those defects must be removed, and that when they are removed, the reorganisation of secondary education becomes as inevitable as it is desirable.[31]

Learning to live provided the occasion for another debate on secondary organization at the 1958 Conservative Party conference. The chairman of the Conservative teachers' association first of all pointed out the increasing recognition of the importance of education by the Conservative Party and conference. There were thirty-four resolutions from all parts of the country on the agenda concerned with education. He attacked the 'doctrinaire approach' of the Socialists and cited the 'technical ladder' as the 'greatest triumph' of the Conservative administration. He accepted that the eleven plus was not perfect but was not prepared to abandon it 'until we are absolutely sure that the other system is better'. Enough experimentation with comprehensives was already going on.[32]

A local councillor delegate was more critical of the existing system, and impatient of simple abuse of the Socialist policy. He saw the answer in the provision of more grammar school places: 'The basis [of selection] must be ability, not availability'.[33] Another delegate also warned that 'we have quite wrongly become obsessed by the brainy child'.[34]

The minister's reply was complimentary to existing comprehensives, though he was wary of their large size. He committed himself no further than to say 'we are encouraging this experiment and the other experiments as experiments'.[35]

Secondary organization was not again discussed at the Conservative Party conference for some years, though there was increasing disquiet at the number of local authorities planning reorganization. At the instance of the Hornsey Conservative association, the annual meeting of the Conservative central council called on the minister, in 1959, 'to safeguard the grammar schools of the country in accordance with the election promise of the Party'. The Home Counties North branch of the Conservative teachers' association approached the minister in furtherance of its opposition to reorganization in Middlesex, which had also included 'writing to local papers and contacting parents' associations and as many teachers as possible'.[36] As early as 1957 the chairman of the association had been active in opposing plans for comprehensives, addressing a meeting of

> Conservative Councillors, members of the teaching profession and others interested in education, to consider a threat to abolish the grammar schools in favour of a comprehensive barracks.[37]

The reaction of teachers' organizations to *Learning to live* was more sympathetic than to earlier proposals. Only the IAHM regarded the proposals as a direct challenge:

> Every member had a duty to make his own contribution to the discussion, to use his influence and prestige at this time of crisis for the grammar schools. Members of Parliament whose position has special significance in this matter are sensitive to public opinion, particularly when it reaches them in the form of cogent and reasoned argument stated in letters from persons of some position in the world, such as Headmasters.[38]

The Joint Four concentrated its efforts on the prospective election in 1959 rather than attempting once again to reverse Labour's policy through the party organization. The IAAM compared *Learning to live* unfavourably with the Conservative government's new white paper on education[39] which left room for continued opportunity for experimental development.[40] NUT comments were rather more friendly:

> The approach to the problem [of comprehensive reorganisation] is less dogmatic, more tolerant and more realistic than that put forward by some elements in the past.[41]

The changing reactions of educationists' and teachers' organizations to proposals for comprehensive schools are partly to be explained by changes in the technical conditions of policy-making and by growing reactions to the acknowledged problems and anomalies of the existing secondary school system. The government and the Conservative Party were not immune to the pressure of evidence and of organizations.

The pace of secondary building increased as the 'bulge' passed into secondary schools. The absolute number of comprehensive schools increased rapidly, while remaining only a very small proportion of the total. The parliamentary secretary to the minister of education claimed that:

> Informed comment was that it was too early to gauge the success or failure of these schools. If that were true it was equally true that it was too early to gauge the success or failure of the existing organisations into separate grammar, modern and technical schools.[42]

Lord Hailsham said that 'the decision on comprehensives lay with the local authorities' and 'it was a little early to condemn them'.[43]

Despite its efforts to promote the tripartite system, the government failed in its attempts to damp down the growing disquiet over the selection procedure, articulated through the Labour Party, through individual educationists and even within their own party. The education sub-committee of the Conservative Party post-war policy central committee had testified in 1947 to the efficiency of the eleven plus in selecting the brightest children. The Conservative teachers had found positive merit in entrance examinations, though they were critical of the intelligence test. They wanted the emphasis to be on tests of attainment.[44]

Miss Horsbrugh, as Conservative minister of education, maintained a neutral pose on the question of selection procedure:

> I think it is best that I should leave local education authorities to work out methods of determining the most suitable secondary education for each child.[45]

She admitted to advising local authorities who approached the ministry that limited coaching might be allowed in primary schools, but later she disclaimed all responsibility for the tests.[46] Sir David Eccles expressed outrage at the introduction of the eleven plus as a political issue. At the same time Conservative ministers remained confident that time was in favour of the tripartite system because 'selection procedures were improving' and 'the construction of new schools would do much more to narrow the gap in provision'.[47]

But in 1958 the Conservative teachers reported that the Press sometimes exploited the eleven plus 'in a way leading parents to suspect that selection is undemocratic and unfair, and causing them to regard with sympathy propaganda in favour of the comprehensive school', and that

> unless the public have clear and constant evidence of efforts to improve the efficiency and impartiality of selection, there is a danger that the advocates of the comprehensive school may meet with ever increasing sympathy.[48]

Perhaps because of this the government began to take a more conciliatory line; Mr Butler in a party political broadcast expressed his sympathy 'with any of you who may be parents who are anxious about the 11+ examination'.[49] Sir Edward Boyle was in entire agreement with

> the Hon. Members that the present system of selection causes a great deal of anxiety in many quarters, and it would be both foolish and wrong simply to remain content with it.[50]

However, he found difficulty in suggesting any solution, regarding selection as an essential part of the education system, and thinking it too difficult to make any radical alteration in the existing 'piecemeal system':

> I should have thought that it would be better here to accept selection and to remedy its disadvantages by providing in all types of school opportunities for work beyond school leaving age, and where appropriate, the transfer to other schools offering different types of courses.[51]

The changed attitude to the eleven plus may be judged from the exchange between Sir Edward Boyle, then minister of education, and a former parliamentary secretary to the ministry, Sir Kenneth Thompson. Thompson put the emphasis on the necessity of selecting the appropriate children for admission to the grammar school, while Boyle defended the movement by local authorities towards more informal methods of selection, and to a less rigid conception of the role of the grammar school.[52]

By 1963, Boyle was openly following rather than leading public opinion on selection. He was still, however, leading Conservative opinion. He welcomed the LCC's abolition of the written examination for the eleven plus: 'I am glad therefore to have the opportunity of saying that in my view the general public welcome given to the LCC proposal is fully justified'.[53]

As comprehensive schools continued slowly to expand, the numbers of teachers working in them grew correspondingly. Though not yet significant as a mass group, they and those leaders who acknowledged their potential influence began to constitute a new feature in the deliberations of educational groups. By 1956 at the NAS annual conference there was unanimous support for a call to study the merits of existing comprehensives; the proposer assumed that:

> in the event of its merits meeting with your approval, our National Education Committee and Local Association Committees up and down the country would feel obliged to see that the NAS plays its part in the study for which the motion calls.[54]

There was still enthusiasm for the secondary modern school within the union, and recurrent opposition to the abolition of the eleven plus. But by now there was pressure from the supporters of comprehensive schools, as in Birmingham, and in 1959 the executive was accused of not keeping pace with the current developments in this sphere throughout the country.[55]

By 1955, teachers were beginning to realize that comprehensive schools were challenging the tripartite system in practice, and were no longer merely an idea that had been momentarily popular in the post-war euphoria; by 1958, the basis of the tripartite system was being questioned. Within the NUT, the grammar schools' committee persuaded the education committee to send out a questionnaire to LEAs asking for their plans on forms of secondary education being provided and envisaged for the future; a panel was set up to analyse the replies.[56] The initiative again came from the grammar schools' committee when the executive agreed to co-opt representatives from both comprehensive and bilateral schools in 1959.[57]

Before a committee was introduced into the official organization of the NUT specifically to deal with problems of comprehensive and bilateral schools, the union was organizing meetings of heads and teachers in these schools. In 1957, Birmingham and London were the scenes of conferences of assistant teachers, and three meetings of principals in London led to the production of *Inside the comprehensive school* under the imprint of the NUT.[58] This was a symposium written by the heads of comprehensive schools in different parts of the country, and presented a most encouraging introduction to this type of school. The activities of heads of comprehensive schools under the guidance of the NUT continued in 1958, with, among other events, an address on the Leicestershire experiment by S. C. Mason, and the compilation of 'year to year information about the growth and structure of the comprehensive schools'.[59] Secondary education sectional meetings at the end of the year were almost exclusively concerned with organization; the secondary modern section agreed that secondary education should be flexible, so as to provide a variety of courses 'each based on a general education'. A joint session of secondary and further education teachers considered various methods of organization, while the technical teachers voiced anxiety for the first time at this new threat to their identity.[60]

This controversy was aired in a more muffled form at the national sectional meeting in January 1960. For the first time, as a result of the union's reorganization of its system of articulating sectional demands, a meeting of teachers from comprehensive and bilateral schools was held; they too were in disagreement over the usefulness of streaming. Some members also called for a campaign to explain the philosophy of comprehensives to all members of the union. At the secondary modern school meeting a motion was proposed that aimed to demote reorganization along comprehensive lines from its place as the most satisfactory remedy for the defects of the tripartite system:

> This meeting greets with gratification the opening of fifth and sixth forms in secondary modern schools and looks forward to the day when all such schools will have facilities for extending the school life of every pupil who deserves it and is worthy by reason of enthusiasm and behaviour for inclusion in the scheme. We feel this to be the best way of achieving true parity of esteem and real desire for education throughout the whole ability range of the schoolchildren of this country.

It was agreed in an amendment to omit the second part of the motion, from 'and is worthy'.[61]

It was not until 1960 that the first executive member teaching in a comprehensive school was elected, but since then representation of comprehensives has been maintained and increased to two in 1964, and then three in 1965.[62]

The IAAM was later than most teacher organizations in recognizing the existence of a growing body of its members working in comprehensive schools. Not until 1959 did it hold a conference of these teachers to discuss the practical problems of large non-selective schools. It had concentrated on its 'responsibility to keep the argument essentially directed to the service of a truly educational end'. It had been critical of party political commitment to comprehensive schools, but the secretary warned in 1959 that:

> Plans founded on educational ideas should not be condemned on superficial considerations or be confused with those emanations from party political ideology.[63]

By 1957 the AMA had reconsidered its attitudes to comprehensive schools sufficiently to recognize that 'they had begun to play an important part in the educational system and that an increasing number of our members are serving in them'.[64] From then on its policy began to unfreeze and adapt itself to a new situation. There was also some realization that resistance to comprehensives was still strong among the leaders of the association, a minority of the delegates to the 1959 conference supporting a motion deprecating prejudice against comprehensives in AMA pamphlets and editorials.[65]

At the 1957 AMA conference it was proposed on behalf of the London association that the time had come for the executive to undertake a full report of the 'practical, professional and educational' problems of the comprehensive schools. An overwhelming majority supported this move[66] and the education sub-committee went ahead with arrangements for a conference of members in comprehensive schools in Birmingham and London.[67] The resulting pamphlet was still critical of the dangers of a general policy of comprehensive schools, instancing the possibility of parents who could afford the fees removing their children to the independent sector of education, and neighbourhood bases producing less socially heterogeneous schools than the present grammar schools.[68] But further meetings of comprehensive school teachers were held in 1958, and by May 1959 *A first report on teaching in comprehensive schools* was ready for publication. The annual general meeting in 1959 demonstrated the new division of opinion within the union: a motion opposing 'hasty and ill-considered schemes of comprehensive secondary education' was amended to delete the more inflammatory comments on existing comprehensive schools and was opposed unsuccessfully by the supporters of comprehensive schools.[69]

Neither did the IAHM remain unaware that the system was changing round them while they argued. In 1959 they viewed the prospect of 'selective schools in a comprehensive system', and some support for comprehensives was expressed.[70]

The development of thought and practice was entering a new phase. Despite the opposition or reluctant neutrality of teachers' organizations in their public utterances, they had only slowed down, not stopped, the growth of comprehensive schools. Now the pace of development was quickening, and new attitudes had to be worked out by groups as well as by the individual teacher in the school, for whom reorganization was no longer a matter for academic discussion, but an imminent possibility. Reactions of approval or disapproval were already largely determined by each organization, but they had to be translated now into the acceptance of change and a concern to salvage something of their former policies.

The most immediate problem for teachers'· associations was in the localities where official plans for comprehensive schools were being made. Loath to be excluded from consultation by national doctrine, local branches followed their own policies in response to local circumstances. The necessary emphasis was often on participating constructively in reorganization. Members of the AMA in Scunthorpe took the step of dissociating themselves from the national policy of opposition to the abolition of grammar schools, so that they might be included in the teacher consultation on reorganization in the area.[71]

In Carlisle, in 1955, a plan was announced by the Labour council to organize secondary education in three comprehensive units.[72] Opposed by the Conservatives and the local evening newspaper, the plan was condemned by large majorities in all local teachers' associations. A swing against Labour in the local elections that year and in the general election (the seat was lost) was followed by a petition signed by 500 parents to the minister of education protesting against the plan.[73] The minister eventually refused his consent.

In 1959, the year of another general election which might have produced a sympathetic Labour minister of education, another plan by the Labour council found the teacher opposition in Carlisle smaller and unprepared. Though it was known that reorganization was being discussed, the teachers did not approach the council and the council did not go to them, so that their first knowledge of the plan was through the Press. The Joint Four were not till then separately organized in Carlisle, but they immediately set up a local committee.[74] However, the NUT and the National Association of Head Teachers were not prepared to cooperate with the Joint Four in a public protest, and the latter had eventually to accept the plan with as good a grace as possible.

> There may well be some of our members who will think that the Joint Four should take a firm stand against any change, but the Committee feel that this would be an unrealistic and untenable position to take up. One reason for the change is the desire to abolish the 11 + examination and the tide of public opinion is running strongly in favour of such a move.[75]

The junior college plan in Croydon re-emerged in 1961, though the initial problems provoking discussion were different: 'they were the unreliable selection procedure and the apparent waste of grammar school places'.[76] As such, they were issues being debated nationally; Croydon's particular contribution was the work of its chief education officer in campaigning for the junior college as the answer to the problems now recognized. Even this recognition was in part due to the papers prepared by the education officer since 1956 which 'all showed concern at the quality of response to grammar school opportunity as evinced by those with a poor record in examinations for the General Certificate of Education'. Despite the support the chief education officer received this time from outside educational consultants, he once again failed to commit the education committee before opposition could be organized. Given the greater general awareness of the need for change in secondary education, the local teachers' associations were not in a position to oppose every suggestion, but the imminence of local government reorganization gave the council the opportunity to avoid putting the opposition to the test.

By 1959 the pressure of local reorganization plans was beginning to alarm Conservative backbenchers. At a meeting of the party education committee at the House of Commons they expressed their fear that the minister of education (then Geoffrey Lloyd) 'might be going beyond the criteria set out in the 1958 White Paper on Education'. Mr Lloyd explained that:

> Local authorities under Labour control seem to have misunderstood the degree of sympathy for comprehensive school proposals and that his own record as Minister of Education on this subject was as respectable as the backbenchers could wish.[77]

He made it clear, however, that the government still did not exclude experiments with comprehensives. Labour spokesmen were suggesting in 1961, probably in an attempt to spread dissension in the Conservative ranks, that the minister had begun to favour the comprehensive schools.[78] Certainly Sir David Eccles admitted that:

> the comprehensive school is having a good run. Some of these schools are doing well but we have enough experience now to know that the large comprehensive school puts an exceptional strain on the teachers.[79]

He went on to warn that a proposal to reorganize the whole national system on comprehensive lines 'raises much wider problems, and nobody has yet explained what this would involve for the existing schools'.[80] Nevertheless some backbenchers were trying to block local reorganization plans. A private member's bill was introduced in 1964 to provide that any proposal 'to change the status or nature of a secondary school should require the approval of the Minister of Education'; it was defeated by 24 votes only (152 to 176).[81]

By 1963 the rationale of Conservative policy on selection had collapsed; and the ministerial attitude to comprehensives had radically changed. Boyle made it clear in the Conservative pamphlet *Educational opportunity* that:

> none of us believe in pre-war terms that children can be sharply differentiated into various types or levels of ability; and I certainly would not wish to advance the view that the tripartite system, as it is often called, should be regarded as the right and normal way of organising secondary education, compared with which everything else must be stigmatised as experimental.[82]

Boyle could say this now, not because of his own impregnability as minister, or simply because of the recognition of the electoral dangers of too rigid a secondary education policy. Support for comprehensive schools, always to be found in a tiny minority of the population, had grown hesitantly among a wider public to sufficient strength to legitimize his reorientation of policy.

A Conservative Party ideologist, T. E. Utley, had warned as early as 1956 that:

> in a just reaction against egalitarians, we tend to be more and more obsessed with the interests of the secondary grammar school.[83]

There were, of course, Conservative authorities who had established comprehensive schools in rural areas as the only solution. And the Conservatives in London were more wary in their opposition when it 'became increasingly obvious that more and more voters seemed to be enthusiastic about the comprehensive school programme'.[84] But it was the Bow Group which crossed the threshold to open support of the comprehensive school. In 1959 their comments were tentative in the extreme, but their initial assessment of comprehensives was untinged by any political prejudice; they only went so far as to say that 'Despite many imperfections the comprehensive school may sometimes be preferable to a rigid system of allocation'.[85] Some Conservative backbenchers too were calling for a modification of government policy on secondary organization. *The Times* reported that:

> In the past few years Conservative backbenchers have tolerated rather than encouraged 'comprehensive school' experiments, but they have also been basically suspicious of the development out of the fear that the grammar schools would be imperilled. Today some of those backbenchers who are best informed about education are clearly occupying a new position. They are no less determined to preserve the grammar schools but they believe that the logic of the fulfilment in the near future of the policy of secondary education for all means that the value of the Kidbrooke type of school should now be more realistically recognised in the Conservative Party.[86]

The strongest support for comprehensives came in a second Bow Group pamphlet which suggested that the present tripartite system of secondary education should be progressively superseded:

> When there is an opportunity to plan new schools, for example in rural areas or in new towns in development areas, then, in our view, the local authority would be wise to plan such new schools on comprehensive lines.[87]

Even the Conservative teachers' association changed the tone and direction of its attack.[88] In 1959 the chairman claimed that Labour councils were trying to reorganize without consulting the teachers, and accused them of intimidation.[89] A more plaintive and conciliatory note was struck in 1964:

> Is it right that local education authorities should continue to build comprehensive schools in areas where other types are still maintaining excellent results? Conservatives must be progressive, but to be progressive does not mean revolution. Let tradition and experiment work together side by side without pressure being brought to bear by subtle innuendoes and sharp practice.[90]

The attention of the teachers' organizations increasingly centred on adequate consultation with teachers during the planning of reorganization. In 1959 the NUT executive submitted to conference a statement of the union's attitude to reorganization. They outlined the growth of the secondary system away from the rigid tripartism of the Norwood Report, and welcomed the flexibility and diversity of the present system. In its educational criteria for judging reorganization plans, the defects and advantage of segregated and comprehensive education were neatly balanced. The statement went on to concentrate on the necessity for consultation:

> Satisfactory development of any kind however depends on more than local and national policies; it depends on the willing co-operation of teachers.[91]

It argued that many of the local conflicts would have been avoided if there had been the opportunities and incentives for such cooperation; and on the main issue it explicitly refused the responsibility for a decision:

> The National Union of Teachers is not called on to decide whether all children should go to the same school or whether there should be a measure of segregation; that is for the elected representatives of the people to determine.[92]

Within this formula the executive was able to reconcile the various and conflicting interests and ideals within the union, while permitting the maximum freedom of action at local and sectional levels. There was no doubt that there was little enthusiasm at the annual conference for many of the plans proposed, and that the leaders of the union displayed a variety of attitudes to educational development. The 1959 president claimed that:

> the comprehensive schools are also showing what can be accomplished when the slower child has the incentive of working in the same environment as the more gifted.[93]

The general secretary told the North of England education conference:

> the great illusion of our time is that the stumbling block to equal opportunity is the 11 plus examination. It is not; the stumbling block is an inadequate education system.[94]

By 1964, the NUT was cooperating with the Joint Four in producing a common statement on the reorganization of secondary education which concentrated on the procedures for consultation and the protection of the professional interests of teachers.[95] This latter point had been raised at the 1959 NUT conference, when one speaker said: 'before the time of the next conference there is going to be a growing army of disgruntled and discontented teachers'.[96] The discontent arose from the consideration that if four modern schools and a grammar school were combined to make one comprehensive school, four heads stood to lose at least authority and status. A year later the executive reacted strongly to the proposal of one local education authority planning reorganization to limit the headships of secondary schools to graduates in future.[97] Some local associations negotiated their own satisfactory agreements on teacher protection during reorganization, but the law and tenure committee prepared, for the guidance of others, an approved policy of acceptable arrangements for the displacement of head-teachers, and the transfer of assistant staff.[98] By default, the substantive issue receded into the background. This may have coincided with a growing acceptance of comprehensives as the inevitability of their wide establishment became plain. The NUT's evidence to the Plowden committee came out strongly in favour of them.[99]

The logical conclusion of the meetings for comprehensive school heads held by the NUT in 1957 and 1958, and of the continued growth of the proportion of teachers working in comprehensive schools, was the expansion of the union's system of sectional committees and conferences. In 1959, an advisory committee for comprehensive and bilateral schools was set up, and the grammar schools' committee also co-opted members from these schools. Educationally there appeared to be some indecision about the new committee's role. At its first meeting the committee examined in detail the problem of building in as short a time as possible a working agenda which would be based on the real needs of the types of school in whose service it had been created. The committee noted that:

> it would have to face rather more difficult problems in the organisation of its work than would seem to be the case in respect of the other types of secondary schools, which are of a more homogeneous character. It was therefore necessary to pay particular attention to the sharing of experience as between area and area. It noted too that its considerations might well be concerned with problems of internal organisation to a greater extent than other committees. In many respects it was felt the Agenda of the Grammar School Advisory Committee would be relevant to the new Advisory Committee while

liaison with all the secondary committees would need to be fully established at an early date.[100]

This lack of clear educational *raisons d'être* suggests that other motives were behind the setting up of the committee: the desire or need to recognize the new strength of comprehensive schools, and the desire to provide an organizational structure which would encourage further membership from those schools straddling the boundary between the traditional territories of the NUT and the Joint Four. The headmaster of one comprehensive school made the matter plain: 'Education needs a Union, a Union that can fight for the whole profession, not just some sections of it'.[101] He had been a member of other teachers' associations but he found that only the NUT sought to serve all teachers. In December 1964, responsibility for the organization of the union's advisory committee passed from the membership committee to the education committee.[102] But the former had already agreed that there was a prima facie case for the establishment of a single advisory committee for secondary education, a further step in the membership movement which had distended the union's organization temporarily only to reunify it with a wider catchment area. Nevertheless sectional organization provided the opportunity for sectional reactions to the reorganization of secondary education.

In 1960 some of the comprehensive school teachers called for a campaign to explain the philosophy of comprehensives to all members, but nothing came of this. On the other hand a motion was proposed at the grammar school teachers' meeting expressing unwillingness for

> [grammar] schools to be merged into much larger units unless adequate and convincing educational reasons are given and sufficient time is allowed for discussion by all parties concerned.[103]

Some of those present wished to go further in defence of grammar schools, but the motion finally approved was restricted to a demand for full consultation with the grammar school staffs involved in reorganization, and denied any opposition to 'the comprehensive school as such'. There had been a move too at the secondary modern schools' meeting to support fifth and sixth forms in secondary modern schools as the best way of achieving true parity of esteem, but this too was unsuccessful. *The Schoolmaster* described the function of sectional meetings of the NUT in the following terms:

> They are the working meetings of a profession which likes to formulate its policy from below; for though this is not a policy-making

conference in the formal sense of the term, the views expressed and the conclusions reached are placed before the Executive and play an important part in shaping policy both at Executive level and at the annual Easter Conference.[104]

Nevertheless the executive's concern was to walk a tightrope of neutrality, and to avoid commitments that would jeopardize the cherished unity of the profession.

The IAAM had adopted the same strategy as other teacher groups, investigating existing comprehensive schools at the end of the 1950s, in an attempt to retrieve the development initiative for educationists:

> We do not actively recruit members holding only basic qualifications and working in other schools [than grammar schools], but a number of these do join us, so that the body of members has a growing interest in different forms of secondary education.[105]

Sections of the 1960 conference agenda were reserved to 'the experimental types of secondary school'. This did not mean that the assistant mistresses had come out in favour of comprehensives; the 1960 conference concerned itself with motions put forward by the executive as a result of meetings of members working in comprehensive schools, but:

> Some individual members found difficulty in supporting the resolution lest they should be thought thereby to be in favour of the development of comprehensive schools.[106]

A consensus was once again reached in a call for adequate consultation, and the setting out of the essential facilities of a comprehensive school.

The NUT made clear its strategy of attracting the new comprehensive school teachers away from other unions in a *Schoolmaster* editorial commenting on the AMA annual conference in 1959:

> In their conference at Harrogate last week the Incorporated Association of Assistant Masters in Secondary Schools seems to have scant regard for the feelings of their members serving in comprehensive schools judging from the spirited attack on the comprehensive school made by the retiring Chairman . . . with the enormous staffs which must necessarily be concentrated in comprehensive schools, it seems absurd that teachers' membership of professional bodies should be spread over several associations.[107]

But despite strong conference feelings against comprehensives, the AMA executive were trying in different ways to make known their recognition of the important part comprehensives were beginning to play. Conferences of members working in these schools held over a period of several years led to the publication of a survey of problems, as much as of the solutions to them, of the existing comprehensives. The chairman of the association in 1960 recognized that:

> Emotional terms like barracks, factories, mass production, are no substitute for careful enquiry into what is going on. But this does not imply headlong adoption of comprehensive schools regardless of the effect on grammar schools. It does imply some shift of emphasis. At all costs we must safeguard the essential qualities and achievements of the grammar school as we have ourselves defined them. Essential content is of more vital importance than organisational form.[108]

But the association was prevented from shifting its emphasis officially by the terms of its agreed policy which opposed reorganization schemes 'which involved the disintegration of established grammar schools'.[109] By 1963, protests were heard, and they came to a head at the annual conference: it was claimed that the local education authorities assumed the inevitable opposition of the AMA and therefore excluded them from consultation. The conference eventually agreed that the executive committee should give 'further consideration to Association's policy towards educational reorganisation'.[110] The executive too put the emphasis on gaining the cooperation of the teachers:

> Teachers were ready to work any scheme which was demonstrably decided upon by law. They recognised the right of the people to decide the general structure of education through the franchise.[111]

The AHMI put greater emphasis on the validity of the case for change, as well as the advantages of change which had been collectively agreed:

> I think we would accept that there are areas where the present situation is less satisfactory, and where change would be to the advantage of the majority.[112]

But sometimes they found that 'the matter is treated much more like a battle'.[113]

The AHMI were inevitably concerned with the effects on their professional interests reorganization might have, and the executive joined that of the IAAM to discuss the position of women in the mixed school.[114]

When reorganization plans became common among local authorities, the IAHM first reacted as though there were a battle to be fought. Its legal committee advised affected headmasters that:

> At least while the policy is still under consideration [they] should not feel themselves muzzled by any threat to their right of free speech. They can organise local opposition by meetings, and it is a good idea to get a colleague of standing from outside the area to speak at such meetings.[115]

By 1962, this emphasis on freedom of speech had been superseded by the view that:

> While we [deplore] rash and ill-considered policy statements by headmasters on Speech Day and other public occasions, we [are] very conscious of the lack of proper consultation in some quarters. The establishment of adequate consultation machinery [will] be our immediate aim.[116]

The council of the association debated reorganization in 1963, reaching

> a notably high standard. Readiness to consider change was balanced by a wise determination to preserve what is good in existing systems; babies are more important than bathwater.[117]

The headmasters took their own action in pressing their demands for consultation, but the main instrument of external pressure remained the Joint Four. The Joint Four's hostility to the comprehensive school had never been so strong as that of the IAHM alone. Their statement of policy at the time of the 1959 election made a strong plea for the grammar schools but left the door open for a change of view:

> The Joint Four is convinced that it would be most unwise in the national interest to undertake a hasty and wholesale recasting of secondary education, at any rate before greater and larger experience of new types of secondary school has been gained.[118]

The committee took the lead in pressing for consultation on local reorganization plans, circularizing local authorities and local authority associations and advising local Joint Fours on what action to take; in some cases local Joint Four committees had to be reconstituted to deal with the plans.[119]

In many local authorities group commitment was tested. Nationally teachers had already accepted that the ultimate decision lay with the 'people' or their representatives. Locally, consultation was an opportunity to retreat or advance from that position. The relative strengths of different groups were also brought out by such negotiations. A typical consultation process would be that taking place in a divisional executive where the overall decision to reorganize had already been taken at county level, and might expect endorsement by central government, but where the implementation of that decision was still an open question. In Lancashire's Division 9, a working party of divisional executive members and teachers was set up to decide between the possible future patterns of secondary education laid down by the county education committee. Opposing groups were formed out of the grammar school teachers, with support from the Conservative councillor on the one hand, and the Liberal and Labour nominees, supported by the NUT representatives, mainly primary school teachers, on the other. While the divisional education officer concentrated on the alternatives favoured at county level, opponents of reorganization consistently produced schemes which would preserve selection in one form or another or defer the completion of reorganization for the foreseeable future. Two supporters of reorganization, a Labour councillor and a former Liberal councillor, attempted to have adopted a scheme for a sixth-form college with feeder secondary schools for the age range eleven to sixteen; they were well satisfied with the airing this idea received although it was finally abandoned in favour of all-through comprehensive schools. The greatest disagreement occurred over the transitional plans rather than the long-term plans, but eventually a scheme for immediate change was accepted, receiving the support of the NUT representatives.

In this small-scale encounter, postures of neutrality were impossible if not irrelevant for the teachers' organizations: nearly all lined up consistently in support or opposition to proposals for change. Interestingly the only initiative to widen the debate over the educational alternatives offered by reorganization came from political representatives on the working party rather than teachers. However one might evaluate the specific commitments of teachers in the debate and the quality of decisions eventually reached, it remains true that teachers' organizations did not, from their professional base, contribute any extra dimension to the decision-making process.

While Labour remained in opposition its opportunities for developing comprehensive schools were restricted to local authorities where it was in control, and then to those occasions when a Conservative minister would allow experiment. Dismay at the apparent lack of interest of local groups was expressed as early as 1950 at party conferences. But by now the efforts of committed comprehensive supporters such as the NALT, the drift of party policy and of non-political educational thought, and, above all, the favourable publicity given to comprehensive experiments such as in London, Coventry and Leicestershire, led to a more positive attitude on the part of Labour-controlled education committees. Secondary school building was now a priority, and whenever a general election approached, with its promise of a sympathetic Labour minister in Curzon Street, plans for comprehensive schools would suddenly increase. The Labour Party's local government conference in 1959 concentrated on the means by which 'local education authorities could implement Labour Party policy by creating a comprehensive system of secondary education'.[120] The NALT conference in July the same year called for the preparation of plans along these lines. It is not surprising, then, that after the third successive general election defeat of Labour in 1959, the head of the government's education inspectorate could tell headmasters that the danger for the grammar schools was past and they could look forward to a long period of stability.[121] Even in 1964 Anthony Greenwood warned Labour local authorities that the party planned the abolish the eleven plus:

> But how many local authorities have got down to the practical details of applying the comprehensive principle in their own area?[122]

At national level, the unity of the party behind its educational policy was well assured. The right-wing revisers of economic policy priorities were loud in their insistence on the necessity for radical social and educational change. Anthony Crosland charted and predicted the line of policy development:

> We therefore need to select now a limited number of key issues and propagate them insistently and purposefully for the whole period up to the next election. . . . the issues which are most outstanding are, surely, first education . . .[123]

This was the direction in which Labour propaganda moved.

Signposts for the sixties[124] concentrated on five themes, one of which was equality of educational opportunity. The plans were not restricted to secondary education: they included points on teacher–pupil ratio in primary education, and the broadening of university entrance. Harold Wilson was already using the idea of a scientific revolution and 'a broader avenue of educational advance from the primary school'[125] at the 1960 annual conference. By 1963 he had already accomplished the integration of the comprehensive school policy with the wider theme of national revival:

> But to train the scientists we are going to need will mean a revolution in our attitude to education, not only higher education, but at every level. . . . As Socialists, Democrats, we oppose this system of educational apartheid, because we believe in equality of opportunity. But that is not all. We simply cannot as a nation afford to neglect the educational development of a single boy or girl. We cannot afford to cut off three-quarters or more of our children from virtually any chance of higher education.[126]

The importance of this sketch of the development of Labour's educational policy lies not so much in any effect it may have had on the electorate's sympathies as on its illustration of the way in which a policy at first almost totally rejected by the party leadership may be pressed on them from below. It also demonstrates the way in which a policy was transformed from a liability into an asset, an integral part of a concerted propaganda campaign which may well have contributed to Labour's return to power in 1964.

Chapter Seven

THEORY into practice: the Labour government 1964–70

Although issues play a limited role in the winning or losing of general elections, in 1964 both politicians and the electorate were more concerned about the issue of education than ever before. As early as 1957 the Labour Party had conducted a survey of public opinion on educational issues which concluded that, at that time, the electorate had little interest in either the public schools or comprehensive education. Party antagonism towards the techniques of the advertising world inhibited further testing of public opinion in this way, but in late 1962 an attempt was made to isolate a sample of 'floating voters' with the intention of testing these voters' attitudes towards political issues and Labour's stand on them. It was then found that Labour's educational policy attracted considerable support.[1] In the middle of the 1964 election campaign, National Opinion Polls found that the issue of education ranked second only to the cost of living in the minds of the electorate. It would seem that Labour's commitment in their election manifesto to a policy of abolition of the eleven plus and the reorganization of secondary education along comprehensive lines did not, at the very least, damage their prospects of victory.

The Conservative policy for the organization of secondary education in the general election of 1964 was necessarily vague. They continued the attack on Labour's 'doctrinaire' plans for secondary reorganization, branding them as involving the destruction of the grammar schools. For themselves they could only put forward the general aspiration to provide 'opportunities for all children to go forward to the limits of their capacity in good schools of every description'.[2] A commitment to the raising of the school-leaving age and to a general expansion of the education system did not differentiate their policy from that of other political parties in the election. The limits of their flexibility had been reached and the forward ground was already occupied by the Labour Party. The Conservative government had unintentionally contributed to its own defeat by acknowledging and fostering the increasing importance of education, by tolerating the comprehensive schools until they were too important to ignore, and by failing to convince the interested public that it had an alternative answer to the 'bogey of the eleven plus'.

Although the first speech from the throne prepared by the Labour government gave no specific commitment to early comprehensivization,[3] the Conservative opposition and the pace of policy development in the localities allowed no respite to the new secretary of state for education, Michael Stewart. In October 1964, the Liverpool authority, now under Labour control, decided on full comprehensivization within a year. The local Conservatives did not press home their opposition to the scheme but pupils at Liverpool grammar school and their parents were soon vocal, and the voluntary aided schools, which catered for 40 per cent of pupils, opted out of the scheme. Liverpool parents coordinated their pressure on the national government with similarly-minded parents in Bristol, and enjoyed the support of Liverpool teachers' associations in opposition to the particular proposals, if not the principle itself. Groups of children marched and counter-marched in opposition to reorganization and parents planned to raise so many objections with the secretary of state that a public enquiry would have to be held.[4] Bristol parents had a spokesman in Parliament in Robert Cooke, who claimed 'this seems to be part of some sinister national plan of the Labour Party – most sinister indeed – to destroy fine schools which are doing a splendid job of work and to impose unwanted on the country a pattern which is only just beginning to be effective'.[5] Although the minister understandably required time to prepare a considered policy on secondary school organization, the submission to him by Bristol of its own plan for reorganization prompted both ministerial discussion of alternatives and parliamentary consideration of policy before it was carried out. The promise was given that a general statement of policy would be put to the House of Commons and it was said that arrangements were being made for consultation with the national teachers' organizations on this issue.[6] The minister's clear intention was to play for more time and to continue to hold the middle ground in the debate:

> I think that this process [of grammar school change] has to continue. I do not say that this can be done without anxieties and heart-searching among many people. I was myself a sixth-form master in a

grammar school and I know well how some people who have served these schools very well indeed must naturally feel . . . if we approach them reasonably I think we shall get a reasonable answer.[7]

One of the Conservative members for Bristol proposed a motion in November which attempted to steal back the middle ground while defending Bristol's grammar schools.[8] Even so, the secretary of state was able to keep his options open, coming down firmly in favour of a national policy but adding 'I would reject any plan for educational reorganisation which imagined it had become meritorious merely because it had abolished selection. . . . I would rather wait a bit for a good comprehensive system than try to push a sham version in its place'.[9]

Criticism of her own school by one of the teachers at Kidbrooke in December 1964[10] provided another opportunity for a former Conservative minister of education, Geoffrey Lloyd, to attack the government's commitment to secondary reorganization by asking for a review of well-established comprehensive schools.[11]

Although opinion had moved a long way towards support of Labour's policy on secondary education, there was still scepticism of the value of the change to comprehensives among teachers' organizations and strong criticism of the haste with which some local authorities were setting about reorganization. Lack of consultation with local teachers was the recurring complaint at teachers' conferences in January 1965, and, according to a report in *The Times*, the AMA council 'seemed to divide between a sympathy, of the heart perhaps, for the diehard supporters of the grammar school and a forward-looking appreciation of what was said about the need to develop education to meet modern requirements. Both were listened to and well applauded'.[12] Total opposition to reorganization was still expressed at the IAHM conference:

> The grammar school, which had no class barriers and provided equal opportunity for all who were capable of profiting from it, was one of the most potent democratic influences in our society. . . . A neighbourhood comprehensive school which abandoned intellectual segregation would put social segregation in its place.[13]

It was no surprise, then, that the opposition front bench should take up the issue once more, choosing to use one of the supply days in January 1965 to debate education. A motion, in the names of Quintin Hogg and Sir Edward Boyle, recommended discouragement of local schemes for comprehensive schools carried out at the expense of grammar schools, and rejected the case for a national policy. In opening the debate, Quintin Hogg called for a bipartisan policy based on the views of non-political educationists. The secretary of state was prepared to accept a bipartisan policy if the opposition clearly rejected segregation at eleven plus:

> The rejection of separatism means that in time – and in pursuit of agreement I will go a very long way over the question of timing and method – we will not have schools whose entry is based upon selection and presumed judgement of a child's abilities at the age of 11.[14]

Almost immediately after this debate in Parliament, Anthony Crosland became secretary of state for education. Clearly a change of minister would tend to delay publication of a detailed policy on secondary reorganization; nevertheless, the new minister was quick to comment:

> The complete establishment of comprehensive secondary education will take a considerable time. I believe, however, that in five years such progress could be made that the comprehensive system would be accepted as the normal pattern, towards which all local authorities were working though necessarily at different speeds.[15]

He also made it clear that plans for change must be constructive and not 'any old makeshift scheme'. Protests over local schemes for comprehensives were now being heard from Luton parents and from teachers in Manchester.[16] Crosland's first public response was to tell Liverpool that time would be needed to consider their plans and that therefore selection for secondary education would need to continue for another year.[17] As a junior minister in the Department of Education and Science said, 'We would rather wait a little longer for a good scheme from a particular area than have a local authority rush in with an ill-considered scheme'.[18] In Liverpool, Conservatives and Liberals joined together in an unsuccessful attempt to make the local authority reconsider its plans. The Conservatives still did not ask for a rejection of comprehensives but called for a 'genuinely representative working party' to devise a less disruptive scheme.[19]

While dealing with individual local authorities, the minister had at the same time to produce, after consultations with teachers' organizations, a national policy. It was understood that a departmental circular was in preparation and Crosland rejected the case for compulsion disingenuously put to him by Conservative members of Parliament, expressing his confidence that local authorities would respond to a request for submission of plans.[20]

Clearly the minister wanted to move only a little ahead of the consensus of opinion: it would appear that he had the explicit backing of the cabinet for a policy of voluntary guided reorganization.[21] His negotiations with teachers' organizations and local authority associations were therefore long and detailed. At the beginning of May 1965, he claimed that

> discussions have now gone a considerable way, and I think it is important to say that there has been a very marked degree of agreement on our basic approach. The tone of the negotiations has throughout been extremely cordial. There has been no dog-fight, nor anything remotely resembling it, between my department and the local authorities.[22]

Even so, it was reported later in May that a draft of the circular sent to local education authorities for comment was being revised to make it sound more advisory and less directive.[23]

Crosland's first decisions on plans submitted by local authorities were a considerable blow to the hopes of Labour councils for a speedy reorganization. After seeing a delegation of parents from Luton opposed to their local plan, the minister rejected it and offered to discuss the matter with Luton councillors. The scheme had been rejected ostensibly because it involved closing one school only to reopen it a year later, which would necessitate a long legal process under Section 13 of the 1944 Education Act. Local Conservatives who had organized a petition of 11,000 signatures could be well pleased with their apparent success. Reaction on the Labour side was shocked and bitter, but talk of defying the minister's wishes soon subsided; as the chairman of the education committee said, 'We just want him to think again'.[24] By October the local authority had revised its plans on the advice of the ministry and were almost ready to re-submit them.

Stoke-on-Trent had its plans accepted in principle but rejected in detail, while Liverpool's were partly accepted and in large part disapproved. In April Crosland saw members of the Liverpool education committee to discuss objections raised to their scheme. In June no decision had been announced despite pressure from the local authority. In July it was announced that three of the proposed mergers were acceptable, another seven were given conditional approval and thirteen were rejected. Liverpool education committee immediately decided to go ahead with the three approved mergers, despite an attempt by Liberal and Conservative members to have the whole scheme withdrawn. The other proposals were revised and submitted again to the secretary of state with full approval from the city council.

In other local authorities where Conservatives were in a minority they reacted strongly to local plans for reorganization. In Manchester, Conservatives opposed the Labour scheme as 'unworkable' and circulated 75,000 leaflets condemning it during the local election campaign of 1965. Birmingham's scheme was characterized by the Conservatives as 'reckless, expensive and unnecessary'. Bournemouth, under Conservative control, decided that comprehensive schools were 'unnecessary and undesirable';[25] this was the first local education authority in the country to reject outright any move towards reorganization of secondary education after Labour had come to power nationally. Brian Redhead, minister of state for education, discussed the situation with the Labour minority on Bournemouth's council but refused to commit the government to any use of compulsion against the authority.[26]

Circular 10/65 was published on 12 July 1965. It described in detail alternative schemes of reorganization that would be acceptable in principle, and asked that plans should be submitted within a year, and should contain both a general statement of the authority's long-term proposals and a detailed plan for change over three years starting not later than September 1967. At the same time, by both its tone and its content, the circular attempted to reassure the less enthusiastic local authorities that the government understood the need for local variety, and to restrain the precipitate enthusiasm of some Labour authorities.

Four out of six model organizations of secondary schools were proposed by the ministry as fully comprehensive in character. Ideally, all-through comprehensive schools catering for an age range of eleven to eighteen should be set up. A two-tier system in which pupils attended a junior comprehensive school from eleven to thirteen or fourteen and then all transferred to a senior school was also acceptable: although such a system would require close cooperation between junior and senior schools in matters of curriculum, syllabus and teaching methods, there were distinct advantages in fitting such schools to the capacity of existing buildings. A three-tier system covering both primary and secondary education (five to eight/eight to twelve/twelve to eighteen *or* five to nine/nine to thirteen/ thirteen to eighteen) would be acceptable in a few cases only, although fully comprehensive in character. This was because the Central Advisory Council was currently considering the age of transfer to secondary education and any widespread adoption of a middle-school system would present the council with a *fait accompli*. A system of secondary schools covering the age range eleven to sixteen and followed by a sixth-form college drawing on a number of schools would only be acceptable occasionally. It was argued that successful experience with such colleges was very limited and, although they might have both educational and economic advantages for those who attended and those who provided them, there would be disadvantages of a similar nature for the schools deprived of sixth forms and the fullest range of specialist teachers.

Two other sorts of reorganization were acceptable as a transitional arrangement, but not as part of a long-term plan since they both retained selection at some stage. There were two-tier plans, with either transfer to the senior school for some at the age of thirteen or fourteen while the remainder completed their secondary education in the junior school, or transfer at thirteen or fourteen for all to specialist senior schools.

The main consideration in all these alternatives, including the compromise transitional plans, was the relative inadequacy of existing buildings to the demands of comprehensive schools which would cover the full range of ability and, it was argued, would need to be a minimum six-form entry size. The most disappointing aspect of the circular was its statement that

> It would not be realistic for authorities to plan on the basis that their individual [building] programme will be increased solely to take account of the need to adapt or remodel existing buildings on a scale which would not have been necessary but for reorganisation.

The circular received immediate criticism from the Joint Four secondary associations but other teachers' organizations gave it a general welcome. The NAS said they would 'co-operate with local education authorities who act in the spirit of the circular',[27] the NUT supported the policy but commented 'in the union's view there is one big question mark about the entire circular. If the government is going to ask local authorities to go comprehensive it will have sooner or later to provide the money for the job'.[28] *The Times Educational Supplement* made the same point in an editorial,[29] and a fortnight before, at the AEC conference, the chairman of Coventry education committee had claimed 'It's cash that counts'.[30] Support for a comprehensive policy voiced at the AEC conference was echoed at the annual conference of divisional executives for education in September, where delegates voted overwhelmingly in favour of comprehensive schools while again pointing out that reorganization would be delayed if the necessary funds were not available.[31]

It had always been the rank and file at Labour Party conferences who had evinced the greatest enthusiasm for secondary reorganization. In December 1964 the first conference for many years was held with a Labour government in power. Amidst the euphoria of oratory it almost passed unnoticed that the new prime minister, Harold Wilson, expressed no clear and substantial commitment to educational reform. Debating the party leader's speech, David Rubinstein drew attention to the possibility that in education 'above all else, we can in a relatively short time do something to work for socialism'.[32] In 1965 an emergency motion on immigration cut short the intended debate on education, where a motion had been tabled pressing the government to speedier action in reorganizing secondary education. The proposer was well aware, as were all others interested in education inside and outside the party, that reform required finance if it was to be successful. In 1964 Rubinstein had cautioned: 'until we have housing estates which represent all classes in society, until our schools are socially as well as intellectually comprehensive, they are not being properly comprehensive'.[33] A year later delegates were warned: 'the educational system can only become genuinely comprehensive if the practice of selection (i.e. streaming) is actively discouraged'.[34] Attention was moving from the externally visible marks of a selective secondary school system, to the less obvious problems of internal organization and demographic setting of secondary schools. Such subtleties were, understandably, absent from the government's own summary account of its progress. The prime minister reported that a 'purposive start on the ending of the 11-plus selection and the creation of a truly comprehensive system'[35] had been made, and the parliamentary report asserted that 'about two-thirds of the secondary school children in the country are living in the area of authorities who have already decided to go comprehensive in all or part of their territory'.[36]

Debate at Conservative Party conferences in 1965 and 1966 provides clearer evidence that the political initiative in secondary education remained with the Labour government. In 1965 a long motion defended the previous Conservative government's record in education, but acknowledged 'that comprehensive schools have an important part to play in the education system'.[37] The proposer was able to mock the government's plan for research into comprehensive education as 'Socialist science' where 'you do the main project first and have the pilot scheme afterwards',[38] but the next speaker pointed out that 'a rigid system of testing ability which has a finality about it cannot provide the equal opportunity we demand for our children. For this reason, the Party must welcome the move away from such an inflexible system of selection as the 11-plus'.[39]

Lena Townsend, a Conservative member of the Inner London Education Authority, thought the motion 'wishy-washy', but Sir Edward Boyle in replying to the debate had no difficulty in reconciling the views expressed by delegates with his own moderate policy: 'Let us firmly stand by our ideal of secondary education for all and do not let us ever give the impression that we are interested only in the secondary education of one section'.[40]

In 1966 the attack on Labour was more general, and criticism of the comprehensive school policy oblique. Kathleen Ollerenshaw, the leader of Conservative educational opinion on the Manchester city council, saw concentration on secondary reorganization impeding plans for the raising of the school-leaving age. While many local authorities were still firmly under Labour control and the national government had been returned with a much larger majority only six months before, there was little opportunity for potentially successful political opposition to the comprehensive policy. As long as this was so, the gap between feeling in the grass roots of the party and Sir Edward Boyle's national lead could be bridged or tolerated.

From Labour's conference delegates, especially those from counties traditionally under Conservative control, there was a welcome for a proposal in 1966 for legislation to compel local authorities to reorganize their secondary schools. At the very least it was felt that with more money 'the rate of reorganisation could be speeded up'.[41] Despite opposition, Jennie Lee, for the national executive, successfully persuaded delegates to remit the proposal to the executive with an account of progress made in reorganization throughout the country:

> Do not underestimate that we have won the intellectual argument against the 11-plus, do not underestimate that it is becoming more and more difficult for any civilised man or woman, whatever their politics, to put up an impressive and convincing case against the comprehensive principle.[42]

Although the Labour government did its best to turn aside the accusation that they were forcing local education authorities to reorganize secondary education, the Conservative election campaign in 1966 had made a good deal of the issue of local freedom. The Conservative leader referred at his press conference to 'an arbitrary interference with the power of local authorities to put forward proposals which they believe to be right in themselves'.[43] The issue was particularly topical in that a DES circular had just been published which implied that capital loan sanction would only be available for secondary building on comprehensive principles; 'council officials seemed to accept that as the Government had laid down a policy line on comprehensive schools the latest circular was a natural consequence';[44] and the minister argued that to follow Mr Heath's policy would amount to accepting the extension of the eleven plus into new areas where building was needed.[45]

With its increased majority after March 1966, the Labour government made every appearance of progressing steadily with its policy of secondary reorganization. In August 1966 it was reported that only three authorities had explicitly refused to send in plans for reorganization, fifteen local authorities had had their plans approved in full, another fifty-two had received partial approval and a further sixty-eight authorities had submitted plans for approval. Where Conservative controlled local authorities showed some willingness to plan for reorganization the secretary of state went to great lengths to encourage their cooperation by persuasion, one of his strongest weapons being control of building plans.

Surrey's first submission to the DES in response to Circular 10/65 proposed large secondary schools similar in scope to comprehensive schools, but existing alongside small grammar schools offering highly academic courses. The proposals did not fall within the six alternative models for reorganization suggested in Circular 10/65, and the minister rejected the Surrey plan along with those of Richmond and Kingston-upon-Thames in December 1966. The Surrey teachers called on the county education committee to abolish all selection for secondary education and claimed that the continuing delay was undermining parent, teacher and pupil morale in the county.[46] Later in 1967 an education committee working party which had discussed possibilities with a ministry official reported back to the committee in favour of ten- to twelve-form entry comprehensives topped by sixth-form colleges. The education committee rejected this plan by twenty-six votes to fourteen, despite its need to win DES approval for essential secondary school building in the county.[47] The minister deferred his decisions on proposals for seventeen Surrey schools. A meeting between the chairman of the county council and the minister preceded a further revision of the working party's plan, the only substantial alteration being the deferment of the date for implementation to 1971, and in October 1967 the Surrey education committee accepted the proposals.

In the local elections in 1967 the dissatisfaction of the electorate with the performance of the national Labour government showed itself decisively. Many Labour local authorities were lost to the Conservatives, including some which had put forward controversial plans for school reorganization. *The Times Educational Supplement*, which had never been more than lukewarm in its attitude to comprehensive schools, commented:

> To construe the results as a vote of confidence in the tripartite system would be excessive. What can be said, however, is that all the talk about the wave of public indignation at the existence of selection in education is nonsense. It is just not there; it does not show itself on the chief measuring rod that politics provides. For the ordinary voter other things come first.[48]

Although there might be some truth in this, it was also true that the development of comprehensive schools was by no means abandoned as a result of the change in control of so many local education authorities. Schemes of reorganization for the whole or part of at least twenty-two authorities of which the Conservatives won control in 1967 had already been approved. Approval had also been given to seventeen other schemes submitted by Conservative controlled authorities, and in a similar number of Conservative authorities schemes were under consideration. Only in a small minority of authorities was reorganization likely to be completely halted. In some of these cases the secretary of state might well have been glad to see further revision of plans. It seemed unlikely that the change of power locally would provide a widespread confrontation with the government. Much more likely was a slowing down of the rate of change; as *The Times Educational Supplement* had itself suggested in 1966, the

> wisest attitude for those who oppose comprehensive policies as harmful to education will be to regard the campaign against them as having to be long drawn out, to be waged for a generation and through the lifetime of several governments. . . . A diplomatic resistance, the skilful use of delaying tactics, a certain haziness in plans presented for the future are weapons which local authorities can use to effect when satisfied that their present provision of secondary education is efficient and just.[49]

The old LCC had been one of the first authorities to provide comprehensive schools in its area; although steady progress towards reorganization was being made, the large number of voluntary aided grammar schools with some powers of self determination impeded the completion of the change. The ILEA, set up in 1964, was Labour controlled during the first three years of Labour government nationally, and it determined to increase the number of comprehensive schools to 113 by 1970, bringing in a large number of county and voluntary aided grammar schools. Early in 1966 the Association of Governing Bodies of Greater London Aided Grammar Schools announced its opposition to such proposals:

> We are of the opinion that a universal comprehensive system of secondary education cannot be justified in the light of experience. The time allowed for proper consideration and discussion of the fundamental proposal for reorganisation is deplorably and unrealistically short.[50]

When the ILEA's plan was announced in November 1966, diocesan authorities, both Anglican and Roman Catholic, who had overall responsibility for many aided schools, were reported to be eager to cooperate; outright and powerful opposition could be expected to come from the individual governing bodies of grammar schools sponsored by the churches.[51]

The situation changed dramatically when the ILEA was unexpectedly captured by the Conservatives in the 1967 local elections. The leader of the Conservatives on the ILEA was vehemently opposed to comprehensives and was thought to be willing to encourage a confrontation with the government on their policy.[52] Anthony Crosland's reaction to Labour's local election reverses was cautiously optimistic. The secretary of state was prepared for a slowing down in the pace of change but did not expect any new direction for change. He reiterated a warning: 'I have said all along that if it came to a confrontation . . . it would be quite proper to settle it by legislation'.[53]

However the new Conservative majority on the ILEA avoided confrontation on this issue by simultaneously appointing as alderman and electing as leader Christopher Chataway. He hoped to 'do what we think is right with some give and take on both sides'.[54] The ILEA immediately moved to withdraw for further consideration the existing London plan; the deputy chairman, Lena Townsend, said:

> We intend to look at every proposal on its merits . . . we have no intention of breaking up existing comprehensive schools . . . we also allow that when plans for amalgamation or expansion of a grammar school have gone too far we may not be able to put these plans into reverse . . . we feel that schools and children, unlike the steel industry, cannot be nationalised then denationalised, then nationalised again.[55]

The Times carried letters at this time criticizing the Conservative leadership on the ILEA for not carrying out its promise to save grammar schools. Within less than six months a new plan was made public under which the number of comprehensives in London would rise from thirty-one to seventy-eight by 1975. There would then still be forty grammar schools in London catering for 10 per cent of the secondary school population.

A complex situation arose in Manchester in 1966 and 1967, where conflict surrounded not the principle of comprehensive reorganization but the Labour majority's particular proposals and went beyond party alignments. Co-opted members of the education committee refused to vote for the Labour nominee for deputy chairman and instead elected the Conservative spokesman on education, Kathleen Ollerenshaw. Although it was immediately arranged that the clear Labour majority on the full council would later overrule the education committee's decision, in the meantime Dr Ollerenshaw accompanied the Labour chairman and officers at their meeting with the minister to discuss the Labour submission under Circular 10/65.[56] In objecting to the submission the Conservatives had proposed their own alternative three-tier system which Dr Ollerenshaw was in a position to discuss. Shortly afterwards the secretary of state approved a good part of the Manchester submission but rejected the proposals for creating six comprehensive schools, 'regarding many of the objections made to these proposals as being valid'.[57] The Labour education spokesmen pointed out that only 11 per cent of the scheme had been rejected, but the Conservatives replied that 'the limited approval received will give the education committee an opportunity to have a new long look at the best manner in which now to proceed'.[58] In May 1967 the Conservatives won control of Manchester, but their new chairman of the education committee, Dr Ollerenshaw, thought it unlikely that the committee would be able to alter the plan approved by the department to start comprehensive schools throughout the city.[59]

The non-party groups of parents and others who were opposed to reorganization had earlier taken steps to make their campaigns in localities more effective and set the pace for overt Conservative opposition. In October 1965 the National Education Association was formed, 'to safeguard parents' freedom of choice in secondary schooling', with an inaugural meeting of representatives of some sixty parents' protest committees, old boys' associations and heads and governors. Based on a federal structure the association hoped to coordinate and fund local opposition including legal action where necessary.[60]

Parent opposition in Ealing gained national publicity when the borough education committee announced that it was going ahead with a pilot comprehensive scheme in Acton. A committee of parents which had been negotiating with the borough decided to take legal action and sought an injunction in the High Court against any precipitate reorganization. The case was heard at the end of July 1966, and a decision had to be reached quickly as Ealing was planning to introduce its pilot scheme the same September. The parents argued that no regard had been given to the principle of educating children in accordance with their parents' wishes as required under Section 76 of the 1944 Education Act. Counsel for the borough of Ealing argued that the proper remedy for the parent was through the ballot box and that the council had not exceeded its powers in any way. In giving judgement against the parents, and charging them the costs of the action, Mr Justice Goff said that the aspects of education which were covered by Section 76 included such matters as religious instruction and curriculum but not the size of school or conditions of entry.[61] In October the parents' committee decided to give up their fight against the council because of the heavy costs involved. The NEA, which now had about 100 local groups affiliated to it in order to fight plans for reorganization, commented that the Ealing case was 'the wrong action at the wrong time'. Their spokesman added that the association would be 'fighting further actions on entirely different grounds'.[62]

Enfield parents organized a petition of 10,000 signatures opposing the borough's plan for comprehensives. When the secretary of state rejected part of the plan, the borough revised its proposals without, according to the parents' joint emergency committee, any further consultation.[63]

In April 1967, the emergency committee consulted Geoffrey Howe (a Conservative member of parliament and barrister) and launched an appeal for potential legal fees of £5,000. By June, £4,000 had been collected and solicitors had been instructed to serve a High Court writ on the borough preventing reorganization in September 1967.[64] The High Court rejected the parents' case on the ground of 'balance of convenience'; the chief education officer had testified that chaos would follow if the writ were granted.[65] However, the parents appealed against the decision and a temporary injunction was given against the opening of eight out of sixteen comprehensive schools in Enfield because the borough had not complied with the requirements of the 1944 Education Act. The DES had told Enfield that notices of changes in the character of some schools had to be published and a formal procedure for considering objections followed; but, the borough argued, in the case of some other schools the ministry had advised that formal procedures were not necessary. The Court of

Appeal pointed out that the ministry's advice was not law and decided that the requirements of the Education Act had not always been carried out by Enfield. The case also raised the question of approval of 'new schools' which did not conform to the requirements of the school building regulations. The ministry had only applied such requirements to schools that were newly built.[66]

While the case attracted considerable publicity, was regarded as a victory by the parents and encouraged parents in other areas to consider taking similar action, its effects on Enfield's plan for reorganization were limited. The borough council immediately reaffirmed its determination to reorganize and began the statutory process of obtaining approval for the change of character of the schools affected by the court decision. Under its plan, twenty-eight out of thirty secondary schools were to become sixteen comprehensives. Only eight existing schools due to form three comprehensives were affected by the parents' action, and only some of the children allocated to the schools or comprehensives had to be reallocated.

Enfield parents fought another rearguard action over the reorganization of Enfield grammar school as a comprehensive. They argued this time that the articles of government of Enfield grammar school, which required a selective intake for the school, were being flouted, and judgement was given to them. At the request of the Enfield borough council, the secretary of state, then Patrick Gordon Walker, moved immediately to initiate the procedure for changing the articles of government of the school. Only a few days were allowed by the minister for objections to be made to him concerning the proposed new articles, and a combined application by a governor, a teacher at the school and the secretary of the parents' committee was made to the High Court requesting a declaration that the minister was illegally restricting the time for objections to be lodged. This was granted and the minister had to back down and allow a further month for objections.[67] Even so, after this period had elapsed Mr Gordon Walker approved the change. The Conservatives nationally responded strongly to these cases. It was announced that the leader of the opposition had asked the leaders of Conservative groups in local councils to see if parents had been given their full right of objecting to school reorganization; if not, local Conservatives should consider whether they could 'prevent the implementation of ill-thought-out schemes'.[68] The Conservative spokesman on education, Sir Edward Boyle, called the minister's action in arbitrarily restricting the time for representation to be made to him 'deeply regrettable. The opposition will certainly want to debate this'.[69]

As early as 1966 *The Times* commented on the uncertain future of direct grant schools, noting that some were to continue to provide a selective education for a small minority of pupils. In late 1967 the comprehensive schools' committee produced its own report on the government policy and claimed that local schemes had been approved which would retain selection until 1980 and beyond, hardening the existing system into a small, highly selective group of schools and a large number of creamed comprehensives.[70]

Successive Labour secretaries of state had made it clear that as a last resort they would be prepared to legislate to compel local authorities to reorganize their secondary education. The 1967 Labour Party conference debated a motion calling for just such compulsory reorganization and compulsory integration of independent schools to the state system. The proposer wanted to know 'How is it that after three years of Labour Government so many selective systems still exist?' Another speaker from Derby recognized that it was not only national government that was content to move slowly: 'I sit on an Education Committee where the local council has been Labour controlled for thirty years and yet they are still talking about comprehensive schools.' When Alice Bacon, for the NEC and the government, asked the conference to remit the resolution the proposer insisted on a vote. The motion was lost, but only by a small margin indicating the extent of grass-roots disillusion with the government's progress.[71]

The Conservative conference further served to indicate the polarization of attitudes. Local Conservative groups were now in control of many authorities and extensive opportunities to frustrate the government's policy were in principle available. The resolution under debate condemned the 'hasty and ill-considered imposition of a comprehensive system of education', but the tone and content of the proposer's speech was favourable to the principle of reorganization. Other speakers were of a different mind. Dr Hall of north-west Leeds was adamant: 'I wish we could forget some of this bunkum we hear about equality of opportunity in education.' Another speaker from Yorkshire pointed out that:

> we are to condemn 'hasty and ill-considered' imposition of a comprehensive system – not the Socialist principle itself. Presumably if it is not hasty and ill-considered we will accept the imposition . . . this is a pale pink Motion and it recommends pale pink policies.[72]

Despite these strong words a clear majority of the delegates supported the motion. Christopher Chataway, leader of the ILEA, spoke in its favour, as did Sir Edward Boyle in summing up the debate. For the first time the motion on education went to a vote, 1,302 delegates voting in favour and 816 against. In 1968, a motion was put forward for debate which completely ignored this area of controversy. The chairman of the conference debate would not at first allow any amendments, but when this ruling aroused strong resentment among delegates, Angus Maude was eventually allowed to propose an addendum condemning government pressure on local authorities and giving the party's full backing to local Conservative groups who resisted reorganization.[73] The extended motion was passed by an overwhelming majority, but not until after it had become clear that the intention of the party leadership had been different. The chairman of the party's national advisory committee on education pleaded: 'Let us not confuse the issue. Let us not have another occasion like last year.'[74] Sir Edward Boyle admitted 'I had thought today we might have devoted a larger share of the time to other subjects' and claimed that:

> there is a very wide measure of opinion in this country, including a great deal of Conservative opinion, which is not happy – has not been happy for a long time over selection into separate schools at the age of eleven and which believes that a gradual rational sensible approach to change is right. ... I am sorry if this view is not sufficiently right-wing for some or sufficiently left-wing for others. I will only say that I think it is the sensible view educationally.

In the latter part of the Labour government's period of office it became clear that consideration was being given to the introduction of a major new education bill, which would include provisions for compulsory reorganization of secondary education as a comprehensive system, but which would also include many other modifications of the 1944 Education Act. It was no doubt tactically wise to attempt to submerge the particular issue of comprehensive schools amidst a wide range of legislative changes which would most probably receive quite general approval. However, it became increasingly clear to ministers that the necessary minimum period of consultation with those involved in education, such as teachers' organizations and local authorities, over the precise terms of a major bill would effectively prevent its preparation and successful introduction before the next general election, due by March 1971 at the latest. The pressure from backbenchers and from the party for legislative action on the specific issue of secondary reorganization was not to be resisted, and in February 1970 the new secretary of state for education, Edward Short, introduced his bill to compel local education authorities to reorganize their secondary schools as comprehensives. He based his case for legislative compulsion on the arguments that the House of Commons had resolved in favour of comprehensive secondary education as long ago as 1965, and that while most authorities were reorganizing in the light of the overwhelming evidence against selection at eleven plus, there were a few authorities who still resisted both the evidence and national policy. The bill itself was straightforward in enunciating the principle of comprehensive organization for normal secondary schools, and in converting the call, in Circular 10/65, for the submission of reorganization plans according to certain procedures from an administrative request to a statutory requirement.[75] As the new education spokesman for the Conservatives, Margaret Thatcher denied that equality of opportunity in education would be achieved by reorganization, citing the differential effects of neighbourhood on school success. She went on to claim that comprehensive schools and grammar schools could exist successfully side by side, giving London's current system as an example, and pledged the Conservatives to repeal the legislation when next in power.[76] Labour speakers tended to criticize the bill, not for its principle of compulsion but for the slowness with which the principle might be effectively implemented. Sir Edward Boyle, speaking from the backbenches, attacked the idea of compulsion but made it very clear that he was in favour of the comprehensive principle.[77] In summing up the debate, the minister of state, Alice Bacon, pointed straight to the undeniable divergence of views in the Conservative Party between those who had moved, like Sir Edward Boyle, to a position of general support for a system of comprehensive secondary schools, and those like Mrs Thatcher, who were prepared to resist the trend. Miss Bacon demanded to know whether the Conservatives were in favour of abolishing selection or not.

In committee the bill, although containing only eight clauses, met with further detailed criticism from the Conservative members, and also from some Labour educationists who wanted to see its provisions strengthened. Christopher Price and Stanley Newens were two Labour members of the committee who voted against their government in support of an amendment making selective sixth-form colleges illegal.[78] They were also concerned to improve the bill in various other ways, sometimes receiving the oral support of the opposition members. Unfortunately for the government, three of its supporters were absent from the committee's eighth sitting, when a vote was taken on the main principle of the bill, establishing compulsory reorganization. The government were defeated by one vote leaving the secretary of state temporarily bewildered by the almost unprecedented situation. The committee adjourned and met again only to agree to discontinue consideration of the bill. One of the Labour absentees, Mr Mahon, explained that illness had kept him away. William Price had in fact only left the committee momentarily to attend another committee, but also apologized for the consequence of his absence. Christopher Price did not comment when an opposition member claimed: 'We are told that the Hon. Member for Birmingham, Perry Bar [Christopher Price], was away in Copenhagen. I hope that he does not think the price of his being in Copenhagen too high.'[79] Understandably the opposition were delighted with their success and explained Labour members' absences in terms of disillusion with the bill before them.[80] When the government proceeded to try to obtain the agreement of the house to the reinstatement of the vital clause by means of a recommittal of the bill to committee, the opposition challenged them with an extraordinarily large number of points of order to the Speaker; nevertheless the government were successful in restarting the process of considering the bill in committee.[81] On this occasion the declaration of a general election precluded the completion of committee discussions and the bill fell along with the government.

On the return to power of the Conservatives under Mr Heath, Mrs Thatcher became secretary of state for education and science, holding the post throughout the three and a half years of Conservative government. Her first political initiative, taken immediately on assuming office, was to withdraw Circular 10/65. She did not call a complete halt to plans for secondary school reorganization, but acted consistently with the belief that comprehensive schools and grammar schools could co-exist, and she gave great weight to the opinions of objectors to particular schemes of reorganization when having to take decisions under the provisions of Section 13 of the 1944 Education Act.

The return of a Labour government once again, as a result of the general elections of February and October 1974, implied a re-acceleration of the pace of reorganization. While it is too soon to detect any substantial evidence of this through statistics of the proportion of the school population in different types of school, the new secretary of state, Reg Prentice, has already taken action in issuing a further circular to local education authorities similar in intent to that of Circular 10/65 and is understood to be contemplating legislation compelling reorganization. He has also announced the cessation of direct grants to the small number of schools throughout England which were able to remain selective by virtue of their independence of local education authorities.

The pattern of secondary schools 1954–72, with particular reference to grammar schools and comprehensive schools

Year	Pupils					Schools				
	All secondary school pupils	Grammar school pupils		Comprehensive school pupils		All secondary schools	Grammar schools		Comprehensive schools	
	No. in '000s	No. in '000s	Col. 3 as % of col. 2	No. in '000s	Col. 5 as % of col. 2	No.	No.	Col. 8 as % of col. 7	No.	Col. 10 as % of col. 7
1	2	3	4	5	6	7	8	9	10	11
1954	1,822	518	28	12	—	5,054	1,181	23	13	—
1955	1,915	528	27	16	—	5,144	1,180	22	16	—
1956	2,057	544	26	27	1	5,262	1,193	22	31	—
1957	2,186	559	25	42	1	5,380	1,206	22	43	—
1958	2,331	599	25	75	3	5,550	1,241	22	86	1
1959	2,593	641	24	107	4	5,715	1,252	21	111	1
1960	2,723	673	24	129	4	5,801	1,268	21	130	2
1961	2,829	697	24	142	5	5,847	1,284	21	138	2
1962	2,836	708	24	157	5	5,890	1,287	21	152	2
1963	2,781	722	25	179	6	5,891	1,295	21	175	2
1964	2,830	726	25	199	7	5,894	1,298	22	195	3
1965	2,819	719	25	240	8	5,863	1,285	21	262	4
1966	2,817	713	25	312	11	5,798	1,273	21	387	6
1967	2,833	695	24	408	14	5,729	1,236	21	508	8
1968	2,895	656	22	606	20	5,576	1,155	20	748	13
1969	2,964	632	21	773	26	5,468	1,098	20	962	17
1970	3,046	605	19	937	30	5,385	1,038	19	1,145	21
1971	3,144	574	18	1,128	35	5,295	970	18	1,373	25
1972	3,251	540	16	1,337	41	5,212	893	17	1,591	30

Sources: DES statistics and Ministry of Education annual reports for appropriate years.

At the local authority level the pace of change is perhaps quickening as a result of two distinct factors. The Labour Party has recovered in many areas from the large-scale electoral defeats of the late 1960s and, where local control has been regained, has been quick to initiate plans for the reorganization of secondary schools. The second factor has been the general reform of the structure of local authority areas and powers. With executive effect from April 1974, many areas retaining a selective secondary education have been brought under the control of education authorities, counties or metropolitan districts, which also contain areas where the abolition of selection at eleven has already taken place. While in principle it would be possible for such unavoidable mergers of conflicting educational policies to be resolved by the imposition of one policy or the other equally, the political impracticability of reintroducing selection in areas where it has been abolished has meant that the trend towards comprehensives is dominant.

It can be seen from the table on page 148 that the movement towards reorganization both pre-dated the Labour government of 1964–70 and continued after its demise. The pace of change would seem, however, to have been significantly affected by the issue of Circular 10/65 and by the policy of persuasion. It is not until plans drawn up under Circular 10/65 begin to be implemented that the proportion of all secondary pupils in grammar schools begins to decline, and that decline continues up to the latest month for which statistics are yet available. At the same time it is important to note that the proportion of schools still designated 'grammar' has declined at a slower rate; in other words it has always seemed politically attractive to leave existing grammar schools unchanged for as long as possible. While supporters of the comprehensive school might claim, with some justice, that the general argument has now been won, their opponents have by no means retired from the fray and many battles still remain to be fought over the future of particular grammar schools.

Chapter Eight

The development of educational policy

This historical account of secondary education policy has been aimed at a better understanding of the process of policy-making in English education. It was clear at the outset that the initial pressure for reorganization of secondary education into comprehensive schools did not come from the top. It was not so clear that there was any groundswell of opinion among the electorate that forced reform upon central government. Rather, the organizations which mediate between governors and governed – the teachers' organizations, associations of local authorities and, above all, political parties – structured the attitudes of parents and ministers, producing different results and policies at different times. All those engaged in these para-governmental activities are, of course, electors, parents and individuals, and as such they may have contributed to developing policy; organized parents have now begun to play an active role in this sub-government of education. But the links of the sub-government with politics and political ideology generally have been made through one political party, and the sub-government remains for the most part answerable only to itself.

The study of the politics of comprehensive schools over the last twenty-five years is as much that of the struggle to bring the issue into the political arena as it is a study of executive decision-making. To delineate the structural constraints on the emergence of the issue, it has been necessary to concentrate on the organized groups within the sub-government of education. The supporters of the comprehensive school have had to straddle the boundary between education and politics in order to maintain even a foothold in the education policy process.

The response of the teacher groups to the development of comprehensive schools was first and foremost a sectional response, just as the 1944 Education Act and its immediate aftermath was a sectional victory for the old elementary schools and their teachers. Given the context of sectionalism, support for comprehensive schools had great difficulty in finding an institutional base. The apparent paradox of early support among grammar school teachers in the NUT is easily explained: by their very presence in the union of the mass of teachers they demonstrated their atypicality, their break with sectional aims and institutions. Even then, support within the NUT was short-lived and can be positively associated in part with political rather than educational allegiance. This does not mean that there was no cross-current of opinions within the teacher groups, only that there was a failure in the present period to dominate any one group, apart from the 'promotional' New Education Fellowship, where the ideals of experiment and the sociological perspective were reconciled by the social unifier of the comprehensive school. We cannot doubt the conviction of individual headmasters that the IAHM was never against comprehensive schools, but we must compare this personal experience with the expressed policy of the association and draw our conclusions about internal group pressures from that. We can perhaps attribute the apparent hostility in part to the consequences of the decision to make a reply to the Labour Party's proposals for secondary education. A coherent statement involved the abandonment of neutrality or indecision on the value of various aspects of the secondary education system; the consensus which could be reached, and which was indeed reached in 1954, was bound to harden the policy of the secondary associations in the direction of the inviolability of the grammar schools. A contrasting process can be seen in the NUT, where no firm stand was taken at any time during the period, and where maximum internal flexibility was preserved.

The polarization of opinion between habitual opponents may have been part of the reason for the sceptical neutrality of the NAS, especially in London. The London teachers' association from the very first supported and even pushed the LCC and its plan for comprehensive schools; the London branch of the NAS remained sceptical of them.

There can be no doubt either that in the larger teacher groups considerable tactical skill was employed, both by those whose loyalty was to comprehensive schools, and those whose major concern was to preserve group consensus. It seems likely that the policy of encouraging or undertaking investigation into the success or otherwise of existing comprehensive schools fulfilled several group objectives, as well as making a substantial contribution to knowledge of the educational system. It enabled the later discussions – often ignorant, always emotional – to be based on better information than the occasional snippet from American high schools. For the supporters of comprehensive schools, aware of their own numerical and strategic weakness, such investigations were an opportunity to keep the issue open, and to gain a foothold in group machinery. Finally, for the uncommitted leaders of groups, the investigations provided the opportunity for channelling the energies of these supporters in directions not destructive of the groups, while avoiding the danger of alienating the mass of members, and thereby losing their own positions.

The connection between the attacks on the eleven plus and those on the tripartite system is more clearly seen in the activities of the political groups, but within the teachers' organizations there were clearly attempts to associate the two. Criticism of selection, whose obvious corollary was the advocacy of the common school, focused on the eleven-plus examination, and within that on the intelligence test. Success in convincing groups of the inefficiency as well as the inequality of these tests might, it must have been thought, pay dividends in support for the common school. But while distrust of the selection process grew, not only among teachers but among the general public, there is little indication that this in itself led to support for the comprehensive school. Nowhere is this more clearly seen than in the early attitude of the headmasters, whose criticism of the eleven plus took an entirely different form. They and others argued in favour of a more comprehensive selection process in which the IQ test would be relegated to a minor role, rather than the abandonment of the whole system because the one supposedly objective ingredient had been judged inadequate.

The intention of Sir Fred Clarke, the first chairman of the Central Advisory Council, had been to make the council an independent source of policy initiative and as such it might well have taken up the issue of secondary school organization. As it turned out, the council came to be reconstituted virtually afresh with every new assignment, and never took its own initiatives. Even so, the subjects of its enquiries provided opportunities for favourable comment on the growing role of the comprehensive school in the secondary education system. While the Scottish and Welsh equivalents of the council did come out strongly in favour of the comprehensive school, the Central Advisory Council for England did no more than help to confirm the tone and the language of educational debate.

The repeated requests of the IAAM for an enquiry into the different types of secondary education were refused by successive ministers; the association accepted that it had been 'impractical', despite the fact that this topic was quite within the advisory council's basic terms of reference. The impracticability to which ministers referred was that of expecting a committee to reach a decision which went any way beyond the consensus existing among the educational public on so controversial a subject, not the impracticability of having the topic investigated at so early a stage in the development of comprehensive schools. The most the council could and did do was to give some legitimacy to the eclecticism of ministers and to the local confusion.

J. A. G. Griffith claims that:

> it is difficult to exaggerate [the local authority associations'] importance in influencing legislation, government policies, and administration and in acting as coordinators and channels of local government opinion.[1]

But the local authority associations, led by the AEC, had made their attitude clear on the procedural issue early in the debate. Having asserted in conference the freedom of local education authorities to determine the structure of secondary education in their own locality, they pressed home their policy on the minister through a deputation:

> The deputation explained to the Minister the circumstances in which the resolution had been passed by the Association. They explained that the Association was in the fullest sympathy with the importance of experiment in this field. At the same time they were convinced that no final decision on any particular problem of secondary education could be made for a substantial period of time, probably ten years. It was therefore of the greatest importance that individual local education authorities should be free to experiment as they felt best in the interests of their own areas and they sought an assurance that the Minister would not lay down any precise pattern until full experiment had been conducted and a proper evaluation made.[2]

It seems unlikely that the AEC, which had no further internal debate on comprehensive schools throughout the period, was in a position to influence the minister's substantive policy on secondary organization.

On the occasion of the minister's refusal to sanction the closure of Eltham Hill girls' grammar school, the AEC felt that the general principle it had pressed was being undermined. Substantial publicity was given in the association's journal to the history of the approval of the London School Plan, implying that the ministry was deliberately attempting to thwart the LCC's legitimate intentions. Leading members of the AEC accompanied the LCC deputation to the minister; they left satisfied that general principles of procedures in streamlining and coordinating the approval of development plans and closures of schools were agreed with the minister. But this had no effect on the particular case of the LCC and Eltham Hill, or soon afterwards on the refusal to permit closure of Bec boys' grammar school in London. Concerning Manchester education committee's plans to open three comprehensive schools in 1956, the AEC executive

> adopted the Education Advisory Committee's recommendation that
> . . . in their view it is unnecessary to make further representations to
> the Minister of Education, having regard to certain assurances already
> made by the present Minister and by his predecessor in office.[3]

The association assumed that Manchester did not want them to take action in their particular case, but only on the general principle, and thus avoided the possibility of a direct clash with the ministry on the issue of secondary reorganization.

Unless some secret process was in existence which it is impossible to document at all at the moment, relations between organized interest groups and the Ministry of Education appear then to have excluded the topic of comprehensive schools until the 1960s. The larger groups had internal disputes with which to deal first before being able, if ever, to put positive pressure on the ministry in this area of policy. Moreover, it was not their traditional role to assume responsibility for the more abstract items of educational policy. Only among the smaller organizations were there those who were oriented towards or forced into an explicit philosophy of education. The NEF stood consistently for the comprehensive school. The IAHM individually, and through the Joint Four, stood for the preservation of the grammar school and consequently a philosophy of secondary school segregation. On the other hand the subject associations like the Association for Science Education adopted the same neutral pose as the NUT. The impact of these smaller organizations as pressure groups must have been very limited. The Joint Four secondary associations, the only groups having their main numerical strength in the grammar schools, consistently over-reached themselves in their opposition to the comprehensives, so that even a sympathetic Conservative minister gently rebuked them. The balance of pressure between these groups must have been very even; their indirect impact through education of the public into active attitudes was probably greater. Opposition has focused very largely on the abolition of grammar schools rather than the establishment of comprehensive schools. Sympathy for the comprehensive idea percolated through to officials in the ministry, partly as a result of the 'education' given to inspectors and visitors in comprehensive schools run by committed supporters of them; in the same way the public was educated by the books, pamphlets, articles and news items that comprehensive schools and their supporters increasingly produced.

Despite their diffidence over coming to an agreed view on the local organization of secondary education, the pressure of the larger teachers' organizations was probably the cause of the ministry's increasing emphasis on flexibility in school organization. In 1953, Miss Horsbrugh had already abandoned one of the main planks of the tripartite theory and the early policy of the ministry when she told the AEC that she 'rejected the idea that the main purpose of the grammar school was to educate the small proportion of pupils likely to be capable of going to a university. That was not practical politics.'[4] Flexibility of purpose in the other types of school was encouraged by the removal of the ban on external examinations, and freedom given to secondary modern school heads to experiment with special courses at the top end of their schools. The development of the secondary modern was a prime interest of the NUT, a considerable number of whose members came from these schools. In 1955 they drew up a report[5] on their work which found 'real hope for the future' in the development of special courses. They found that the driving force behind this was the teacher in the school rather than the local education authority or the ministry. The line of communication and of influence was in this case upwards, still within education but dependent for success on the support of parents.

The new awareness of greater attainment potential among the mass of children, and the shift of the main stream of an increased child population to the secondary schools, led to the white paper of 1958, *Secondary education: a new drive.*[6] This attempted to keep open all the options for development, including comprehensives. The main problem which it tried to face was:

> That there are today too many children of approximately equal ability who are receiving their secondary education in schools that differ widely both in quality and in the range of courses they are able to provide.[7]

To the extent that this was an attempt to find a formulation of the problem that would receive assent in all quarters, the white paper represented roughly equal success for all educational groups in making their views known. It also represented the Conservative government's recognition of 'the concern that is currently felt over what has come to be known as the 11-plus examination'. The white paper reduced the problems of inequality to one of buildings, and its solution was therefore a promise of massive action to replace all-age schools and inadequate secondary moderns. Rebuilding of grammar schools was also to 'figure prominently in the five-year programme'. In summary, ministry policy on secondary organization up to 1965 can be explained in terms of an administrative stereotype: a combination of precedent and pragmatism led the ministry to abandon any plans it may have had for the coherent development of secondary education. The white paper *Secondary education: a new drive* seems to be little more than an attempt to put a bold face on a situation which was already out of control. Ministerial policy can be said to have done little more than move from aggressive to defensive neutrality between 1944–65.

If central government was unconsciously laying the base for a stronger argument for secondary reorganization – in partnership with teachers and those few local authorities which had originally rejected, and the larger number who had by no means fully accepted, tripartism – it was the Labour Party which was mainly responsible for keeping the comprehensive school issue explicitly alive during the 1950s. It is difficult to believe that without it the educational research on comprehensive schools could have received such backing and publicity, or even perhaps that there would have been sufficient schools in existence for the research to take place. The complex of political, teacher and academic influence on the development of the comprehensive schools idea can be seen most clearly in the case of the LCC's schools which achieved an international fame during the period. The modifications which appeared in Labour's policy, the greater emphasis on local choice and on educational evidence, seem to be due to a process of influence internal to the party rather than to the direct pressure of outside organizations. Those groups which attempted to tackle the Labour Party as a party on the issue were opponents of the comprehensive school who could take little comfort from the policy which emerged as a result of their efforts.

The force behind support for the comprehensive school came from the rank and file of the party under the leadership of the NALT. Neither of the two ministers of education in the post-war Labour government showed much sympathy for the comprehensive school or any understanding of the ideology behind it. Parliamentary supporters of the comprehensive school at this time were vociferous but still a very small minority; for the majority of Labour MPs secondary education was not an issue. Only at conferences of the party and of the NALT was there consistent and definite support for the comprehensive school. And yet by 1953 the Labour leadership had effectively capitulated to the comprehensive school lobby. It is possible to explain the capitulation as an exchange of influence between leaders and led. In a period of internal party disorder, the leadership was prepared to buy rank and file loyalty in more important policy areas by yielding in the traditionally less important policy area of education. This is perhaps more probable than that the leadership simply yielded to pressure from below. Even so, a more important role for Labour's extra-parliamentary party organization is indicated by this account of policy-making than standard studies of the distribution of power in British parties usu lly allow. The final conversion of the leadership to support for the comprehensive school in the late 1950s and early 1960s may have something to do with the change in political generations and party political leadership which occurred in the mid-1950s. But it probably also reflects the realization that the party organization was providing accurate intelligence of the trend of parent opinion which might, at last, be turned to electoral advantage.

A similar pattern in the policies of educational groups can be discerned during the period 1944–64; variations and different rates of development occur from group to group but the basic pattern is the same. This pattern cannot be entirely explained in terms of the internal life of the groups; there appear to be three main phases in the development of secondary education in England which had repercussions within each group, as well as for the activities of each group in relation to its outside contacts. The second half of the 1940s was a period of reconstruction, when the whole of the educational world was evaluating and re-evaluating national educational policy and local development plans. This atmosphere pervaded the conferences and discussions of the teacher groups. No less, the more settled atmosphere in politics in the late 1950s, and the opportunity to begin to evaluate and even reconsider some of the plans for the 1940s which were now in operation, is reflected in the research and reassessments of the teacher groups. The last phase is perhaps the one in which the activities of the teacher groups have been most obviously affected by outside influences; this is the phase of reorganization, beginning at the end of the 1950s and quickening in pace through the 1960s.

With full and positive commitments within the Labour Party nationally and success for the party locally in municipal elections in the early 1960s, a considerable impetus was given to demands for executive action in reorganizing secondary schools. Against these demands a flagging Conservative government made no very coherent response. A minister sympathetic to the case for comprehensive schools, Sir Edward Boyle, was prepared to accept practical proposals for change, but his party's record and current stand made it impossible for him to seize the initiative. With the advent of a Labour government, national and local policies came largely into line, and Circular 10/65 seemed an acceptable progression of policy to many in education who were not ardent supporters of reorganization. While teachers' organizations eventually moved towards acceptance of the comprehensive principle, they remained able to sidestep the main issue by concentration on the details of reorganization plans and the consequences for teachers themselves. Once the general commitment to change became specific to individual schools, a focus for local opposition was provided. The multiplicity of pressure from localities in turn supplied a basis for national Conservative opposition.

If the Labour government's policy seemed increasingly dilatory to its supporters, especially as the local political reverses of 1967 and 1968 returned Conservatives to power in many authorities, the Conservative Party was for the first time seen to be seriously divided on the issue. Many Conservative local authorities acquiesced in Labour's policy, some seemed happy to seize the opportunity for change, while only a handful remained adamant. The party political initiative slipped even further from Sir Edward Boyle's hands. The fierce debates on education policy at Conservative conferences in the late 1960s indicated the frustration of the party's grass-roots at the seeming indecisiveness of the leadership. Although Mrs Thatcher's first act as the new secretary of state for education in June 1970 was to withdraw the Labour circular, her three and a half years of power did no more than slow down slightly the rate of reorganization, an indication of Labour's success in confirming a pro-comprehensive consensus. By this time the main teachers' groups were in favour of the completion of reorganization. Sponsoring bodies such as the churches were in many cases already committed to elaborate planning and phasing of change; even Conservative controlled local authorities like Leeds were well ahead with their plans, to which time, money and building programmes were already committed, and were determined not to be frustrated.

This history began as an examination of certain organized groups and their role in the policy process in English education. The examination has shown that groups have played an important part in the development of comprehensive schools. But it has also been seen that the mechanics of the group process are by no means the whole story. The groups operate in a particular political context to whose creation they are part contributors but by which they are also constrained. Within the groups too there are ideological constraints on policy and action which permit manoeuvre but inhibit radical about-turns of policy.

To a considerable extent the dispute centred on the abolition of certain aspects of the English educational system which were the manifestation of traditional values of English education not in dispute. Segregated secondary education, especially in the grammar schools, was under attack; the concept of 'excellence' was not. There were, of course, other conflicting traditional values such as the emphasis on 'character development'; but the ambiguities and mutual contradictions of simultaneously held values were not such that they were perceived as exclusive alternatives; rather they provided the opportunity for variations of value emphasis from time to time.

The attempt of the Ministry of Education to restrict the role of the grammar school to that of academic hothouse by means of its educational advice and direct pressure in the immediate post-war period had only limited success. It undervalued the importance to English educationists of educational success in non-academic terms. But similarly unsuccessful were the attempts of the advocates of comprehensive schools to ignore the recognized problems of provision for the intellectually able in small unselective schools.

Later the tactics of supporters of the comprehensive school were to change. Once some of these schools had been in operation for the minimum necessary period of time, their advocates concentrated on an evaluation of their success primarily in terms of the grammar schools' criterion of 'ordinary' and 'advanced' level GCE passes. Success with children who would not have gone to a grammar school under a selective system thus came to be measured in terms of examination achievement. Only the more perceptive and persistent observer would not be satisfied with this indicator of success. This is not to suggest that comprehensive schools were not providing a 'sound' secondary education. What it does suggest is that the emphasis in publicity for the comprehensive school increasingly came to be on the narrow criterion of examination success; that this in turn was due to the traditional emphasis on academic excellence in English education and among the educational public; and that this remained largely unquestioned by opponents or supporters of the comprehensive school.

Two related values, one political (local freedom) and one educational (variety in education), have also had an impact on the development of the comprehensive school. Both have made it difficult to advocate a complete ban on comprehensive schools or a complete reorganization along comprehensive lines. Even the IAHM was prepared to accept the occasional comprehensive school. They disputed the point at which experiment became wholesale reorganization. Local authorities whose plans for comprehensive schools were rejected by the ministry phrased their protests the opposite way round. They said there was no educational variety and no local freedom when they could not go ahead with experiments in their area.

The political values of variety and local freedom have their structural expression in the system of local and central educational government set up under the 1944 Act. Whatever the secular trend to greater centralization of control of education, the governmental structure put the initiative for development firmly in the hands of the local education authority. The official frame of reference for decisions about the establishment of comprehensive schools has always been the ministry and the individual local authority; thus the cumulative effect of various similar initiatives in secondary organization on the national political debate was largely uncontrolled by any established national political mechanism until the Labour government initiative in 1965. Both political parties made use of these values 'variety' and 'local freedom'. Both changed sides in using them whenever it suited. Although consensus on the importance of such values tends to disappear when they are related to a particular controversial issue, they do provide common ground across 'issues' and with those only marginally concerned with educational policy. They were thus valuable weapons in the debating armoury of politicians and educationists. They were the common property of all the groups, the parties and bureaucracy, and as such could be used to create or emphasize areas of agreement. They were values which aroused a positive response from opponents and supporters of comprehensive schools and as such they shaped the decisions and policies of both.

Within the different organized groups, their different traditions and value-emphasis have affected either their policy on secondary education or their strategy in reacting to policy originating elsewhere, or both. The NUT is dedicated to the unification in one union of the teaching profession; whilst this might be thought to have encouraged sympathy for the comprehensive school, at first it led to caution in dealing with an increasingly divisive issue. Once the comprehensive school had established itself, none was quicker than the NUT to realize its potential as a recruitment mechanism, and leadership support was able to come into the open.

The policy of the IAHM was framed by an entirely different tradition, one of distrust of government bureaucracy, and idealization of the status of the independent schools. With this tradition it was likely that the association would oppose a 'system' rather than an 'institution' perspective in secondary education policy-making. Opposition to the comprehensive school was complementary to the association's successful emphasis on the special needs of grammar schools in staffing and equipment. The AMA falls into much the same tradition as the IAHM, but the other two secondary organizations have been, historically, much more concerned with attacking the *status quo* than defending it. This helps to explain their less aggressive attitude to the comprehensive school, and suggests that they may have been a restraining influence in the deliberations of the Joint Four.

The scepticism and hesitant acceptance by the NAS follows a similar pattern to that of the NUT. The slight time-lag may be due to the earlier alienation from the official policy process and some of its priorities characteristic of the union.

All teachers' organizations came to acknowledge their subordination to electoral decisions in favour of comprehensive schools, but an accurate assessment of their power must take into account the perpetual readiness of these organizations to place limits on their own range of competence and thereby increase the arbitrary power of other agencies of policy-making. This may spring from the acceptance of the subservience of pressure groups to legitimate government, national and local, or from a reluctant realization that outright challenge would be self defeating in a wider political context of pressure group subordination. Either way this diffidence plays an important part in the political development of the comprehensive school issue.

The structure of the educational groups largely reflected the traditional, institutional structure of English education: on the one hand, the secondary associations, drawing their members almost exclusively from the staffs of the selective secondary schools; on the other, the NUT and the NAS, much more accurately representative of the teacher population as a whole, their centre of gravity in the primary and non-selective secondary schools. With such a system of teacher groups it is difficult for general educational policies to emerge from their internal policy processes; it is much more common for sectional interests to prevail openly. The comprehensive school cuts across the basis of the educational interest group systems. As such it gained support largely from those atypical grammar school teachers who found their home in the NUT.

For the 'promotion groups' the story is only slightly different. The ASE, for example, had a concern for the comprehensive school as it did for all secondary education, but its place in the structure of groups intermingling with government precluded it from taking any position on so controversial an issue. The NEF had no such constraint, but correspondingly no very significant place in the structure of groups.

A study of policy-making in education shows that there can be no simple measure of pressure. It is necessary to distinguish between intention and effect in discussing the pressures of educational groups in England. While support of or opposition to the comprehensive school is a continuous variable, the weapons at hand to express this support or opposition are analogous to a discrete variable; they can only assume a finite number of values. An obvious example of this is the distinction between the level of support for the main political parties in England and its expression in terms of the English electoral system. This leads to two further conceptions: firstly, of a threshold above which support for a policy must rise if it is to make any impact at all; secondly, of a snowball effect whereby the expression of support for a policy may increasingly overstate the actual level of support. In this way it is possible to explain the growing commitment to wholesale secondary school reorganization while recognizing that the level of support for comprehensive schools was never so high. Neither the 1945–51 Labour government nor subsequent Conservative governments gave much support to the comprehensive school, but within both parties there was sufficient interest to keep the issue above the threshold level of support. On the other hand, within the NUT the supporters of comprehensive schools never managed to generate sufficient interest to force the executive to take any positive action during the 1940s. In the later phases of the history, the Conservative government itself, in recognizing as real the problems which the comprehensive school was said to solve, gave greater currency to that particular solution. Within the NUT the strategy of neutrality led to the recognition of a new sectional interest, the comprehensive school teacher, which in turn precluded the union from opposing the comprehensive school. The translation of opposition by the Joint Four into a demand for consultation, far from being simply a recognition that the battle was lost, was very likely an important factor in the loss of the battle. And yet, the Joint Four might retort, what else could be done? In order to remain an effective force at some level of educational decision-making, the more peripheral educational groups must cooperate with government. Under a committed national government, groups opposed to comprehensive reorganization were restricted to fighting procedure for planning and implementing change.

I have emphasized the importance of the cultural, structural and technical constraints contributing to the development of the comprehensive school as a political issue. At the national level it is difficult to find evidence of any leadership domination of circumstances until the Labour government of 1964–70. The measurement of immediate group pressures provides no more satisfactory explanation of the issue. The explanation probably lies in the interaction of a secular trend towards higher educational expectations on the part of the mass of parents and voters, and the circumstances outlined above which have given particularity to these higher expectations. Organized groups have been as often caught between these forces as they have been part of them.

A note on
sources

The greatest difficulty in writing contemporary history is lack of access to internal papers of departments of state. While I am conscious that eventual access to such papers may promote amplification or modification of the interpretation of policy provided in this volume, I hope that the public statements of government and the indirect sources of government thinking have been cautiously interpreted so that no outright reversal of major conclusions will be made. A search through *Hansard*, through *The Times* and through all the major educational journals such as *The Times Educational Supplement*, *Education* and *The Teacher* for the period 1940–70 has provided the basis for the study.

In local government, problems of sources have been only slightly simpler. The local equivalents of a newspaper of record like *The Times* rarely exist, and though in the studies of particular reorganization plans such newspapers have been consulted, particular caution has been exercised in interpreting the evidence they provide. On the other hand, it has proved easier, as in the case of Manchester, to obtain access to internal working papers of the local education authority.

Since the original emphasis of the study was on teacher pressure groups, all materials by way of journals and other semi-publications available from the headquarters of various associations, such as the NUT, the NAS and the Joint Four secondary associations, have been examined. Their journals often contain very full accounts of conference and executive debates.

Political parties produce reports of conferences and of activities as well as policy statements. While I have virtually ignored the Liberal Party after some initial investigation of its concern with this particular policy issue, I have been grateful to receive the cooperation of both Labour and Conservative Party organizations, nationally and locally, in facilitating my investigations.

There is an obvious incentive in studying contemporary history to use active participants as a major source of information. I have indeed interviewed numerous people in teachers' associations, in local government, in politics, but rather to amplify and corroborate (or otherwise) material gathered in other ways than to provide major substantiation of the story told. Participants, with the best will in the world, are liable to a partial view of events, modified by hindsight and blurred by distance in time. I am, of course, very grateful to them for their helpful cooperation.

At the time I began the investigation little or nothing was written on this theme from the same perspective of political studies. It was necessary to read the large literature of secondary education, but only as the research progressed to consider the various published accounts of policy formulation and implementation in individual local authorities or political parties. We still await any detailed study of a Conservative-controlled local authority's reaction to Circular 10/65. The following is a list of the more useful studies that have been made and which may supplement my own account:

R. Barker, *Education and politics: a study of the Labour Party*, Oxford University Press, 1972.
R. Batley *et al.*, *Going comprehensive*, Routledge & Kegan Paul, 1970.
D. Peschek and J. Brand, *Policies and politics in secondary education: case studies in West Ham and Reading*, Greater London Paper No. 11, 1966.
R. Saran, *Policy-making in secondary education: a case study*, Oxford University Press, 1973.

Notes and references

Introduction

1 e.g. D. Rubinstein and B. Simon, *The evolution of the comprehensive school 1926–66*, Routledge & Kegan Paul, 1969.

2 D. Easton, *A systems analysis of political life*, Wiley, 1965, p. 99.

Chapter 1

1 In the debate on the bill it was suggested that it would be much simpler to have a ministry than a board, and the Duke of Devonshire said, with characteristic candour, that the point was mooted when the bill was first proposed, but he was quite unable to recollect the reasons which weighed in favour of a board rather than a ministry. See Sir Lewis Selby Bigge, *The Board of Education*, Pitman & Co., 1934, p. 15.

2 It is striking that when Arthur Henderson was brought into the 1915 coalition cabinet to represent Labour he was given the post of president of the Board of Education as a sinecure. It seems unlikely that Churchill thought he was substantially forwarding R. A. Butler's political career by making him president of the Board of Education in 1941.

3 *Education Act 1944*, Section 7.

4 It did not, of course, eliminate private education, but it made the grant-aided secondary school the exception rather than the rule.

5 P. H. J. H. Gosden, *The development of educational administration in England and Wales*, Blackwell, 1966, p. 111.

6 Unfortunately for education it was slightly too early in its growth as a government concern to set the precedent of 'ministries'; Lord Salisbury defended his preference for a Board of Education by calling ministries 'an undesirable innovation in official phraseology' and it was left to the Ministry of Munitions in 1915 to start the fashion.

7 *Education Act 1944*, Section 1.

8 'This constitutes a greater restriction upon the autonomy of local authorities than had been contained in any previous local government statute.' G. Taylor and J. B. Saunders, *The new law of education*, Butterworth, 6th edn 1965, p. 84.

9 *Hansard*, 18 July 1944, Vol. 132, cols. 960–1.

10 *Education Act 1944*, Section 4. There was to be a further advisory council for Wales and Monmouthshire.

11 Gosden, op. cit., p. 116.

12 *Education Act 1944*, Section 4.

13 Sir Fred Clarke, 'Central advisory councils for education', *Political Quarterly*, 1949, p. 156.

14 The minister went on to indicate that secondary reorganization might be a suitable topic for consideration by the advisory council, but he specifically excluded 'administration' from its terms of reference. Members were very dissatisfied with the rigid distinction between the theory and practice of education and its administration.

15 Clarke, op. cit.

16 *Education Act 1944*, Section 4 (iii).

17 It was probably also intended to reduce the preponderance of university-based educationists in the membership of the council. The consultative committee had been required to have not less than two-thirds of its members qualified to represent the universities.

18 *Central Advisory Councils for Education Regulations*, S.R. and O. 1945, No. 152, 7 February 1945. The regulations were amended to make all members of the council serve for the same three-year period by S.I. 1951, No. 1742.

19 The 'Part III' authorities, named after the part of the 1902 Education Act which created them, were those municipal boroughs with a population exceeding 10,000 at the 1901 census and those urban districts with a population exceeding 20,000 at the 1901 census. The 1902 Education Act gave them responsibility in their area for elementary education, an administrative definition abolished by the 1944 Education Act.

20 It was the removal from local government of responsibility for hospitals and for electricity supply and the new drive for post-war reconstruction which made education now the major concern of county boroughs and county councils, not any favourable distribution of powers within the state education system.

21 Part One of the First Schedule to the 1944 Education Act does make provision for the creation of a joint education board of two or more councils where they would have been separate local education authorities but for the unjustifiable costs or inefficiency involved. One joint board for the Soke of Peterborough and the City of Peterborough was set up.

22 Particular categories of co-opted members were required under the 1902 Education Act and to this extent control of local practice in co-option was being relaxed. See Political and Economic Planning, *Councils and their schools*, 1948.

23 These committees are in an anomalous position since the members owe their loyalty to the local authorities from which they are drawn, rather than to each other, to the division or to the county authority. One critic suggests that over the twenty years since its creation the divisional executive has introduced another tier into the administration which results in delay on occasion, complicates the structure of local educational government and offers many opportunities for friction (Gosden, op. cit., p. 201).

24 *Education Act 1944*, Section 88. My information is that no minister has ever exercised this power.

25 Cmd 6523 of 4 May 1944.

26 It would be wrong to assume too easily that this means that legislative powers of Parliament are being usurped. 'It is an accepted constitutional principle in Britain that choice of policy within the powers given by statutes is a matter for the government not for the Commons, subject to the right of the courts to quash an illegal use of powers, and

subject to the right of the Commons to express a general lack of confidence in the government and so discuss it.' W. J. M. Mackenzie and J. W. Grove, *Central administration in Britain*, Longmans, 1957, p. 382.

27 *Ministry of Education staff*

	1 1/4/39	2 1/4/44	3 1/4/46	4 1/4/48	5 1/4/60
Administration	76	67	142	179	n.a.
Professional	27	18	28	32	n.a.
Executive	57	46	58	127	n.a.
Clerical	657	400	882	1,395	n.a.
Total	815	531	1,110	1,733	2,738
Inspectorate	349	308	424	502	n.a.

Sources: Cols. 1–4, *Ministry of Education Report*, 1947. Col. 5, D. Butler and J. Freeman, *British political facts 1900–1968*, Macmillan, 1969, p. 174.

28 e.g. Gosden, op. cit., p. 107; R. K. Kelsall, *Higher civil servants in Britain*, Routledge & Kegan Paul, 1955, p. 41.

29 W. L. Guttmann, *The British political élite*, MacGibbon & Kee, 1963, p. 335. Of nine civil servants in the Ministry of Education in these categories between 1950 and 1964 only one had received a state secondary education.

30 Quoted in Gosden, op. cit., p. 107.

31 K. C. Wheare, *Government by committee*, Clarendon Press, 1955.

32 'At one period when I was Chief Education Officer in Ealing, I knew that if I gave them half a chance the dominant group on the Town Council would have had my blood . . . the lesson is that if an officer has patience reactionary groups pass away with the years.' A. L. Binns, 'The chief education officer and his task', *Journal of Education*, 1957, p. 140.

33 'Return – Schools for Poorer Classes in Birmingham, Leeds, Liverpool and Manchester 1870', quoted in Gosden, op. cit., p. 128.

34 J. Vaizey, *The costs of education*, Allen & Unwin, 1958, p. 67.

35 J. R. S. Ross, *Parliamentary represen-*

tation, Eyre & Spottiswoode, 1948, pp. 400, 407, 411.

36 ibid., table 92.

37 J. G. Bulpitt, *Party politics in English local government*, Longmans, 1967.

38 ibid.

39 'After the London Labour Party captured control of the LCC in 1934, a series of organizational directives was issued to all Labour councillors. During more than a quarter of a century of unbroken rule, these directives hardened into a system of iron discipline. The kingpin of the LCC Labour hierarchy was the Leader of the Council, and his big lever of power was his authority to appoint all chairmen and vice-chairmen of the LCC committees. In turn, these committee leaders paid due homage to the Council leader by re-electing him to his leadership post each year.' F. Smallwood, *The politics of metropolitan reform*, Bobbs-Merrill, 1965, p. 304.

40 Bulpitt, op. cit.

41 H. Heclo, *The recruitment of Manchester city councillors*, unpublished M. A. thesis, Manchester University, 1966.

42 cf. W. E. Jackson, *The structure of local government in England and Wales*, Longmans, 1960, pp. 180–1, and H. V. Wiseman, 'Local government in Leeds, Part 1', *Public Administration*, 1963.

43 Heclo, op. cit.

44 B. E. Lawrence, 'The work and spirit of a local education authority', *Adult Education*, 1958, p. 97.

45 T. L. Reller, *Divisional administration in English education*, University of California Press, 1959, p. 166.

46 J. Picker, *The part played by teachers' organisations in the administration of education at the local level*, unpublished M.A. thesis, Manchester University, 1957.

47 Lawrence, op. cit., p. 89.

Chapter 2

1 N. Hans, *Comparative education*, Routledge & Kegan Paul, 1949.
2 A. V. Judges (ed.), *Pioneers of English education*, Faber, 1952, p. 13.
3 Sir G. Williams, 'The first ten years of the Ministry of Education', *British Journal of Educational Studies*, Vol. 3, 1954–5, p. 101.
4 J. M. Prest, *Jowett's correspondence on education with Earl in 1867*, Supplement to the Balliol College Record, 1965, p. 6.
5 R. Jenkins, *Sir Charles Dilke*, Collins, 1958, p. 54.
6 ibid.
7 R. Jenkins, *Asquith*, Collins, 1964.
8 ibid.
9 Part III of the 1902 Education Act permitted those borough councils with a population exceeding 10,000 and urban districts with a population of over 20,000 to become local education authorities with control over elementary education only.
10 Clause 25 of the 1870 Elementary Education Act had already provided the opportunity for indirect subsidy of church schools.
11 *Education Act 1936* – this sanctioned the payment of 75 per cent grants by local education authorities to non-provided schools for the provision of senior school places in return for the surrender of some control of the schools.
12 Given Morant's personality it seems fair to talk of his 'policy', although he was not the political head of the Board of Education.
13 *Regulations for secondary schools*, HMSO, 1904.
14 J. T. R. Graves, *Policy and progress in secondary education*, Nelson, 1943.
15 *Report of the Board of Education*, HMSO, 1938.
16 *Report of the Consultative Committee on Secondary Education*, HMSO, 1938 (reprinted 1952), p. 2.
17 Quoted in the Spens Report, apparently with complete approval.
18 ibid., p. 123.
19 ibid., p. 124.
20 ibid., p. 124.
21 *Hansard*, 5 October 1939.
22 Secondary Schools Examinations Council, *Report of committee* (Curriculum and examinations in secondary schools), HMSO, 1943.
23 C. Burt, 'The education of the young adolescent: implications of the Norwood Report', *British Journal of Educational Psychology*, Vol. 13, 1943, p. 131.
24 Secondary Schools Examinations Council, op. cit., p. 2.
25 ibid., p. 6.
26 ibid., p. 3.
27 ibid., p. 3.
28 The figures are taken from a review of Blackwell's 'List of educational research' in *British Journal of Educational Studies*, Vol. 1, 1952–3.
29 F. J. Schonell, 'The development of educational research in Great Britain', *British Journal of Educational Psychology*, Vol. 17, 1947.
30 *Psychological tests of educable capacity and their possible use in the public system of education*, HMSO, 1924.
31 M. L. Jacks, *Modern trends in education*, Melrose, 1950, p. 31.
32 H. M. Knox, 'Research in educational theory', *British Journal of Educational Studies*, Vol. 1, 1952–3, p. 53.
33 H. R. Hamley, 'Research in education', in National Association of Head Teachers, *The first fifty years*, 1947, p. 150.
34 ibid., p. 153.
35 Jacks, op. cit., p. 32.
36 cf. Burt in n. 23 above.
37 *Report of the Consultative Committee on Secondary Education*, p. 124.
38 F. J. Schonell, 'Development of educational research – Part II', *British Journal of Educational Psychology*, Vol. 18, 1948.

39 G. Thomson, *A modern philosophy of education*, Allen & Unwin, 1929, p. 272.

40 In 1949 1,250,000 Moray House tests were sold.

41 'We shall consider persons intellectuals in so far as they devote themselves to cultivating and formulating knowledge. They have access to and advance on a cultural fund of knowledge which does not derive solely from their direct personal knowledge.' R. K. Merton, *Social theory and social structure*, Free Press, 1963.

42 A. Pinsent, 'Psychological and sociological principles for the reorganisation of secondary education', *British Journal of Educational Psychology*, Vol. 14, 1944.

43 J. C. Flugel, 'Popular views of intelligence', *British Journal of Educational Psychology*, Vol. 17, 1947.

44 C. Burt, 'Selection for secondary schools', *British Journal of Educational Psychology*, Vol. 17, 1947, p. 71.

45 Jacks, op. cit., p. 73.

46 C. Burt, 'Ability and income', *British Journal of Educational Psychology*, Vol. 13, 1943, p. 98.

47 J. N. Blackburn, *Psychology and the social pattern*, Kegan Paul, 1945, p. 168.

48 C. M. Fleming, *Adolescence*, Routledge & Kegan Paul, 1948, p. 120.

49 *The Times*, 21 December 1940.

50 H. C. Dent, *Education in transition*, Kegan Paul, 1944.

51 ibid.

52 A major impetus was generated with the appointment of R. A. Butler as president of the Board of Education.

53 Dent, op. cit., p. 202.

54 NUT, *The Hadow Report and after*, 1928; AMA, *Annual conference report*, 1925.

55 A. Tropp, *The schoolteachers*, Heinemann, 1957, p. 124.

56 NAS, *Special report on the 'Spens' report*, submitted to annual conference, 1939.

57 NUT, *Report of the executive*, 1942.

58 IAAM, *The multilateral school* (education committee report), 1942.

59 IAAM, *Annual general meeting report*, 1942.

60 'Memorandum on the white paper', *IAAM Newsletter*, October 1943.

61 'Report of commission on the school child post primary', *New Era*, September/October 1943.

62 'Report of ENEF summer conference on white paper on educational reconstruction', *New Era*, September/October 1943.

63 NUT, *Annual conference report*, 1943.

64 *Education*, 27 October 1943.

65 Joint Four, *Report*, 1942.

66 Joint Four, *Report*, 1943.

67 IAAM, *Annual general meeting report*, 1943.

68 *Education Act 1944*, Section 8.

69 *Education Act 1944*, Section 2.

70 *Education Act 1944*, Section 35.

71 Ministry of Education, *Circular 192*, December 1948.

72 Ministry of Education, *Report*, HMSO, 1958.

73 Ministry of Education, *Secondary education: a new drive*, HMSO, 1958.

74 Based on Ministry of Education reports for the appropriate years.

75 Ministry of Education, *Report*, HMSO, 1947, p. 50.

76 ibid., p. 51.

77 Ministry of Education, *Secondary education: a new drive*.

78 Ministry of Education, *Report*, HMSO, 1966, p. 28.

79 See Ministry of Education reports for appropriate years.

Chapter 3

1 F. Williams, *A prime minister remembers*, Heinemann, 1961, p. 80.

2 *Hansard*, 26 April 1955.

3 Williams, op. cit.

4 *New Statesman*, 18 August 1945.

5 See J. Thompson, *Secondary education for all*, Fabian Research Series, No. 118, 1947, and *Secondary education survey*, Fabian Research Series, No. 148, 1952.

6 Extract from first draft of East Riding development plan for secondary schools quoted in: East Riding education committee, *The first five years. An account of the operation of the Education Act of 1944 in the East Riding of Yorkshire from 1945*, 1950.

7 *The Times Educational Supplement*, 3 August 1946.

8 ibid.

9 *The Times Educational Supplement*, 19 October 1946.

10 *The Times Educational Supplement*, 26 October 1946.

11 Over the period 1939–50 the Middlesex secondary association, which contained a very strong left-wing element, more than doubled its membership. Though it was still not the largest NUT local association in Middlesex (third out of thirty-five in 1950 as against ninth out of thirty-three in 1939) the total membership of the NUT in Middlesex only grew by one-third in the same period.

12 NUT, *Education committee report*, 1948.

13 Letter from the secretary of the Middlesex technical association in *The Times Educational Supplement*, 9 November 1946.

14 Joint Four, *Annual report*, 1948.

15 *AMA Journal*, March–April 1947.

16 K. Lindsay, reported in *The Times Educational Supplement*, 29 May 1948.

17 *Education*, 12 March 1948.

18 *The Times Educational Supplement*, 7 February 1948.

19 *The Times Educational Supplement*, 18 September 1948.

20 ibid.

21 Report in *The Times Educational Supplement*, 18 September 1948.

22 *The Times Educational Supplement*, 7 August 1948.

23 *Education*, 28 May 1948.

24 B. Simon (ed.), *New trends in education*, MacGibbon & Kee, 1957, p. 83.

25 *The Times Educational Supplement*, 19 February 1949.

26 *The Times Educational Supplement*, 26 March 1949.

27 *Education*, 2 February 1951.

28 *Education*, 5 August 1949; *The Times Educational Supplement*, 25 November 1949.

29 *The Times Educational Supplement*, 11 May 1951.

30 IAHM, *Headmasters' Review*, July 1944.

31 AHMI, *Annual conference report*, 1945.

32 London teachers' association conference, 2 September 1945.

33 *Education*, November 1944.

34 IAHM, *Multilateral and comprehensive schools, statement approved by the executive*, November 1947.

35 IAHM, *Annual conference report*, 1949.

36 NAS, *Special report on the comprehensive school*, submitted to annual conference, 1946.

37 NUT, *Executive meeting report*, 1 July 1945.

38 W. P. Alexander, *Education*, 23 July 1948.

39 NUT, Presidential address, *Annual conference report*, 1946.

40 IAHM, *Annual conference report*, 1947.

41 *AMA Journal*, June/July 1946.

42 IAHM, Presidential address, *Annual conference report*, 1948.

43 C. R. Morris, vice-chancellor of Leeds University, addressing NUT summer school, August 1949.

44 IAHM, *Annual conference report*, 1949.

45 NUT, Higher education conference, 1946.

46 *Education*, 20 September 1946.

47 IAHM, *Annual conference report*, 1945.

48 AMA, Presidential address, *Annual conference report*, 1948.

49 IAAM, Presidential address, *Annual conference report*, 1946.

50 IAHM, *Report of council*, 1947.

51 *An examination by the conference of headmasters and headmistresses of the*

LCC's maintained secondary schools of the proposal to institute multilateral schools in London, 1 August 1944.

52 Editorial, *AMA Journal*, June/July 1945.

53 IAHM, Presidential address, *Annual conference report*, 1946.

54 '[The multilateral's] buildings will dwarf the countryside and will be visible for miles around. . . . It will have its own aerodrome and pupils will arrive by commercial transport plane. . . . From an eyrie in its control tower the supreme headmaster will be able to tune in by television and telephone to any classroom.' AMA, *Annual conference report*, 1945.

55 R. B. McCallum and A. Readman, *The British general election of 1945*, Oxford University Press, 1947.

56 'The Party Conference in 1946 had demanded a statement of Party policy – such a statement was produced by what we have termed the consultative-determinative core. This policy statement was accorded formal status through ratification by the leaders of the Party. Neither the Parliamentary (as a group) nor the mass party had played any real part in the policy-determining process.' J. D. Hoffman, *The Conservatives in opposition*, MacGibbon & Kee, 1964, p. 153.

57 Q. Hogg, *The case for Conservatism*, Penguin, 1947, p. 144.

58 D. Eccles in *The Times*, 22 June 1946.

59 H. Linstead, *About education*, Conservative Political Centre, 1949, p. 4.

60 ibid., p. 5.

61 Article in *The Schoolmaster*, 8 May 1947.

62 *Hansard*, 31 July 1947.

63 *Hansard*, 1 July 1946.

64 R. A. Butler, *Hansard*, 31 July 1947.

65 *Hansard*, 22 July 1947.

66 Article by H. Linstead in *The Schoolmaster*, 8 May 1947.

67 Article in *The Right Angle* (journal of the Conservative teachers' association), Vol. I, No. 2, 1949.

68 'During periods of Labour Government, it would appear that the existing policy of the Board of Education was the chief determinant of Labour policy, with emphasis and variations being determined by the personal preferences of the President of the Board, subject to the control of the Cabinet.' J. Schofield, *The Labour movement and education, 1900–1931*, unpublished M.Ed. thesis, Manchester University, 1964.

69 *Education*, 2 October 1945.

70 AEC, *Annual conference report*, 1946.

71 Labour Party, *Secondary education for all*, 1922.

72 *Hansard*, 11 June 1945.

73 ibid.

74 Ellen Wilkinson, introducing education debate at Labour Party conference, *Annual conference report*, 1946.

75 'This Conference in view of the fact that many educational development schemes are being based on the pamphlet *The nation's schools* urges the Minister to repudiate this pamphlet, and urges the present Minister to reshape educational policy in accordance with Socialist Principles.' Labour Party, *Annual conference report*, 1946, p. 195.

76 *Hansard*, 1 July 1946.

77 ibid.

78 ibid.

79 ibid.

80 *Hansard*, 6 June 1946.

81 Williams, op. cit., p. 81.

82 F. Blackburn, *George Tomlinson*, Heinemann, 1954, p. 6.

83 ibid., p. 169.

84 *Hansard*, 31 July 1947.

85 *Hansard*, 5 July 1949.

86 Ministry of Education, *The new secondary education*, Pamphlet No. 9, HMSO, 1947.

87 *Hansard*, 31 July 1947.

88 *Hansard*, 15 July 1948.

89 *Hansard*, 4 May 1950.

90 W. G. Cove, *Hansard*, 4 May 1950.

Chapter 4

1 *Co-operative News*, 12 April 1947.
2 Labour Party, *Annual conference report*, 1947, p. 198.
3 ibid., p. 204.
4 Labour Party, *Annual conference report*, 1948, p. 8.
5 ibid., p. 156.
6 ibid., p. 158.
7 Labour Party, *Annual conference report*, 1949, p. 45.
8 J. Thompson, *Secondary education survey*, Fabian Research Series, No. 148, 1952, p. 11.
9 ibid., p. 20.
10 A NALT deputation had been to see Ellen Wilkinson to protest against her secondary education policy only two days before she died.
11 Labour Party, *Annual conference report*, 1950, p. 95.
12 ibid.
13 ibid., p. 92.
14 Labour Party, *Annual conference report*, 1947, p. 10.
15 Fabian Society, *Annual report*, 1949–50, p. 10.
16 J. Thomson, *Next steps in education*, Fabian Society, 1949.
17 ibid., p. 13.
18 ibid., p. 11.
19 Fabian Society, *Annual report*, 1949–50, p. 10.
20 Fabian Society, *Annual report*, 1950–1, p. 9.
21 Fabian Society, *Annual report*, 1951, p. 8.
22 *The Right Angle*, Vol. 1, No. 1, 1948.
23 *The Times*, 13 March 1948.
24 Conservative Research Department Library, *Leaflets and pamphlets*, 1949.
25 *The Times*, 13 February 1949.
26 Central committee of Conservative teachers' association report in *Conservative Party conference report*, 1949.
27 Report in *The Right Angle*, Vol. 1, No. 1, 1948.

28 Report in *The Right Angle*, Vol. 1, No. 3, 1949.
29 Quoted in *Education*, July 1949.
30 *The Right Angle*, Vol. 1, No. 3, 1949.
31 Address to AMA annual conference, 1950.
32 *Hansard*, 24 July 1951.
33 NUT, *Annual conference report*, 1944.
34 AEC, *Annual conference report*, 1948.
35 Kandel was British-born but had spent his whole academic career in the USA; on retirement from his post as professor of education at Teachers' College, Columbia University, he returned to England in 1949, and his criticisms of the efficiency of the comprehensive high school system at various conferences were given considerable publicity.
36 *Education*, 16 January 1948.
37 *Education*, 6 January 1944.
38 Pamphlet dealing with technical education in Welsh secondary schools, 1944.
39 IAHM parliamentary committee report, *Headmasters' Review*, July 1946.
40 NEF, *New Era*, April 1945.
41 NUT, *Annual conference report*, 1946.
42 NUT higher education conference, 1946.
43 *The Schoolmaster*, 8 June 1944.
44 NUT higher education conference, 1947.
45 NUT, Chairman's address to higher education conference, 1946.
46 *Special committee report* to NUT executive committee, 14 December 1946.
47 NUT executive committee, 7 June 1947.
48 NUT executive committee, 5 June 1948 and 3 July 1948.
49 NUT, *Education committee report*.
50 London teachers' association annual conference, February 1945.
51 London teachers' association annual conference, February 1947.

52 NUT, *Annual conference report*, 1948.
53 NUT higher education conference, 1947.
54 NUT higher education conference, 1948.
55 NUT secondary sectional meetings, January 1950.
56 This concerned the distribution of a Young Communist leaflet to union members.
57 NAS, *Annual conference report*, 1946.
58 cf. *Report of commission on 'The school child – post-primary'*; NEF, *Summer conference report*, 1943; Conference on purpose and content of education, April 1944.
59 NEF, *New Era*, March 1945.
60 NEF, *The comprehensive school*, 1950.
61 IAAM, Presidential address, *Annual conference report*, 1946.
62 IAAM, *Annual conference report*, 1947.
63 IAAM, *Annual conference report*, 1948.
64 AMA, *Annual conference report*, 1945.
65 AMA, *Annual conference report*, 1947.
66 Editorial in *AMA Journal*, June–July 1946.
67 IAHM, *Annual report of the council*, 1945.
68 *Headmasters' Review*, May 1949.
69 Joint Four, *Annual report*, 1948.
70 Joint Four, *Annual report*, 1951.
71 D. E. Butler, *The general election of 1951*, Macmillan, 1952.
72 ibid., pp. 111–12.
73 Address to Conservative teachers' association annual conference, 1952.
74 *The Times*, 19 June 1953.
75 *Hansard*, 25 March 1954.
76 ibid.
79 *Hansard*, 15 July 1954.
78 *Hansard*, 14 March 1957.
79 R. T. McKenzie, *British political parties*, Heinemann, 1955.
80 S. Rose, 'Policy decision in opposition', *Political Studies*, 1956.
81 *Labour News*, October 1953.
82 R. H. S. Crossman (ed.), *New Fabian essays*, Turnstile Press, 1952, p. 108.
83 ibid., p. 110.
84 Fabian Society, *Chairman's annual report*, 1951, p. 5.
85 *The Schoolmaster*, June 1952.
86 *Labour News*, April 1953.
87 Labour Party, *Annual conference report*, 1952, p. 171.
88 ibid., p. 173.
89 ibid., p. 174.
90 ibid., p. 176.
91 *Hansard*, 30 October 1952.
92 *The Times Educational Supplement*, 5 January 1954.
93 Letter to joint committee of the four secondary associations, April 1954.
94 *The Times*, 25 April 1958.
95 *Hansard*, 15 December 1955.
96 Labour Party, *Challenge to Britain*, 1953.
97 Fabian Society, *Annual report*, 1952–3, p. 1.
98 Quoted in Conservative Research Department, *Notes on current politics*, No. 15, 1953.
99 ibid.
100 *The Times*, 20 June 1953.
101 Labour Party, *Annual conference report*, 1953, p. 174.
102 ibid., p. 166.
103 ibid., p. 172.
104 ibid., p. 173.
105 ibid., p. 168.
106 ibid., p. 171.
107 ibid., p. 176.
108 ibid., p. 177.
109 There was an article attacking Labour's *A policy for secondary education*, entitled 'Second rate education for all', in *The Right Angle*, Vol. 3, No. 1, 1951.
110 Conservative Party, *Annual conference report*, 1952.
111 Conservative Party, *Annual conference report*, 1953.
112 *Education*, November 1953.
113 The 1954 annual conference of the Conservative teachers' association called on the minister to abandon the proposals.
114 Report of Conservative teachers' association annual conference, 1954, in

The Conservative Teacher, Vol. 1, No. 3, Summer 1954.

115 Conservative Party, *Annual report*, 1952.

116 Report in *The Right Angle*, Vol. 3, No. 6, 1953.

117 *The Conservative Teacher*, Vol. 1, No. 2, 1954.

118 ibid.

119 *The Conservative Teacher*, Vol. 1, No. 3, 1954.

120 ibid.

Chapter 5

1 NAS, *Annual conference report*, 1954.

2 Quoted in *The Times*, 31 May 1954.

3 NAS, *New Schoolmaster*, April/May 1953.

4 NAS, *New Schoolmaster*, May 1954.

5 AMA, *Annual conference report*, 1951.

6 AMA education sub-committee, *Report on comprehensive schools*, 1957.

7 IAAM, Presidential address, *Annual conference report*, 1951.

8 'Organisation of secondary education', *IAAM Journal*, Summer 1954.

9 IAAM, *Annual conference report*, 1953.

10 IAAM, *Annual conference report*, 1954.

11 Article by a teacher in a comprehensive in *IAAM Journal*, Autumn 1956.

12 NUT, *Transfer from primary to secondary schools*, 1949, p. 14.

13 NUT, *Executive meeting report*, 17 March 1951.

14 NUT, *Annual report*, 1953–4.

15 NUT, *Annual report*, 1954–5.

16 NUT grammar schools sectional meeting, January 1955.

17 NUT, *Executive meeting report*, July 1959.

18 NUT, Presidential address, *Annual conference report*, 1962.

19 NUT, Presidential address, *Annual conference report*, 1956.

20 IAHM, *Annual conference report*, 1952.

21 IAHM, Group discussion on transfer to and from grammar schools, *Annual conference report*, 1954.

22 IAHM, Debate on 'Equality of opportunity in education', *Annual conference report*, 1957.

23 Address to North of England education conference, 1956.

24 IAHM, Debate on 'Equality of opportunity in education', *Annual conference report*, 1957.

25 AHMI, *Annual conference report*, 1954.

26 AHMI, Presidential address, *Annual conference report*, 1957.

27 NEF, *Annual report*, 1956.

28 *Education*, 5 March 1954.

29 Letter to the author from the secretary of the AEC.

30 *Education*, 7 May 1954.

31 Letter from the secretary of the AEC to the chief education officer in Manchester, 28 March 1956.

32 IAAM, *Annual conference report*, 1953.

33 IAAM, *Annual conference report*, 1959.

34 *The Schoolmaster*, January 1954.

35 *AMA Journal*, November/December 1955.

36 AMA, *Annual conference report*, 1953.

37 ibid.

38 *AMA Journal*, June/July 1954. The difficulty presumably arose from a lack of members working in comprehensive schools, through whom information could be gathered.

39 IAHM, *Annual conference report*, 1954.

40 Report in *The Schoolmaster*, December 1955.

41 *The Times*, 25 September 1953.

42 *The Schoolmaster*, June 1953.

43 *Education*, 19 June 1953.

44 *AMA Journal*, February 1954.

45 *IAAM Journal*, Summer 1954.

46 Joint Four meeting, 2 October 1953.

47 Joint Four, *Annual report*, 1953.

48 *The Schoolmaster*, 12 November 1954.

49 *Education*, 22 November 1954.

50 *The Schoolmaster*, 12 November 1954.

51 *The Times*, 8 November 1954.

52 *Headmasters' Review*, March 1955.

53 *The Times Educational Supplement*, 15 October 1954.

54 *The Schoolmaster*, 8 October 1954.

55 IAHM, *Annual report*, 1954. However, one of those present claimed in a letter in *The Times Educational Supplement*, 22 October 1954, that there was a complete non-mingling of ideas.

56 Report in *AMA Journal*, February 1954.

57 Joint Four, *The organisation of secondary education*, 1955 and 1959.

58 The IAHM felt it necessary to take their own action separately in 1958, in reply to the Labour Party's new educational policy document *Learning to live*. IAHM, *Report of council*, 1958.

59 *IAAM Journal*, Summer 1955.

60 P. E. Vernon, 'Modern educational psychology as a science', Inaugural lecture at the Institute of Education, University of London, 6 June 1950.

61 F. J. Schonell, 'Development of educational research – Part IV', *British Journal of Educational Psychology*, Vol. 19, 1949, p. 29.

62 J. Floud and A. H. Halsey, 'Sociology of education', *Current Sociology*, Vol. 7, 1959.

63 ibid., p. 167.

64 ibid., p. 169.

65 ibid., p. 183.

66 D. V. Glass (ed.), *Social mobility*, Routledge & Kegan Paul, 1954.

67 J. Floud, A. H. Halsey and F. M. Martin, *Social class and educational opportunity*, Heinemann, 1956.

68 A. H. Halsey and L. Gardner, 'Selection for secondary education and achievements in four grammar schools', *British Journal of Sociology*, Vol. 4, 1953, p. 74.

69 Central Advisory Council for Education (England), *Fourth report* (15–18), HMSO, 1959.

70 In 1963 the percentage of pupils admitted to schools of parents' first choice was 87·3 per cent (first or second choice 96·1 per cent): figures taken from W. E. Jackson, *Achievement: a short history of the LCC*, Longmans, 1965.

71 See, for example, the report on advanced courses in Portsmouth secondary modern schools in *Education*, 20 July 1956.

72 Central Advisory Council for Education (England), *Fifth report. Half our future* (Newsom), HMSO, 1963.

73 NUT, *The reorganisation of secondary education*, 1965, Appendix VI.

74 This account is based on G. C. Firth, *Comprehensive schools in Coventry and elsewhere*, Coventry education committee, 1963.

75 ibid., p. 14.

76 ibid., p. 45.

77 ibid., p. 64.

78 Sir A. Clegg, Address to AHMI, *Conference report*, 1966.

79 ibid.

80 Account based on case-study in D. V. Donnison and V. Chapman, *Social policy and administration*, Allen & Unwin, 1965.

81 'Over the last eighteen months or so I have been turning towards a new method of organising secondary education which, while avoiding selection at 11, would nevertheless retain in a new guise both the secondary modern school and the grammar school, and at the same time, I believe, enhance the status of both types.' Summary of S. C. Mason's report to the Leicestershire education committee in *Education*, 12 April 1957.

82 *The Times*, 25 February 1955.

83 *The Times Educational Supplement*, 2 April 1957.

84 A letter opposing the scheme in *The Times Educational Supplement*, 6 September 1957, comments: 'The general public, as might be expected, were completely ignored. The Governors of the two grammar schools affected were given no advance notice of the scheme and therefore had no chance to comment. County Councillors not on the

Education Committee first saw the scheme in the local Press . . .'

85 See the letter from masters at Guth-laxton grammar school, affected by the scheme, in *The Times Educational Supplement*, 20 September 1957.

86 *Education*, 2 April 1954.

87 *Education*, 12 March 1954.

88 *The Times Educational Supplement*, 13 March 1953.

89 *The Times Educational Supplement*, 2 March 1953.

90 ibid.

91 *The Times Educational Supplement*, 13 March 1953.

92 *The Times Educational Supplement*, 20 March 1953.

93 *The Times Educational Supplement*, 13 March 1953.

94 Joint Four, *Annual report*, 1953.

95 The tone of this speech cannot be conveyed directly. *The Times* commented that it was 'as near incitement as possible'. Quoted in *Labour News*, June 1954.

96 *Education*, 7 May 1954.

97 Manchester education committee, *Education development plan*, 1947, p. 5.

98 ibid., p. 6.

99 Manchester education committee, *Development plan for schools*, 1953, p. 1.

100 ibid.

101 Manchester secondary education sub-committee minutes, 9 March 1953 (Lewis Library Papers).

102 ibid., Appendix II.

103 *Report of the CEO to the secondary education sub-committee*, Appendix (Stages of consideration of proposals for comprehensive schools), 12 September 1955 (Lewis Library Papers).

104 General purposes sub-committee minutes, 19 July 1954 (Lewis Library Papers).

105 *Manchester Guardian*, 22 March 1955.

106 *Manchester Guardian*, 7 April 1955.

107 *Manchester Guardian*, 15 April 1955.

108 *Manchester Guardian*, 26 April 1955.

109 *Manchester Evening News*, 6 May 1955.

110 *Report of the CEO to the secondary education sub-committee*, Appendix (Stages of consideration of proposals for comprehensive schools), 12 September 1955 (Lewis Library Papers).

111 This was explained at the meeting of the Manchester education committee, 20 September 1955.

112 Dated 7 July 1955 (Lewis Library Papers).

113 *Manchester Guardian*, 19 July 1955.

114 *Manchester Evening News*, 2 September 1955.

115 'For months now this comprehensive school business has resolved itself into a political battle. The people most directly concerned – the teachers and the parents – are the least considered. If they do have firm views on the matter they keep them for their own friends.' *Manchester Evening News*, 9 September 1955.

116 *Manchester Guardian*, 14 September 1955.

117 *Manchester Guardian*, 20 September 1955.

118 *Report of the CEO to the general purposes sub-committee*, 17 October 1955 (Lewis Library Papers).

119 *Manchester Guardian*, 20 December 1955.

120 'Undoubtedly the majority of members of the Labour group were in favour of experiments with the comprehensive system, but unlike some of their colleagues on the Education Committee, they were not prepared to push these ideas against a hostile Government and Minister.' J. G. Bulpitt, *Party politics in English local government*, Longmans, 1967, p. 64.

121 'An actor who can perform a requisite action has authority over the action. He may perform it or not, as he likes, or, in the language to be used here, he may give or withold it from the system of activity being concerted towards the adoption of the proposal.' E. C. Banfield, *Political influence*, Free Press, 1961, p. 309.

Chapter 6

1 Article by Conservative spokesman in *The Times Educational Supplement*, 13 May 1955.
2 *The Schoolmaster*, 3 June 1955.
3 Conservative Party, *United for peace and progress*, 1955.
4 Conservative Party, *Campaign guide*, 1955, p. 205.
5 D. E. Butler, *The British general election of 1955*, Cass, 1955.
6 ibid.
7 ibid.
8 'We need not have schools all of one type: there can be an infinite variety. We say that it is wrong to have selection at 11 and would like to see a movement towards the elimination of that system.' *Hansard*, 26 April 1955.
'One solution was the comprehensive school but he did not want to be dogmatic about the worth of this type.' Lord Silkin in House of Lords debate on education, 9 February 1955.
9 One informant explained this in terms of the low priority given to education by politicians.
10 E. Shinwell, *The Times*, 26 June 1958.
11 *Annual conference report*, 1957.
12 ibid.
13 Leader in *The Schoolmaster*, 13 May 1955.
14 Letter from Joint Four to leaders of all political parties, 16 May 1953.
15 *Hansard*, 30 July 1953.
16 R. S. Milne and H. C. M. Mackenzie, *Marginal seat 1955*, Hansard Society, 1955.
17 J. Longland, North of England education conference, 31 December 1958.
18 IAAM, *Annual conference report*, 1955.
19 *The Times*, 27 June 1958.
20 NUT, *Annual conference report*, 1955.
21 *The Times*, 21 April 1958.
22 *The Times*, 14 April 1958.
23 Labour Party, *Annual conference report*, 1958, p. 113.
24 ibid., p. 114.
25 ibid., p. 35.
26 ibid., p. 108.
27 Labour Party, *Learning to live*, p. 5.
28 ibid., p. 7.
29 ibid., p. 25.
30 *The Times*, 5 July 1958.
31 Labour Party, *Annual conference report*, 1958, p. 87.
32 Conservative Party, *Annual conference report*, 1958.
33 ibid.
34 ibid.
35 ibid.
36 *Conservative Teacher*, Vol. 2, No. 5, Spring 1959.
37 *Conservative Teacher*, Vol. 1, No. 11, Spring 1957.
38 President of IAHM at IAHM council meeting, 20–21 June 1958.
39 *Secondary education: a new drive*, HMSO, 1958.
40 IAAM, Surcharge report, *Annual conference report*, 1959.
41 *The Schoolmaster*, June 1958.
42 *The Times*, 15 January 1955.
43 *The Times*, 12 January 1957.
44 Report of committee on school examinations of Conservative teachers' association in *The Right Angle*, Vol. 3, No. 5, Winter 1953.
45 *Hansard*, 6 March 1952.
46 *Hansard*, 25 March 1954.
47 Parliamentary secretary to minister of education, speaking at a grammar school, 14 January 1955.
48 Report on 'Selection for secondary education' in *The Conservative Teacher*, Vol. 3, No. 2, Summer 1958.
49 8 December 1958.
50 *Hansard*, 5 April 1957.
51 ibid.
52 *Hansard*, 11 July 1963.
53 Address to annual conference of AEC, 5 July 1963.
54 NAS, *New Schoolmaster*, April 1956.
55 NAS, *New Schoolmaster*, April/May 1959.
56 *The Schoolmaster*, 11 July 1958.
57 NUT, *Executive report*, 1959.

58 NUT executive meeting, March 1957.
59 NUT, *Annual report of executive*, 1958.
60 NUT sectional meetings, 31 December 1958 and 1 January 1959.
61 NUT modern school sectional meeting, January 1960.
62 NUT. Derived from lists of executive members in appropriate annual reports.
63 IAAM, *Annual conference report*, 1959.
64 AMA, *Annual conference report*, 1957.
65 *AMA Journal*, February 1959.
66 AMA, *Annual conference report*, 1957.
67 *AMA Journal*, June 1957.
68 AMA, *Comprehensive secondary education*, 1958.
69 *AMA Journal*, February 1959.
70 IAHM annual conference, 2 January 1959.
71 Speaker at AMA annual conference, 1963.
72 *The Times Educational Supplement*, 13 April 1955.
73 *The Times Educational Supplement*, 22 July 1955.
74 Report in *IAAM Journal*, Summer 1959.
75 ibid.
76 D. V. Dennison and V. Chapman, *Social policy and administration*, Allen & Unwin, 1965.
77 *The Times*, 11 March 1959.
78 *Hansard*, 20 April 1961.
79 *Hansard*, 17 July 1961.
80 ibid.
81 *Hansard*, 21 April 1964.
82 Conservative Research Department Library, *Leaflets and pamphlets*, January–December 1963, Vol. II.
83 'The Tories and education', *The Conservative Teacher*, Vol. I, No. 10, Winter 1956.
84 F. Smallwood, *The politics of metropolitan reform*, Bobbs-Merrill, 1965, pp. 112–13.
85 *Willingly to school*, September 1959.
86 *The Times*, 20 June 1960.
87 *Strategy for schools*, January 1964, p. 62.
88 Conservative central council executive,

Report of executive committee for period since June 1962, February 1963.
89 Conservative teachers' association, *Conference report*, 1959.
90 *The Times*, 21 June 1964.
91 NUT, *Organisation of secondary education*, 1959, p. 5.
92 ibid., p. 4.
93 NUT, Presidential address, *Annual conference report*, 1959.
94 North of England education conference, *Report*, 1959.
95 NUT and Joint Four, *Reorganisation of secondary education*, October 1964.
96 NUT, *Annual conference report*, 1959.
97 NUT executive meeting, February 1960.
98 NUT, *Law and tenure committee report*.
99 NUT, *First things first*, Memorandum of evidence submitted to the Central Advisory Council for Education (England), 1964.
100 NUT advisory committee for comprehensive and bilateral schools meeting, 12–13 June 1959.
101 NUT, *The Schoolmaster*, April 1962.
102 NUT, *Executive report*, 1964.
103 NUT, Grammar schools sectional meeting, January 1960.
104 Leading article, *The Schoolmaster*, January 1961.
105 IAAM, Secretary's report, *Annual conference report*, 1960.
106 ibid.
107 *The Schoolmaster*, 9 January 1959.
108 AMA, *Annual conference report*, 1960.
109 AMA motion passed at 1959 annual conference.
110 AMA, *Annual conference report*, 1963.
111 AMA, *Annual conference report*, 1964.
112 AHMI, *Annual conference report*, June 1964.
113 AHMI, Quotation from letter read in presidential address, *Annual conference report*, 1966.
114 *IAAM Journal*, Summer 1964.
115 IAHM, *Legal committee report*, 1958.
116 IAHM, *Report of council*, November 1962.

117 IAHM, President's report for 1963, *Headmasters' Review*, December 1963.
118 Joint Four, *Organisation of secondary education*, 1959.
119 Joint Four, *Report*, 1963.
120 Labour Party, *Annual conference report*, 1959, p. 41.
121 IAHM, *Annual conference report*, 1960.

122 *The Times*, 15 February 1964.
123 *The Conservative enemy*, 1957, p. 158.
124 Labour Party, *Signposts for the sixties*, 1959.
125 Labour Party, *Annual conference report*, 1960, p. 151.
126 Labour Party, *Annual conference report*, 1963, p. 136.

Chapter 7

1 D. E. Butler and A. King, *The British general election of 1964*, Macmillan, 1965, pp. 65–9.
2 Conservative education spokesman in *The Times Educational Supplement*, 18 September 1964.
3 'My ministers will enlarge educational opportunities and give particular priority to increasing the supply of teachers.' *Hansard*, 3 November 1964.
4 *The Times*, 26 and 28 October 1964. Four hundred individual objections were received, and one from the Liverpool parents' protest committee. *Hansard*, 12 November 1964.
5 *Hansard*, 3 November 1964.
6 *Hansard*, 12 November 1964.
7 ibid.
8 'This House while mindful of the need to ensure that the abilities and aptitudes of every child are developed to the fullest extent, and while recognising the importance of flexibility and variety in the organisation of secondary education including, in cases where appropriate on educational grounds, the comprehensive principle, would nonetheless deplore the wholesale abolition, whether by closure or by radical alteration, of direct grant or maintained grammar schools.' *Hansard*, 27 November 1964.
9 ibid.
10 *The Times*, 29 December 1964.
11 *The Times*, 31 December 1964.
12 *The Times*, 1 January 1965.
13 ibid.
14 *Hansard*, 21 January 1965. One Labour member, Harold Lever, a former pupil of Manchester grammar school and currently a governor of the same school, voted against the opposition motion but abstained from supporting the government's own amendment in favour of pressing ahead with comprehensive organization.
15 *The Times*, 8 February 1965.
16 A minor diversion was created at this time by Lord Snow, a government spokesman on education in the House of Lords, who defended his decision to send his own son to Eton on the twin grounds that it was unwise 'to educate your child differently from most of the people he knows socially' and wrong to impose 'ideologies I have upon someone who might not have those ideologies'. *The Times*, 11 February 1905.
17 *The Times*, 23 February 1965.
18 *The Times*, 26 February 1965. Reg Prentice speaking at East Ham.
19 *The Times*, 4 March 1965.
20 *Hansard*, 18 March 1965.
21 *The Times*, 7 April 1965.
22 *The Times*, 1 May 1965.
23 *The Times*, 24 May 1965.
24 *The Times*, 27 April 1965.
25 *The Times*, 24 March 1965, 27 April 1965, 3 December 1965, 22 December 1965.
26 *The Times*, 6 January 1966.
27 *The Times*, 14 July 1965.
28 ibid.
29 *The Times Educational Supplement*, 16 July 1965.
30 *The Times*, 2 July 1965.
31 *The Times*, 17 September 1965.
32 Labour Party conference, *Annual report*, 1964.

33 ibid.
34 Labour Party Conference, *Annual report*, 1965.
35 ibid.
36 ibid.
37 National Union of Conservative and Unionist Associations, *Annual conference report*, 1965.
38 ibid.
39 ibid.
40 ibid.
41 Labour Party conference, *Annual report*, 1966.
42 ibid.
43 *The Times*, 15 March 1966.
44 ibid.
45 ibid.
46 *The Times*, 24 May 1967.
47 *Guardian*, 8 July 1967.
48 Editorial, *The Times Educational Supplement*, 21 April 1967.
49 Editorial, *The Times Educational Supplement*, 18 March 1966.
50 *The Times*, 13 January 1966.
51 *Observer*, 20 January 1966.
52 *Observer*, 16 April 1967.
53 ibid.
54 *The Times*, 20 April 1967.
55 *The Times*, 4 May 1967.
56 *Observer*, 19 June 1966.
57 *The Times*, 11 July 1966.
58 ibid.

59 *The Times*, 15 May 1967.
60 *The Times*, 27 October 1965.
61 *The Times*, 26 July 1966.
62 *Guardian*, 29 July 1966.
63 *Daily Telegraph*, 21 April 1967.
64 *The Times*, 23 June 1967.
65 *The Times*, 1 August 1967.
66 *The Times*, 24 August 1967.
67 *The Times*, 18 September 1967.
68 *Sun*, 25 August 1967.
69 *The Times*, 15 September 1967.
70 Comprehensive schools' committee, *Comprehensive reorganisation in Britain*, Survey No. 2, 1967.
71 Labour Party, *Annual conference report*, 1967.
72 National Union of Conservative and Unionist Associations, *Annual conference report*, 1967.
73 National Union of Conservative and Unionist Associations, *Annual conference report*, 1968.
74 ibid.
75 *Hansard*, 12 February 1970.
76 ibid.
77 ibid.
78 *Parliamentary debates, Commons standing committees session*, 1969–70, Vol. I, cols. 163–4.
79 ibid., col. 336.
80 ibid., cols. 327–38.
81 *Hansard*, 22 April 1970.

Chapter 8

1 J. A. G. Griffith, *Central departments and local authorities*, Allen & Unwin, 1966, p. 33.
2 *Education*, 9 March 1953.
3 Quoted in *Report of the CEO to the secondary education sub-committee – secondary school organisation*, Manchester, 9 April 1956.
4 Address to annual general meeting of the AEC, 2 July 1953.

5 NUT. *A memorandum on some aspects of the work of the new secondary schools*, 1955.
6 Ministry of Education, *Secondary education: a new drive*, Cmnd 604, HMSO, 1958.
7 A. F. Bentley, *The process of government*, Chicago, 1908 (new edn, ed. by P. H. Odegard, Harvard University Press, 1967).

Index

About education (1949), 52
Advance in education (1947), 59
'aided' schools, *see* voluntary aided schools
Alexander, Sir William, 66, 89
all-age schools, 25, 27, 41, 42, 104, 156
'all-purpose' schools (*see also* 'combined' schools, common schools, comprehensive schools, multilateral schools), 69
American high schools, 31, 83, 152
Anglicans, *see* Church of England
aptitude tests (*see also* intelligence tests), 28, 32–3
Ashford grammar school, 46–7
Assistant Masters' Association (AMA), 34, 36, 46, 51, 70, 82–3, 89, 115–16, 123–4, 131, 161
Association for Science Education (ASE), 21, 152, 162
Association of Education Committees (AEC), 21, 35, 48, 54, 56, 65, 87–90, 99, 106, 135, 153–5
Association of Governing Bodies of Greater London Aided Grammar Schools, 140
Association of Headmistresses (Incorporated) (AHMI), 70, 76, 87
attainment tests, *see* tests of attainment
Attlee, Clement, 15, 43, 56

Bacon, Alice, 58, 59, 75, 78, 90, 144, 146
bilateral (bipartite) system (*see also* tripartite system), 35, 44, 87, 94, 113, 114, 121

Birley, Dr Robert, 86
Birmingham, 25, 113, 115, 134
Board of Education, 5–7, 10, 12, 25, 34–5
consultative committee of, 7–8, 26–7
president of, 5, 7, 20, 38
Bolton, 19
Bournemouth, 134
Bow Group, 119
Boyle, Sir Edward, 15, 16, 108, 112, 113, 118, 131, 137, 143, 145–6, 158
Bristol, 130–1
building programmes, *see* school buildings, provision of
Burt, Sir Cyril, 28, 30, 32, 33
Butler, R. A., 8, 15, 22, 43, 52, 53, 63, 64, 112

Caernarvonshire, 61
Cardigan, 61
Carlisle, 116
Central Advisory Council for Education in England, 7–9, 19, 94, 134, 152–4
Central Advisory Council for Education in Scotland, 56, 152
Central Advisory Council for Education in Wales, 152
central schools, 26, 27
Challenge to Britain (1953), 76–9, 88, 89, 90
Chataway, Christopher, 140, 144
chief education officers, 10–11, 13–14, 18, 47, 95–7, 99, 100, 108, 117, 142
Church of England, 20, 27, 94, 140
church schools (*see also* Church of England,

religion, Roman Catholic Church), 6, 20, 22, 24–5, 158
Churchill, Sir Winston S., 22, 72
Circular 10/65, *see under* Ministry of Education
Clarke, Sir Fred, 8, 92, 152
Clay, Henry, 56
Claydon, W. A., 90
'Cockerton judgement' (1900), 25
Cole, Margaret, 73
'combined' schools, 70
common (secondary) schools (*see also* 'all-purpose' schools, 'combined' schools, comprehensive schools, multilateral schools), 49, 54, 56, 57, 60, 68–9, 152
Communism, 63–4, 68–9
comprehensive schools (*see also* 'all-purpose' schools, 'combined' schools, common schools, multilateral schools)
  compulsory reorganization into, 145–6, 147
  'experiments' in, 48–9, 57, 64–5, 68–9, 71–2, 75, 78–9, 83, 85, 87–9, 91, 98–9, 102–3, 107–10, 117–19, 127, 151–3, 160
  growth in numbers of, 41, 44–7, 57, 61, 65, 68, 72, 94, 111, 113–14, 116, 121–2, 139–41, 143, 148–9
  in rural areas, 66, 79, 86, 118–19
  opponents of, 36, 45–54, 58–65, 67, 69–73, 79–83, 85–6, 88–9, 91, 95, 97–9, 101–2, 104–7, 110, 112, 114–17, 123, 125, 131, 134, 139–46, 151, 154, 156, 158–62; in Labour Party, 16, 54, 58–62, 78, 81, 105, 141, 156, 162
  qualified support for, 16, 23, 38, 43, 57, 62, 69, 72–4, 78, 80, 82–4, 87–8, 90, 94, 105, 111, 113, 115–16, 118–20, 122–5, 127, 129–32, 136–7, 144, 150–6, 159–63
  size of, 45, 60–1, 64, 91, 97, 110, 118, 123, 142
  supporters of, 22, 43–7, 57–8, 60–3, 67–79, 81–2, 86–8, 90, 93–8, 100–5, 108–10, 112–16, 118–22, 125–30, 132–3, 136–7, 140, 144, 146, 147, 149–52, 154–62; in Conservative Party, 72–3, 79, 96, 102–3, 105, 108, 117–19, 136, 140, 144, 146–7, 158, 162
  teachers in, 113–15, 121–3, 162
Conservative Party (*see also* comprehensive schools, multilateral schools, tripartite system)
  conferences of, 52, 79, 104, 106, 109, 136–7, 144, 158
  in local government, 17, 47, 59, 80, 96, 100–3, 110, 116, 118, 126, 130, 133–4, 137–41, 143–5, 158
  in national government, 16, 34, 52–3, 57, 63–5, 71–2, 75–6, 79–81, 103, 107, 109–11, 113, 117–19, 126, 129–32, 136–7, 142–3, 146–7, 154, 156, 158, 162
  teachers in, 63–5, 72, 79, 80–1, 107, 109–10, 112, 119
Conservative teachers' association, *see* Conservative Party, teachers in
Cooke, Robert, 130
Co-operative Party, 59
County Councils' Association (CCA), 36, 66
Cove, W. G., 55, 56, 57, 58
Coventry, 61, 94–6, 100, 127, 135
Crosland, Anthony, 127, 132–3, 140
Crowther Report (1959), 93
Croydon, 96, 117

Davies, Clement, 15
Department of Education and Science (DES) (*see also* Ministry of Education), 132, 137, 142–3
Department of Science and Art, 5
Derby, 144
direct grant schools, 20, 144, 147

Ealing, 141–2
East Riding, 44
Eccles, Sir David, 15, 73, 107, 112, 118
Ede, Chuter, 43, 55, 76
Eden, Sir Anthony, 64
Education Act (1833), 5
Education Act (1902), 1, 5, 22, 25
Education Act (1918), 6
Education Act (1921), 9, 10
Education Act (1936), 34, 37
Education Act (1944) (*see also* local education authorities), 1, 5–11, 14–18, 20, 22–3, 29, 33–4, 37, 38, 43, 51, 53, 59, 65, 76, 80, 93, 101, 105, 133, 142–3, 145, 147, 151, 160
  passage of, 1, 16–17, 33, 37, 55

education committees (*see also* Association of Education Committees, party politics in education), 9–10, 13, 18–19, 117
co-opted members on, 9, 18–19
education of the adolescent, The, see Hadow Report
Educational opportunity (1963), 118
educational psychology, 28–33, 38, 71, 91–3, 99
educational sociology (*see also* social bias of education, social effects of comprehensives, social effects of intelligence tests, social effects of tripartite system), 66, 92–3, 151
Elementary Education Act (1870), 5
elementary schools (primary, infant and junior schools) (*see also* all-age schools), 6, 16, 24, 25–8, 41, 42, 127, 151, 161
integration with secondary system, 12, 26–7, 33
eleven plus (*see also* intelligence tests, selection), 49, 90, 102, 112, 120, 127–8
opponents of, 63, 74, 76, 80, 88, 97, 102, 105, 112–13, 117, 127, 129–30, 132, 136–8, 146, 152, 156
supporters of, 36, 47, 64–5, 93, 109, 111–13
Eltham Hill grammar school, 80, 98–9, 153–4
Enfield, 142–3
'experiments' in comprehensive and multilateral schools, *see under* comprehensive schools

Fabian Society, 61–2, 63, 73–4, 76, 90
fees, abolition of in maintained schools, 54
Fienburgh, Wilfred, 74
first report on teaching in comprehensive schools, A (1959), 115
Free Place scholarship system, *see* scholarships
further education, *see* universities
future of secondary education, The (1954), 80

Gaitskell, Hugh, 76, 78, 90, 109
Glass, D. V., 93
Goff, Mr Justice, 142

Gordon Walker, Patrick, 143
grammar schools (*see also* selection), 27, 29, 50–1, 60, 65, 68, 84–5, 89–90, 93–4, 96–7, 109–12, 117, 149, 155, 159
closures of individual schools, 46, 47, 80, 87–8, 98–9, 143, 153–4
opponents of, 55, 70, 78, 99, 129–31, 159
supporters of, 36, 44, 50, 53–5, 60, 64, 67, 71–2, 79–84, 86, 88–91, 95, 98–100, 103, 105–7, 110, 115–16, 118–19, 122, 124–5, 127, 129–31, 138, 140, 146–7, 149, 151, 154, 156, 161; in Labour Party, 54, 57, 60, 61, 74, 78, 106
teachers in, 50, 51, 67, 69, 84, 85, 97, 113, 121–2, 126, 151, 162
Green, Miss M., 90
'Green Book' (1942), 34
Greenwood, Anthony, 127

Hadow Report (*The education of the adolescent*) (1926), 26–8, 30, 42, 60
Hailsham, Lord (*see also* Hogg, Quintin), 111
Heath, Edward, 137–8, 147
high schools (*see also* American high schools), 77
higher education, *see* universities
Hogg, Quintin (*see also* Hailsham, Lord), 16, 131–2
Holmes-Morant memorandum (1910), 13
Hornsey, 110
Horsbrugh, Florence, 15, 64, 72, 75, 97–9, 106, 111, 155
Howe, Geoffrey, 142
Hutchings, A. W. S., 71
Hyman, Alderman, 65

Incorporated Association of Assistant Mistresses (IAAM), 35–6, 51, 70, 83, 88, 107, 110, 115, 123, 124, 152
Incorporated Association of Headmasters (IAHM), 21, 48–50, 66, 70–1, 86, 88–91, 110, 116, 124, 131, 151, 154, 160–1
independent schools (private and public schools), 6, 12, 16, 26, 37, 61–2, 74, 79, 86, 90, 106, 108, 115, 129
opponents of, 57, 78, 90, 105–6, 108, 144
supporters of, 57, 78, 79, 90, 106, 161

infant schools, *see* elementary schools
Inner London Education Authority (ILEA), *see under* London
Inside the comprehensive school (1957), 114
inspectorate, 12, 13, 100, 127, 155
Institute of Education, University of London, 92
intelligence tests (*see also* aptitude tests, eleven plus, selection), 30–3, 84, 91
  coaching for, 93, 111
  opponents of, 33, 49–50, 64, 84–5, 92, 93, 111, 136, 152
  supporters of, 28, 30–3, 38

James, Eric, 86, 90
Joint Four secondary associations, 20, 36, 46, 71, 75, 88–91, 98, 106, 110, 116–17, 120, 122, 125, 135, 154, 161–2
  local associations, 46, 71, 98, 116, 125
junior colleges, *see* sixth-form colleges
junior comprehensive schools (*see also* three-tier system), 134
junior schools, *see* elementary schools

Kandel, Professor I. L., 66
Kidbrooke comprehensive school, 87, 90, 98, 119, 131
Kingsmill Jones, Alderman Mary, 101–2
Kingston-on-Thames, 138

Labour and the new society (1950), 62
Labour believes in Britain (1949), 60, 62
Labour Party (*see also* comprehensive schools, grammar schools, tripartite system)
  conferences of, 58–60, 62, 73, 75–6, 79, 95, 105, 108, 136, 144, 157
  in local government, 17–18, 43–5, 47, 57–61, 99, 101, 103, 116–17, 119, 126–7, 130, 133–5, 137–41, 144, 149, 158
  in national government, 16–17, 34, 43–4, 52–6, 58–9, 61, 63, 69, 71, 73, 75–81, 87–8, 90–1, 104–5, 107–8, 111, 116–17, 126–32, 134–8, 144–7, 151, 156–8, 162–3
  National Executive Committee (NEC) of, 59, 61, 63, 73, 77, 89, 108, 144
  teachers in (and National Association of Labour Teachers), 56, 61, 74, 76–8, 81, 105, 107, 127, 156–7

Lancashire, 10, 126
'late developers', 92, 93
Learning to live (1958), 108–10
Lee, Jennie, 137
Leicestershire, 93, 96–7, 114, 127
Let us win through together (1950), 62
Liberal Party, 24–5, 126, 132, 133
Linstead, Hugh, 52–3
Liverpool, 97, 130, 132–3
Lloyd, Geoffrey, 15, 107, 117, 131
local education authorities (*see also names of individual authorities*), 11, 25, 149
  and Assistant Masters' Association, 124
  and intelligence tests, 31, 32, 93
  and 1944 Education Act, 9–10, 37, 43, 44, 48–9, 54, 57–8, 60, 65
  and secondary reorganization (*see also* comprehensive schools, compulsory reorganization into), 5, 7, 9, 14, 37, 43–4, 57–9, 65, 72, 78, 87–8, 91, 99–104, 107, 111, 116, 118–19, 126, 132–5, 137–8, 144–7, 149, 153–4, 160
  subsidies to, 14–15, 135, 137–8
London (*see also* London School Plan, London teachers' association)
  under Inner London Education Authority, 139–41, 144, 146
  under London County Council, 17, 24, 26, 30, 53, 57, 68, 74, 87, 93, 97–100, 113, 115, 118, 127, 137, 139, 151, 153–4, 156
London School of Economics, 93
London School Plan, 48, 51–2, 73, 97, 140, 153
London teachers' association, 48, 68, 151
Luton, 132–3

Manchester, 17, 25–6, 88, 99–103, 132, 134, 137, 141, 154
Mannheim, Karl, 92
Mason, S. C., 96–7, 114
Maude, Angus, 145
middle-school system, *see* three-tier system
Middlesex, 45–7, 57, 68, 110
Middlesex secondary schools' association, 46, 68
minister of education, 5–8, 10–11, 15, 19, 37
  status in government, 5, 15–16, 43, 72

Ministry of Education (*see also* Department of Education and Science), 9–10, 12, 14–15, 20, 37, 44, 50, 59, 65, 71, 94–5, 101, 143
  Circular No. 5, *Schemes of divisional administration* (1944), 10
  Circular 10/65 (1965), 134–5, 138, 141, 146–7, 149, 158
Morant, Robert, 6, 12, 25–6
Morley, Ralph, 55, 58, 67, 77
Morrison, Herbert, 105
multilateral schools (*see also* comprehensive schools), 1, 49, 58, 68, 94
  defined, 1–2
  'experiments' in, *see under* comprehensive schools
  opponents of, 48, 52, 63, 65–6, 70
  supporters of, 34–5, 45, 48, 50, 59, 65–6, 68, 70–1, 96, 100; in Conservative Party, 53, 64

nation's schools, The (1945), 54–6
National Association of Head Teachers of Secondary Technical Schools, 97, 108, 116
National Association of Labour Teachers (NALT), *see* Labour Party, teachers in
National Association of Schoolmasters (NAS), 21, 35, 48, 69, 82, 113, 135, 151, 161
National Education Association (NEA), 141–2
National Executive Committee (NEC), *see under* Labour Party
National Foundation for Educational Research (NFER), 19, 49
National Union of Teachers (NUT), 21, 34–6, 45–6, 49–51, 55–6, 65, 67–9, 71, 83–5, 88–91, 97, 104, 106–7, 111, 113–14, 116, 120–3, 126, 135, 151, 154–5, 160–2
New Education Fellowship (NEF), 21, 35, 66, 70, 87, 151, 154, 162
Newens, Stanley, 146
Norwood Report (1943), 29–30, 32, 36, 44, 52, 71, 120

Oldham, 61
Ollerenshaw, Dr Kathleen, 102, 137, 141
'omnibus schools', 53

parents, role of, 3, 11, 47, 93, 95, 98, 101–2, 106, 110, 112, 116, 130, 132–3, 141–3, 150, 155, 157, 163
'parity of esteem', 1, 42, 55, 68, 114
'partnership', in government of education, 2–3, 22, 156
party politics in education (*see also* Conservative Party, Co-operative Party, Labour Party, Liberal Party, Progressive Party), 3, 15–19, 22, 52, 57–65, 67, 71–3, 76, 80, 88, 94–104, 112, 115, 126, 132, 141, 150–2
Peart, Fred, 58, 60
Pitman, I. J., 79
Plowden committee, 121
policy for secondary education, A (1951), 63, 73
Prentice, Reg, 147
Price, Christopher, 146–7
primary schools, *see* elementary schools
Principles of government in maintained schools (1944), 11
private schools, *see* independent schools
Progressive Party, 94
public schools, *see* independent schools

Reading, 61
Redhead, Brian, 134
religion (*see also* Church of England, church schools, Roman Catholic Church)
  in schools, 11, 142
  influence of education policy, 17, 20, 22, 24, 33–4, 38
Richmond (Surrey), 138
Roman Catholic Church, 20, 27, 94, 140
Royal Commissions, requests for, 72, 83
Rubinstein, David, 136

scholarships, 27, 78
school boards, 5, 25
school buildings, provision of, 39–43, 60, 79–80, 99, 104, 111–12, 127, 135, 138, 156
school-leaving age
  raised to fifteen, 28, 37, 39–42
  raised to sixteen, 37, 94, 129, 137
  voluntary staying-on, 39–40, 89, 94
Scotland, education in, 23, 53, 56
Scunthorpe, 116

Secondary education: a new drive (1958), 155–6
secondary modern schools, 27, 48, 60, 94, 111
  fifth and sixth forms in, 85–6, 93–4, 114, 122, 155
  opponents of, 53, 64, 66–7, 78, 99, 132
  supporters of, 44, 53–4, 60, 75, 79, 84–5, 106–7, 113–14, 155–6
  teachers in, 67, 69, 97
Selborne, Lord, 7
selection at eleven for secondary schools (*see also* eleven plus, intelligence tests), 59, 83–5, 90, 106–7, 111–13, 132, 146
  opponents of, 34, 48–50, 70, 76, 78–80, 84, 88, 93, 97, 99, 111–12, 136, 145–6, 149, 152
  supporters of, 28–9, 71, 80, 83–6, 90, 93, 106–7, 111–12, 126, 152
senior elementary schools, *see* elementary schools
senior schools, 60, 65
Short, Edward, 145
Signposts for the sixties (1959), 127
sixth-form colleges (junior colleges), 96, 117, 126, 135, 146
social bias of education, 17, 31, 93
Social class and educational opportunity (1956), 93
social effects of comprehensives, 115, 131, 136, 146
social effects of intelligence tests, 31
social effects of tripartite system, 59–60, 73, 115, 131
sociology, *see* educational sociology
Southend, 61
Southport, 19
Spens, Sir Will, 7, 27
Spens Report (1938), 27–8, 30, 35
Stewart, Michael, 77, 90, 130
Stockport, 19
Stoke-on-Trent, 133
streaming, 114, 136
subsidies, *see under* local education authorities
Surrey, 138

teachers
  and psychologists, 30
  Communists among, 63, 68–9, 71
  consultative role of, 2, 3, 19, 20–1, 24, 39, 45–6, 68, 77, 91, 97, 102, 116–17, 119–24, 126, 131, 133, 138, 145, 150, 152, 154–8, 162–3
  protection of interests of, 121, 158
  salaries of, 104
  training of, 19, 30, 41, 42–3, 67
technical schools, 5, 6, 27–9, 46, 85, 111
  decline of, 40, 114
  opponents of, 99
  supporters of, 44, 46, 53, 60, 65, 67, 79–81, 94, 104, 106–9
tests of attainment, 111
Thatcher, Margaret, 146–7, 158
Thompson, Sir Kenneth, 112
Thomson, Godfrey, 31
threat to the grammar schools, The (1946), 50
three-tier system, 134, 141
Times Educational Supplement, The, 135, 139
Tomlinson, George, 15, 56–8, 97
Townsend, Lena, 137, 140
Trades Union Congress (TUC), 58, 108
transfers between types of school, 1, 64, 75, 81, 84–6, 112
tripartite system (*see also* bilateral system), 29, 94
  opponents of, 35–6, 55, 59, 63, 66–70, 93, 95–6, 99, 108–9, 113–14, 118–20, 152, 155–6, 159; in Conservative Party, 52, 72, 118–19
  supporters of, 27, 35–6, 44, 46, 54, 57, 68–9, 71, 79–81, 86, 100, 105–6, 108, 111–12, 138, 154; in Labour Party, 54, 57, 60
two-tier system, 135

universities, 6, 24, 67, 81, 106, 114, 127–8, 155
Utley, T. E., 118

voluntary aided schools, 20, 130, 139–40